DES

Instinct demanded it:

The SIXTY-FOOT SHARK rolled back its eyes to protect those precious vision ports and expanded its cavernous mouth, exposing row-upon-row of nine-inch, razor-edged teeth. Erupting through glassy-calm water, the gigantic creature assaulted the 27-foot cruiser with thunderous impact. Flung violently against the hull, Harold Hawkins' head exploded in viscous blood and pasty, grey brain matter. Monstrous teeth split Joe Mason's head like a meat cleaver and their ivory companions sliced him from nose to hip.

Hawkins' legs and right arm, severed by the initial bite, were sucked down a waiting gullet. Those incomprehensible jaws ripped savagely through his head and left shoulder while slamming shut again and again. Flesh, bone, and boat disintegrated under the ferocious attack until the intolerable, aggravating sound that had filled the shark's domain was finally silenced. Ten million years of instinctive, predatory skills destroyed a persistent, throbbing noise that infuriated it so. The brief, but violent commotion ended in seconds and the sea covered her secrets. *Fifty tons of* **Megalodon** and its obliterated victims vanished. **Then . . .** only calm.

QUEST FOR MEGALODON

BY

TOM DADE

SWAN PUBLISHERS
New York * Texas * California

Copyright @ June 1993 by J. Thomas Dade
Library of Congress Catalog Number 92-084088
ISBN 0-943629-06-3

QUEST FOR MEGALODON is available in quantity discounts. Please address to: SWAN PUBLISHING CO., 126 Live Oak, Suite 100, Alvin, Texas 77511 (713) 388-2547

Printed in the United States of America

* Cover shark drawn by Tommy Dade
  Artwork and cover by Glen Clark

FOREWORD

SHARK! The word terrifies every man, woman, and child. The movie **JAWS,** scared millions and kept people from even going *near* the water. That single, fictional Great White Shark spread paranoia across the civilized world, creating an almost permanent phobia of the oceans. But *now*, that despicable beast from **JAWS** pales to insignificance when compared with the *unimaginable* creature man has unknowingly sucked from the depths. *MEGALODON!!!*

Matt Hooper, the Marine Biologist Richard Dreyfuss played in **JAWS,** alluded to a prehistoric shark fifty, maybe even a *hundred feet long.* Hooper presumed it was extinct. No shark alive could possibly be that long!

Yes, author Peter Benchley's book had us believing *Carcharodon Megalodon* was extinct, but he was wrong*! Dead wrong!* Megalodon did not perish. Megalodon is *here!* And while we are searching for it, *it,* is hunting *us!*

For a hundred million years, the world's optimal hunting and feeding creature evolved, expertly forged for survival. Throughout countless ages, these colossal beasts have existed while continually adapting, developing, and refining carnivore skills unapproached in the animal kingdom.

In **JAWS**, Hooper's adversary was a terrifying, man-eating shark, weighing maybe four tons. Try to imagine a *shape changing, sixty ton, hundred-foot monstrosity* five times as long and fifteen times as heavy as the shark in **JAWS**. Like some runaway missile, this colossal creature explodes through its seven-mile-deep lair, brutally devouring all it encounters with row-after-row of foot-long teeth in its gigantic tunnel-of-a-mouth. Ruling the oceans, its savage instincts and killing tactics have been honed to perfection over 10,000 generations. Today's world has been spared confrontation with this epitome of all creatures—*until now!*

More than a shark, *Megalodon* is a specter of unreality; a rare, but dreadfully real aquatic monstrosity unequaled as a hunting, killing, and eating machine. Mankind's intrusion into its watery domain is unleashing devastation of unfathomed proportion. Proving it's real is the challenge facing a marine biologist, a physician and a Hall of Fame baseball player. Together, they seek to show the world this gigantic beast exists. Join with them on their *QUEST FOR MEGALODON.*

TABLE OF CONTENTS

DEDICATION

To Willy and Sandy, the lifelong fishing buddies who inspired Doc Smitty and Red in this book.

To Pete Billac, a new friend whose inspiration and guidance saved this tale from the trash can. His participation has been instrumental in my creation of what you are about to enjoy.

To my wife, Lois, whose faith and support have kept me going the past five years.

And to Carcharodon Megalodon, the monster shark that I know is still roaming and ruling the uncontested depths of the world's oceans.

Chapter One

IT BEGINS

THAT MORNING - SEPTEMBER 1964

"Come on skipper, can't we fish a little longer? Just till the sun's up," the lanky middle-aged man pleaded, frustration creeping into his tired request. Without realizing it, he deftly pushed the wire-rimmed glasses back in place. "A few more minutes can't hurt anything."

"Okay Joe," Captain Fishy Hawkins acceded, "but we pick 'em up at seven sharp. Been a long night and I got family coming for dinner at noon."

The twenty-seven-foot MONEY HOLE rocked gently on a placid, predawn sea as two exhausted men shuffled around her cockpit. Harold *Fishy* Hawkins, her captain, had been running charter boats for going on thirty years, the last fifteen out of Lauderdale. Steel blue eyes and a sunburned, wrinkled face concealed the older man's lack of faith in the newfangled sonic device his client was hanging over the side. It was some sort of *Hi-Tech* fish teaser.

"Charley would probably love the shit out of this gadget," the skipper muttered, thinking about his brother-in-law, Charles McMasters, who had a PhD in Marine Biology and was teaching at the University of Miami just down the coast. Concluding his thought, "Me, I don't give a gnat's ass for these Buck Rogers' contraptions. Zero results too!"

"Gonna drop the frequency a little for the last minute skipper," Joe Mason advised while glancing to the east. "Man, take a gander at that sunrise. Talk about gorgeous." Joe's fingers caressed twin segmented dials on a black box strapped to the boat's center post, adjusting them slightly. "Can't understand why we haven't gotten any action? Sure thought this frequency would drum up at least a shark or two."

Simultaneously their attention was drawn shoreward by the increasing drone of an approaching outboard. Mason commented, "Looks like someone's getting an early start. Must be dolphin fishing?"

"Yeah, Joe," Hawkins agreed. "Think that's Doc Smith's boat from the shape of her hull. Probably that boy of his and some of his buddies. Bunch of fishing nuts."

"Makes you feel immortal, don't it?" Joe philosophized, looking back at the magnificent sunrise. "God, it's great to be alive. Hell Fishy, it just don't get no better'n this."

"The salty skipper flashed a quick smile, nodded his agreement, and added, "Only if that crazy fish caller of yours will attract something decent in the next few minutes."

Not far below, a massive shape rose effortlessly through the dark water. The absence of an air bladder condemned the monstrous creature to perpetual motion. As the sea parted, ultra-sensitive nerves and timeless muscles rippled beneath a leprous skin and instinctively remolded its hideous appearance. Its prehistoric brutality was being sucked unerringly to the source of an infuriating sound that was now close . . . very close. As the frequency increased, the pulsations became intolerable. Streamlining itself, the malignant shape shot upward. An ageless sensory system formed accurate images of its prey long before sight came into play. As the depths fell away beneath its accelerating bulk, exceptionally keen vision took over. In dawn's early light, Megalodon saw the slender object floating above. *Destroy!!!* Instinct demanded it.

"Fishy, what the hell is that . . .?" Joe screamed in an unfinished question. The monster's grotesque feelers, radiating from its yawning chasm filled with row-upon-row of wicked ivory triangles, hovered over them but an instant as MONEY HOLE was flung clear out of the water. The white veil of death then plunged downward with the boat and her occupants. Nine-inch teeth split Joe's head like a meat cleaver as its ivory companions crudely sliced him in half from nose to hip. Hawkins' legs and his right arm were severed with the initial bite and vanished down a waiting gullet while incomprehensible jaws ripped his head and left shoulder apart as they slammed shut again and again. Flesh and bone, along with fiberglass, aluminum, and wood disintegrated under a ferocious attack until nothing remained. That aggravating sound was silenced. The violent commotion on the surface ended in seconds with the sea quickly covering her secrets. The water was deceptively sedate, marred only by a single floating cushion. MONEY HOLE and two men vanished in less than an eye-blink.

* * *

A half-mile to the west, the red and white outboard raced eastward over the shimmering surface. Countless twinkling stars rapidly faded to oblivion as dawn cast a multi-hued portrait across the lightening sky. Brilliant red arrows knifed upward as three teenage friends headed seaward on one last fishing fling. Each would start college the following day.

"God, look at that!" Scott Thompson exclaimed in awe from the controls of MORE TROUBLE. "You two dick-heads are missin' one helluva matinee." Dozing behind him on twin-padded bench seats were his two best friends, Red Dickson and Peter Smith. Before him the infant sun was peeking over the earth's edge, its red glow blossoming in the east and spreading rapidly across the cloudless sky.

"Looks like someone got out before us," Scott growled in frustration. "Sure thought we'd be first on the weed-line today." In spite of the sun's blinding glow, Scott could see a solitary boat, perhaps a thousand yards ahead, although the morning glare created uncertainty.

As the crimson ball crept over the horizon with expanding brilliance, it divided like an amoeba, splitting and then combining with its own reflection to form an elongating ellipse. Twin balls of fire materialized and quickly moved apart, their contacting surfaces becoming pointed nipples that briefly touched. A dazzling hourglass lay ahead of the speeding boat for a few seconds before the real sun and its reflection slowly parted. A rim of fire, cascading to the north and south an instant before, dulled to magnificent daylight as the sun's daily journey across the heavens commenced. In the center of this monument to beauty, the ocean erupted around an indistinct vessel as a gargantuan creature destroyed the horizon.

"Holy shit guys! Wake up!" Scott screamed. "A giant whale! He ate the boat! *The fuckin' boat's gone!*"

Scott raved in isolation for an instant until his unbridled excitement finally penetrated Red's sleep. His green eyes flicking, Red mumbled, "What'd ya say Scott? Why all the noise?"

Still more asleep than awake, Red slowly propped himself up on his elbows and peered through sleep-encrusted eye-slits toward where Thompson's finger was pointing. "You see something?" he drawled. "Where? I don't see anything."

"Too late!" Scott barked. "Whatever it was is gone! Had to be a whale! The boat . . . it was there one minute and now, it's gone!"

The commotion finally aroused Peter. "What's your problem, Thompson?" he questioned angrily. "Seeing things again, huh?" Straining to reach an upright position, Peter hastily rubbed partially opened eyes with the backs of both hands before probing the pockets of a maroon windbreaker for his glasses. Locating the wire framed bifocals, he shoved them into place while asking, "What kind of shit you think you're seeing now?"

Scott Thompson was silent, his blank, unseeing eyes riveted ahead. In spite of the chilly wind whipping around him from the speeding boat, beads of perspiration were covering his brow. His jaw was hanging slack and his upper lip quivered noticeably. He did see something! Wide awake now, Red and Peter saw the terror and shock in their friend's eyes.

"What'd you see Scott?" They asked in unison, but Scott didn't answer.

Standing up and moving next to his unresponsive friend, Red nudged Scott with his right shoulder and said, "Com'on man, what the hell'd you wake us for? Why all the noise? What'd you think you saw?" Jokingly, he added, "Better be something good, asshole."

"Yeah, don't tell me you got us up for nothing," Peter commented, slipping up on Scott's other side. With his left hand gripping the aluminum support bar on the steering console and his right holding his eyeglasses in place against the whistling wind, Peter demanded, "What the hell is it Scott?"

"Damn it guys," Thompson stammered, "there was some kind of whale or monster . . . and a boat. Yeah, a boat was there. One minute I can see its lights, then it's gone, just vanished. Eaten by whatever it was. Something big as a submarine, tore up the surface for a split-second and took the boat under.

Looking past Scott's strained face, Red glanced at Peter. "A sea monster, huh? Ate a boat, huh?" Red chuckled. "Come on Scott, what's goin' on? You turning *druggie* on us?" Then a huge grin split the redhead's face. Peter was also chuckling. Paying no attention to either, Scott stared at the open ocean while trying to figure out what he *thought* he saw.

With his two friends, now slapping their legs and laughing uncontrollably, the MORE TROUBLE continued to race seaward. Finally, Scott barked angrily, "Laugh away you two creeps. I know what I saw."

Shaking his head, they reached the spot where he *thought* he'd seen the boat disappear. Jerking back on both throttles, Scott spun the steering wheel to the right. The MORE TROUBLE's forward motion halted abruptly on the slick surface. Babbling more to convince himself than his friends that he'd seen something, he mumbled, "It just ate the damn boat. I saw it! *I know I saw it!* Didn't I?"

"Come on Scott," Peter interrupted, "stop this crap. There's nothing here. The ocean's clean."

Red stopped laughing and was scanning the vacant horizon. "You're right Peter," he added. "Scott's gone weirdo on us. Gotta be on drugs, seeing things that ain't there." Watching the area where Scott was pointing moments earlier Red's intense green eyes suddenly lit up and he yelled excitedly, "Look out Scott! There! *There!* It's Godzilla. Christ man, he's got a fuckin' boat in his mouth. And he's eatin' it!" Gut-wrenching laughter consumed Red and he doubled over in pain, grabbing his stomach with both hands as tears streamed down both cheeks. "Fuckin' *Godzilla!* You see it, don't ya Scott?" Peter was also roaring with laughter as he fell off his boat seat. Scott Thompson didn't think it was so funny.

Then a choking, laughing Red, his face shining and tears filling his eyes, pushed himself up and pointed at the open sea. "Oops! He's gone again. Don't see him now? You see him Peter? Maybe *Scott* still sees him. How 'bout it Scott?" He stifled his laughter momentarily and added, "Then you really are nuts, 'cause he's headed back to Japan to stomp a few buildings."

Red was speechless as laughter again engulfed him. Then Peter, attempting to stand up, slipped and fell against the outboard's cowling before sliding back to the deck. The pair's laughter and ridicule continued unabated for a couple more minutes as Peter, unable to get up, just stomped his feet and banged his fists against the deck. When one would almost stop, he'd hear the other and burst out laughing again. Scott, more than a little bit pissed by this time and feeling very foolish, sat somber-faced, still looking at the open water.

Struggling to his feet, Red wiped his eyes with his shirt sleeve and looked over at Scott who was staring in the general direction of the *mystical vanishing boat.* Taking the wheel from Scott, he concentrated on the same area. His now-lucid eyes with their 20/10 vision searched the unrippled surface for anything as the boat made a wide circle. Seeing nothing, he concluded, "Nothin' here Scott. Let's just forget it, get our asses in gear and go catch some fish."

"Yeah, come on Scott, who ya kidding?" Peter pleaded. "I don't see anything either." He too was staring at where Scott's attention was focused. "There ain't nothing there."

Scott Thompson looked at the familiar face and auburn locks of his next-to-best friend. "Jesus Red, something horrible just happened. My eyes saw something big as a house eat a boat, but my brain tells me it couldn't have happened. But I *saw* it, Red. Damn it. I saw it. Shit, I don't know what to believe." Scott reached in front of Red and spun the wheel to starboard. Gunning both engines, he made one last sweep toward where he *thought* he'd seen a monster eat a boat.

"Right about here," Scott guessed as he throttled back both powerful Johnson 75's. Looking to his left, then his right, then left again, he scanned the ocean like a madman, searching and praying for any evidence to prove what he *knows* he saw. But there was nothing to see.

The MORE TROUBLE idled quietly on an empty sea that sparkled and quivered in the summer morning light. Two hundred feet below, an unimaginably large creature milled about, its sensory system coming down from full-alert. The puttering sounds from above no longer concerned it. Instinctively, it regurgitated portions of the hard-skinned prey it had just consumed. Most of the rejected items sank into the limitless depths. A single, lacerated boat cushion rose toward the surface.

Three pairs of eyes searched the placid water. "Over there, what's that? No kidding." Red blurted excitedly, hitting Scott's left cheek with his extending hand. "In the water over there!"

"There it is!" Scott stammered in relief. "I told you shit heads I saw something!" Quickly slipping the port engine in gear, he spun the boat's bow once again to starboard. Thirty feet away was a small, yellowish object, bobbing erratically. Almost invisible beneath it in the early morning glare was a gigantic, brownish mass, an indistinguishable shape that was rising as it undulated grotesquely.

"*Jesus Kee-rist! It's the monster,*" Scott yelled excitedly.

"You *are* on drugs," Peter laughed. "It's a weed-line. Ain't nothin' but grass . . . and a boat cushion."

Then all thoughts of monsters vanished as Red spotted a large school of dolphin swimming beneath the tattered cushion and grass. This new occurrence was far more exciting than a torn boat cushion. "Christ man, look at the dolphin. Fuckin' dolphin everywhere!" Grab the rods man, grab the rods."

One hour later, the still-idling outboard was almost drowned out by screeching seagulls overhead. A lone frigate bird altered its seven-foot wing span, broke out of a tight circle several hundred feet above, and glided swiftly off to the south. They forgot everything as three rods bent and taunt lines sang under the strain of acrobatic dolphin. The boat circled a patch of sargassum weed that sheltered the school of blue-green fish.

Red had spotted the lacerated boat cushion seconds after it popped to the surface amongst the bead-like grass and floated against the eastern edge of the brown mass. But it became unimportant when the school of fish appeared other than to serve as a location buoy for their colorful quarry. The three boys could not see the cushion's underside stenciled with the letters O-N-E-Y H-O. A single triangular-shaped object embedded in the E was also invisible from the surface. With nine-inch sides, its ivory edges were serrated and it had a thickened top. The wake of their boat gently rocked the cushion and the gleaming object slipped out, oscillating slightly as it quickly sank.

"Shit, I hooked the damned cushion," Peter bitched. In a last ditch effort to catch one more fish from the depleted school, he somehow managed to drag a bait across the floating object. "Come on Scott," he badgered, "back down on it. Can't make no headway with this light outfit." And his fishing buddy kicked the port engine in reverse.

"Look at this," Red asked quizzically moments later as he eyed the string of letters. "Wonder what they stand for? And that's a helluva gash in the *E*." He stared at the bottom side of the cushion for a few seconds after extracting Peter's hook. Then he added, "Looks like a boat cushion with both ends chopped off. Wonder how long its been floating? No marine growth, but it sure is torn up. Think this was eaten by your *invisible monster* Thompson?" Red snickered before tossing the cushion over the side. "Maybe it'll bring someone else a little luck."

Hell, let's find another batch of fish. It is our last day, guys. We got college tomorrow!"

MORE TROUBLE, carrying three inseparable friends, glided eastward, leaving a single stained and lacerated boat cushion in its wake, the lone clue to an unknown atrocity.

U *OF M CLASSROOM - OCTOBER 1985:*

It was *Professor* Scott Thompson who sat casually on a corner of his desk at the University of Miami some twenty-one years later addressing nineteen graduate students. Halfway through that Fall semester in 1985, the young professor paused for effect, took a quick sip of water from a plastic cup on the desk next to him, and resumed his Ichthyology 621 lecture.

"The absence of tangible proof documenting bizarre creatures cannot disprove their existence. New species of life are discovered each year. Still, supposedly-knowledgeable scientists categorically deny certain creatures existence because no one has proven it. I reiterate. *The absence of scientific documentation does not prove non-existence!*"

Looking up from his <u>Statement of Position</u>, both hazel eyes were drawn to a hint of white between Karen Korinski's tanned thighs. More of the silky material became visible as the pretty twenty-year-old coed from nearby Boynton Beach repositioned her sculptured legs. Scott blinked hard and cleared his throat before continuing. "Dense jungles such as the Amazon may seclude countless undiscovered species and the world's oceans remain virtually inaccessible, unexplored by humankind. Water covers 75 percent of our planet. With depths of seven miles, we can only *guess* at the secrets awaiting discovery," Scott finished with a flourish of emotion to further convince his students, and himself, of what he already knew *must* exist somewhere in those depths.

Departing from his prepared text, his keen eyes beamed with excitement as he raised a question. "Who knows of an incident where an animal classified as extinct has been encountered?"

Hands shot up, but Chad Brown blurted out the answer. "The *coelacanth* Dr. Thompson. They caught one off Africa in the '30's, said it was extinct. All the experts had it dead and gone for about fifty million years."

"Very good, Chad," his professor replied, concealing his amazement at just how a kid from a Kansas wheat field ended in his marine biology class. Chad was probably his best student.

"A prime example is the *coelacanth*, a strange metallic-blue fish over six feet long which was classified as having been extinct for seventy million years. A living specimen was taken by fishermen in the Indian Ocean in 1938."

Noting the avid attention displayed by Miss Korinski, Scott carefully avoided looking at her legs while glancing around the class before continuing. "Another, even more recent case is *megamouth*, a species of shark similar to a whale shark that has no teeth and feeds on plankton by seining water through its oversized mouth. A fourteen footer was caught several years ago in the deep Pacific near Hawaii. Two other specimens have been encountered since.

"Other creatures *must* exist, incomprehensible in size and adaptability, which we have not met since our ability to penetrate their aqueous world is somewhat limited. But, as we continually transform our environment, some of these animals will be forced into our realm."

Casually placing his notes on the desk, Thompson concluded, "That's it for today gang. Monday we'll talk about my pet project. If you think the Great White's something, just wait till you meet *Carcharodon Megalodon*. See you Monday."

THE EQUATORIAL ATLANTIC OCEAN - TWO YEARS LATER

"Certain low-frequency sounds attract it," Dr. Scott Thompson mumbled to himself over the drone of twin diesel engines purring beneath the slowly moving vessel's deck. Scott momentarily stopped writing in his log. Carefully mouthing each word, his thoughts continued, *"Something so Promethean and unstoppable it defies imagination.* The black, felt-tip pen paused briefly. Focusing on the sheet before him, he gathered his thoughts. As always, words began to flow and speaking as he wrote, Scott started with the date.

"It's July 19th, 1987, our ninth day at sea. Impeccable weather has prevailed, clear skies and virtually no wind. Exceptions are the welcome afternoon thunder showers which moderate sweltering tropical temperatures on deck. Three-digit thermometer readings and paralyzing humidity are the norm. So far it's been more of a vacation than work, but things may be about to change. I can

sense increasing apprehension in my crew. The possibility of finding our quarry increases daily. I am uneasy over it, but I've managed to suppress my fears."

Again his mind wandered. "The University of Miami is sponsoring this expedition, but I am why we are here, trying to find something I think I saw as a boy, something most reputed experts believe is extinct."

Speaking out loud as he wrote; *"Proving its existence through study and research seemed all but impossible until Red told me about that necklace. His chance discovery provided conclusive evidence and gave me the ammunition I was lacking for Departmental support at Miami."*

Scott's attention returned to the pages before him. Black letters formed words, which marched relentlessly across each line, filling the page. *"My theories will be proven in the next few days. This crew will establish that Carcharodon Megalodon exists."*

The sound of Peter Smith and Red Dickson joking near the stern distracted him. Looking up, Scott scanned the glassy blue seascape around him, unable to tell exactly where water ended and sky began. Almost like an extension of himself, the pen moved.

"The means I use to attract this gigantic fish may also solve many unexplained maritime disasters. Confirming my beliefs may head off future catastrophes, possibly save hundreds of lives. But irrefutable proof is required."

Without hesitating, he continued, *"Our vessel seems to shrink daily and each minute tends to increase our vulnerability to this force of nature. Our quest is to find an animal of such staggering size and destructive capability that even our large, well-equipped boat may not withstand the attack. A twenty-five-year-old ghost haunts me, overwhelming probable reality with potential horror."*

Looking up, Scott glanced again at Red and Peter before scribbling a final afterthought. *"It's almost funny. I can sense Megalodon approaching at this very minute and we haven't even started using Doc's sound machine."* He put the cap on his pen, closed the log and rose to go join his friends.

1,000 MILES TO THE EAST

Even as Scott sensed the impending arrival of his quarry, a pair of monstrous shapes swim steadily through intense pressures and frigid waters. Effortlessly, powerful tails drive two huge shark-like creatures through eternal darkness in the limitless ocean depths. Copulation completed, the male's genital claspers relax, pointing astern. Species propagation has been assured and their finely tuned sensory systems spring to life. Soft barbels covering their heads firm to form multi-array antennas, probing the distant waters for telltale signals of prey. Their perennial search for food resumed.

Sixty feet from the male's tail is a prodigious conical head and knife-filled jaws. He is huge by any standard, but the female is half-again as long. Cells inside her womb are already dividing to form dozens of fetuses. As they develop, cannibalism will prevail and only two shall survive to be born alive in thirteen months. Instinct permitted these magnificent creatures to find each other in the vast open sea as nature temporarily camouflaged their aggression and allowed their brief joining.

Despite their differing sizes, each could easily kill or maim the other. Because of this, nature sends them on similar, but divergent paths. With the mating instinct satisfied, both enormous fish renew their search for food. The requirement to replenish energy expended during seventy-two hours without feeding is overwhelming.

The male's migration spans the North Atlantic Ocean but he currently prowls the equatorial waters east of Brazil. Every decade or so, he will depart from normal patterns and forage in other oceans; detours that help insure species' continuity.

Food dictating his schedule, his prey includes tuna, squid, and swordfish during an annual 20,000 mile trek. Nothing in the sea is safe from his preponderant appetite. At home in the impenetrable depths, the giant fish seldom approaches the surface and has never encountered humans. Routines unchanged from 10,000 preceding generations, his yearly travels are shorter than those demanded of relatives during previous ages and in other oceans. His instincts and capabilities are identical.

Momentarily, nature beckons from some remote spot of the boundless, mid-Atlantic Ocean. With faintness approaching nonexistence, the enticement reaches him, sucking at sixty million years of fine-tuned predation. Present for less that one stroke of his magnificent tail, stillness rapidly returns to the surrounding water. However, the gigantic fish's course alters slightly and his pace quickens. *Moments later, she senses it too!*

Chapter Two

JENNIFER'S JOY

SOUTHEAST AUSTRALIA - DECEMBER 1980

Thousands of lights from modern high-rises along the picturesque waterfront created a shimmering reflection on the placid water of Sydney Harbor. An inverted replica of that panorama was enhanced by the beautiful red-orange glow highlighting those tall buildings as a dying gasp of the brilliant red ball nestled beneath the western skyline. A dozen sportsfishermen raced westwardly into the spacious harbor, returning home after a long day on the calm ocean. In contrast, a lone craft departed port, bearing to the south-southeast as it avoided the incoming fleet.

A light evening breeze caressed the crew of JENNIFER'S JOY, bringing a mild, but distinct, chill with it. A single, dark-blue marlin pennant flapped gently at three-quarters mast from a vertical outrigger on the closest homeward-bound fishing boat. Alex Keller, an electrical engineer and the youngest of four passengers on the departing forty-six foot Bertram, waved enviously from his cushioned seat on the flying bridge, acknowledging that crew's success. Beside him, a graying Captain Sharpney, whose aqua-blue eyes provided the only change of color in a deeply tanned and wrinkled face, skillfully guided his craft over the oncoming wake. Without slowing, he readjusted his course to 120 degrees.

In the cockpit below, John Lawtoon, his mate and brother-in-law, prepared a large squid bait. Three remaining passengers were lounging casually in the cozy salon. Harvey MacElroy and Ed Friar, stock brokers from Perth, were carefully sipping hot coffee from wide-based mugs. Otis MacElroy, Harvey's older brother and a twenty-year veteran of the Australian Navy, was already enjoying his first toddy of the young evening.

JENNIFER'S JOY, en route to what her crew hoped would be a fruitful night of swordfishing off the southeastern coast of Australia, felt large and stable to those on board. The experienced crew was making that run for at least the hundredth time.

They would generally catch a swordfish about every third trip with most outings providing action from tuna, sharks, or the occasional marlin. Broadbill swordfish however, was the primary quest. This was the first night swordfishing trip for both Alex and Ed. The MacElroy's were old hands, generally making two or three excursions each season. But tonight's run would be unlike any the six men aboard could ever have imagined.

A two-hour run at approximately twenty-five knots placed the sportsfisherman on the northern edge of an immense submerged mountain peak. Forces of creation had driven this mass up from a mile of water to within 500 feet of the surface. Upwelling, due to the vast underwater structure, steered nutrients to the warmer surface waters. The vital food chain was magnified by this large concentration of its tiniest link. Each of the other elements was generally present in above-normal quantities, including that lengthy chain's pinnacle, the magnificent gamefish.

Great shoals of baitfish flashed on the small CRT screen of the sensitive fathometer. The skipper expertly positioned his vessel for her several-hour drift to the south. She would ride the slow current which overpowered an opposing light breeze. Finally satisfied, Sharpney killed the engines and told his mate, "Okay Johnny, we're on top of 'er. Let's get the bait's wet."

"Ready to go Captain," Johnny replied from the neat cockpit. "Thirty more seconds and we'll be fishing." Hurrying, he spilled some fishy water from his bait bucket on the glistening deck. "Shit, Jenny wouldn't like that" he cursed under his breath and reached for a short-handled mop kept onboard for such situations. "Got to keep her spotless or me-lady'll give me a lit'l hell," and the mop head went into action.

John was referring to Jennifer Sharpney Lawtoon, his wife of nine years and the Captain's sister. Eighteen years younger than her brother, Jenny was the old man's pride and joy. His boat, JENNIFER'S JOY, was named after her. "That's got it," the mate stated and began to whistle *Waltzing Matilda* as he focused on the last bait.

Above Lawtoon on the flying bridge, the Captain's trained ears listened intently to the sudden quiet, broken only by the gentle hum of a small diesel-driven generator powering vital electrical fixtures on the drifting boat. "Well, at least that damned thing's going" the tanned man muttered to himself, thankful the generator was running at all. "Bitch has really been misbehaving the last few weeks. Hope she'll get us through the night." Even his keen hearing didn't notice an almost indistinguishable throb, unknowingly emitting an abnormal, low-frequency vibration. His ears did pick up the subtle splashes of the three baits going over the side.

"All done," Lawtoon commented and three two-foot-long, pinkish-colored squid, carefully sewn around forged steel hooks attached to 300 pound test monofilament leaders, entered the water. Each rig was completed with a chemical glowstick that John activated by flexing its stiff plastic sheath at the top of the leader, twenty feet from the bait. These lights attracted the prized swordfish which prowled the black depths. Three lines were set at different depths, suspended beneath air-filled balloons and intended to locate the thermocline where the fish should be feeding.

"We're all set Captain," he stated confidently. "I got number one at 300 feet, number two at 150, and my top one at less than fifty feet." Fifteen minutes of fiddling with the bait and lines left Lawtoon and Captain Sharpney satisfied.

"Okay mate," Sharpney concurred. "All we can do now is wait. Got lots of activity on my screen."

Then, four anxious anglers, pretending to be calm, settled into preselected seats in anticipation of that first blistering strike. For a long time nothing happened.

The bait went out at 21:00 hours. Almost inaudibly, the first balloon finally popped at 01:45. The mate stirred as a slow, methodical click sounded from the golden Fin Nor reel connected to the deepest bait. All onboard the boat sprang to life as the night's first fish screamed off line.

* * *

Weariness showed on each man's face and the false glow of the predawn hour was a prelude to impending daylight. Sunrise, when the bait would be retrieved for the final time, was less than forty-five minutes away. A highlight of burnt orange fringed the eastern horizon, heralding a beautiful day.

Three good size fish had been boated in less than three hours. A barrel-shaped tuna, with its polished blue body and streaming yellow fins succumbed to Friar thirty minutes after that first strike. Then the baseball-sized eye of the night's only swordfish, preceded by its imposing four foot rapier, glowed vividly as it was led into the spotlight. A single swift stroke with the gaff, followed by a brief commotion alongside the fiberglass boat, and 250 pounds of sought-after prize was safely aboard with Harvey MacElrcy gloating over it. One hour later, a second tuna, longer but considerably leaner than the first, was winched from the deep by Otis MacElroy.

Since then, nothing. Absolute inactivity. JENNIFER'S JOY drifted in quiet solitude through the stillness before dawn. Then, for the fourth time that morning, a clicker sounded. The youngest fisherman sprang to his feet. He grabbed the heavy fiberglass rod and its Penn International 80 Wide reel just as the line began to melt away.

* * *

Three days earlier, abnormal sensations were experienced that demanded the immense fish emerge from its sanctuary of great depth. Never before, as it continually traversed the world's seas, had it accompanied smaller members of a related species. Now, the powerful tail stroked slowly as the giant fish followed its two smaller companions steadily up the sloping undersea mountain. Extraordinary senses drove it toward an irritating low-frequency sound from somewhere far above.

Confused with whales because of its size, this was really a cartilaginous fish whose ancestors survived unaltered for tens of millions of years. At most, one in ten thousand of these giants was sometimes afflicted with an impairment producing uncharacteristic behavior after decades of normalcy. Just such a case, this magnificent male effortlessly carried his fifty-ton weight into the arena of his only potential enemy, those shallow, inshore waters sometimes frequented by the species Homo sapiens.

The irritating acoustical signal intensified, making it easier for the fierce predator to track, even in his disturbed state. Suddenly, the hunting rhythm of the two smaller sharks he was shadowing from afar became erratic. Instinctively, he closed on them with swift strokes of his sickle-like tail. Forward motion amplified the debilitating sound, irrationalizing his behavior even more.

Exceedingly keen eyesight came into play in the limited light of the shallower depth. Rising swiftly, he saw an object on the calm surface which was three times the size of the sharks he followed. The smaller fish's behavior changed dramatically, fleeing from the larger shadow before making a sweeping turn back toward it. The beat of its tail signaled distress and the faint aroma of death tainted the water behind it. Millions of years of inbred hunting instinct took control. Its huge mouth opened and eyes rolled back to protect the precious vision ports as his attention shifted to a frantically struggling object that entered his watery domain just behind the surface shadow. Without slowing, he altered his course and veered abruptly toward the secondary victim.

* * *

Alex Keller sprang to his feet yelling, "*I got it!*" Grabbing the rod, he could see line being ripped off the reel at an alarming rate. Unfamiliar with the gear, he jammed the anodized aluminum striking-lever past the *stop* button locking the reel. As the sole of his left sneaker landed on the slime-coated decking, Keller lost his balance and tumbled forward. Instinctively, his hand tightened on a quivering fiberglass shaft he followed over JENNIFER'S JOY's transom into the dark, foreboding water, screaming as he went.

Relaxing his grip in mid-air, Alex's flailing left hand tangled in the Dacron line streaming off the expensive reel. Slackening for less than a heartbeat, the unforgiving line formed a half-hitch that flipped around Alex's left index and middle fingers. An instant later, both were severed at the second knuckle as the helpless man was dragged under. Cold water closing above him, he gulped for air and got nothing but burning saltwater. Alex Keller realized he was drowning. Releasing the rod, he kicked upward with all his strength. As choking water clogged his nose and stung his eyes, Alex's head broke the surface.

Mate John Lawtoon, Ed Friar, and Captain Sharpney, all saw this abbreviated scenario. The grizzled captain's initial concern for $1,500 worth of tackle disappearing over the side with some blithering idiot changed rapidly to worry when Alex vanished beneath the black water. All sighed with relief when Alex surfaced and began dog-paddling for the lighted stern of the sportsfisherman.

Lawtoon saw it first and spat out. "Christ, what in God's name is *that*?" Four other eyes focused in disbelief on what was appearing ten feet behind the petrified Alex.

A gigantic shadow materialized beneath the splashing swimmer, lifted him into the air, and slammed him savagely against the boat's stern. Alex's unprotected head exploded against the unyielding fiberglass. Dark crimson blood was plastered over the once-clean stern, staining the closing swirl of angry water where a huge snout and gleaming teeth had just been. JENNIFER'S JOY lurched violently. The distinct snapping of fiberglass-layered wooden supports and struts below deck rang through the vessel. Alex Keller disappeared without making another sound. Then quiet, but not peace, returned.

Captain Sharpney spun around, firing both engines that sprang to life. Simultaneously, the diesel generator sputtered and died. Without hesitating, he shoved the twin black-knobbed silver handles on the gear shift levers forward, kicking both engines into gear. In the next motion, two other silver levers topped by small red knobs were jammed full ahead, demanding maximum power of both engines.

JENNIFER'S JOY once comfortable size quickly shrank to something anemically small and inadequate. The creature that pulverized a young man against the hull was twice her size. Worse yet, the boat's lights and the glow of dawn outlined a towering dorsal fin remorselessly tracking them.

The vessel fled on her westerly course at almost thirty knots as the sun rose majestically behind her. The giant fish followed. No one aboard noticed the gorgeous sunrise. All they saw were flashes of that ominous fin, frequently breaking the calm surface of white foam in their wake, pacing their craft.

* * *

Intent on their pursuer, those aboard JENNIFER'S JOY didn't see the small outboard they passed. Its yellow hull bobbed gently on the calm water a quarter-mile to the north as the escaping vessel zipped by to the south. A single white light glowed dimly from a tarnished aluminum standard near the boat's stern. In the early morning light, the faded red flag with its white diagonal stripe hanging limply below the frosted plastic housing of the twelve-volt DC light bulb was almost invisible.

Slumbering unconcernedly across the only seat in the tiny boat was Mary Hastings. The quiet tunes from a transistor radio muted the sound of the large sportsfisherman racing past. Seventy-five feet below, her husband Paul and fourteen-year-old son, Paul Jr., were ending the boy's second night-dive.

The mammoth creature's interest in the fleeing shadow that was JENNIFER'S JOY gradually subsided as the trail of human scent being washed from the boat's stern through the cockpits's rear scuttles dissipated during the chase. As the final traces vanished, the hypersensitive creature detected vibrations of a nearby, struggling fish accompanied by other life forms in the water. Altering direction, it glided gracefully downward, drawn by nature's splendid instincts.

"Damn, almost time to call it quits," Paul Hastings complained around the Scuba Pro mouthpiece as he illuminated his watch with the underwater flashlight. "Where's little Paul?" he added, hating for the peaceful dive to end with a single, partially-filled bag of abalone. "Couple more minutes," he argued, looking around for his son's light.

"God, look at that beauty!" he thought, spotting the large ocean perch halfway between him and his son's beckoning light, clearly visible in the dark, clear water. "Got time to get me a day-saver," Hastings muttered. "Yes sir, gonna get me a day-saver." Carefully lining up his weapon, he squeezed the trigger releasing a four-foot spear from the compressed-gas-driven gun. Two seconds later, twenty pounds of delectable meat was being wrestled toward him as the reddish-brown fish struggled to escape. Looking past the fish, his son's light was still illuminating exquisite reef colors fifty feet away. That was the last thing Mary Hastings' scuba-diving husband ever saw.

Locked in on the struggling fish, the giant shark swooped by, engulfing fish and man. A few oversized teeth snapped off and fell from the massive jaws when they struck the hard metal tank as the huge fish bit down. The imposing terror-of-the-sea swept past the dead-man's son and, circling swiftly, then bore down on the small creature with the light.

Paul Jr. was frightened. His father's comforting light had disappeared. Fear rose, choking his young throat. Desperately scanning the dark water with his inconsequential beam of yellow light, he never saw the whale-sized shark approaching from behind. Its huge jaws were agape like a living vacuum cleaner, sucking the lad in. The confines of its mouth were exposed briefly in the dull yellow glow of the dying boy's light. Bits and pieces of both human and fish-remains were lodged within, including a flaccid torso and head, face mask hanging uselessly around the neck, both eyes empty and lifeless. Then Paul Hastings, Jr. was sucked down the life-ending gullet.

Like an airplane changing the attitude of its flaps to climb, the prehistoric shark flexed its large pectoral fins and angled for the surface. A quick check of the small shadow floating above stirred no interest and it turned toward the open sea. Brushing against an almost invisible nylon anchor-rope, which momentarily hung on its left pectoral fin, the giant fish noticed a momentary restriction to its movement. The minute constraint lasted but a second or two, and the enormous denizen methodically headed northeastward, three feet of its remarkable dorsal fin neatly knifing the surface briefly before it sounded. Slipping silently into the depths, *Megalodon* vanished.

"What was that?" Mary Hastings asked the lessening darkness around her. The yellow-hulled boat lurched unexpectedly. Mary's plastic-cased resistor radio clattered to the deck as she was jerked from semi-comatose to wide-awake. "Something happen?" she wondered, shivering as a chilling sensation of dread sucked at her gut, a response to unexplainable intuition developed over many years of marriage and motherhood? The uncomfortable feeling quickly passed. Glancing around, she saw nothing, although the early morning light might have betrayed an ominous triangular object slicing swiftly through the ocean surface off the starboard bow. Her rapid scan overlooked it, registering nothing. Behind her small boat, and somewhat closer to shore, she noticed a sleek sportsfisherman heading inbound toward the lights of Sydney Harbor.

"Must have been that boat's wake?" she thought, punching the tiny button which lighted her Seiko digital wrist watch. "Good, it's almost time for their dive to be over," she realized. "They should be up in a couple of minutes." Picking up the radio from where it lay, belching out meaningless static on the fiberglass deck of the small cockpit behind her, Mary Hastings adroitly retuned it to her favorite station. Listening to the familiar drawl of a Willy Nelson ballad, she reclined against the ragged boat cushion on the fading fiberglass seat and waited for her men to return.

* * *

Captain Sharpney expertly maneuvered JENNIFER'S JOY into a vacant slot at the Exxon Australia gas dock. She was promptly boarded by a young Coast Guard Ensign and two Sydney policemen, one in uniform, the other a plain clothes detective. When the shark finally gave up its chase and disappeared, Sharpney had regained sufficient sense to radio in a report of the incident to the authorities. The only physical evidence that anything out of the ordinary happened was several cracked struts in the hull and superficial damage to the transom where the crisp urethane paint job was scratched and marred.

"Hey, what the hell is this?" the uniformed officer asked. "Can I borrow your pocket knife for a minute inspector."

Without a word, the plain clothes detective opened his knife and handed it to the young police officer leaning over the transom. "Well, well, what've we got here? You ain't gonna believe this, Walt," the uniformed officer snickered, addressing the detective. "You just ain't gonna believe it."

Pulling himself to a sitting position on the boat's transom, the two-year-veteran of Sidney's police force handed Detective Walter Taylor a pair of human teeth and stated, "These were stuck in the letter 'R.' Christ man, it took one helluva whack to drive 'em into that fiberglass-coated wood like that. Yes sir, one helluva whack."

In spite of the two teeth, little credibility was given to the *shark chase* story by investigators until later that day. A distraught woman, Mary Hastings, reported her husband and son missing during a predawn diving trip. The dive took place in the same area where the supposed giant shark was last seen.

During the next ten days, five more possible shark attacks occurred near Sydney Harbor. No verifiable eyewitnesses came forward. Local shark attacks had been experienced before, but they never continued over such an extended period or were confined to such a localized area. In desperation, a shark bounty was initiated and a *shark expert* summoned to help. It took him five days to get to Sidney. During that time, there were three more attacks.

Chapter Three

FRIENDS FOREVER

"My name's Peter Smith," the thirteen year-old-boy interrupted. "That's my boat we caught it in!" he added, pointing toward the nearby dock. "The MORE TROUBLE, that's her over there."

The female reporter from the Fort Lauderdale Daily News wasn't quite ready for the avalanche of information descending upon her. Addressing all three of the boys in front of her while considering the best angle for her pictures, she asked, "But which one of you boys caught the shark?"

"We all did, sort of," Red Dickson replied. "Mostly Scott there, he saw it first and it ate his stingray. But I shot it."

"Yeah, we all caught it. Used a handline and big hook on a chain." Scott Thompson attempted to clarify the situation. "I saw it, threw the bait, a twenty-pound stingray, to it, and hooked it. After that, it just pulled the boat around for about an hour until Red shot it 4 or 5 times with his .12 gauge shotgun. Then we tail-roped it and dragged it here. Yeah, I guess you can say we all caught it."

"Hey Thompson, 856 pounds! What a shark!" Peter had gone over to watch them weigh in the giant hammerhead while Red and Scott continued relating their story to the reporter. "Guy over here says it's probably the biggest fish ever weighed at Bahia Mar! Maybe in the whole damn county!"

"Hot damn!" Red exclaimed, "told you guys it'd go over 700! What a shark!"

"Can you boys get together by the shark so I can get a shot of the three of you with the fish?" The reporter needed a picture to go along with her story in case the local news editor decided to run it. She felt they would, maybe even the Sunday edition if she submitted it in time. "That's it boys, I want to get a picture of your faces and that thing's funny head."

Three teenage boys struggled to get in the most prominent position and pose for their photo. It had been quite a day, quite a day indeed.

The story took up a full column and included two pictures in the following day's Sunday edition.

* * *

Peter Smith was born in Fort Lauderdale the year before Scott Thompson.   The two boys first met in a third grade class at Croissant Park Elementary School. Young Smith was not athletically inclined like Scott, but leaned more toward music, learning to play several instruments. Despite obvious differences, the boys really hit it off and inseparable pals were born.

In the mid-fifties, southeast Fort Lauderdale was largely undeveloped. The two boys usually ended up on some muddy canal bank, hunting crabs or catching a myriad of species of small fish frequenting the still-clear waterways.   Many nights were spent together camping out in a tent in one or the other's back yard, meticulously planning the next day's crusade.

When sixth grade rolled around, both of their Dads purchased small boats and the two families began taking joint vacations to the Florida keys. Typically, their boats were trailered to Marathon or Islamorada where they would troll for grouper and bottom-fish for snapper. Life-long friendships developed.

Scott Thompson and his older brother, Bobby, became avid scuba divers. While Peter didn't take up the sport, he obediently ran the boat while the Thompson boys scoured the shallow waters of the keys. Plucking lobster after lobster, they would toss the culinary prizes into the boat for its driver to corral. The Smith and Thompson families shared many a good time.

During junior high school, other interests developed which temporarily minimized their time together. Scott participated in school sports, while Peter's musical inclinations found him concentrating on the saxophone. They would still occasionally sleep over at one another's house, typically before an early morning fishing trip. By then, both families were living on island developments with boats docked at their back doors.

Entering ninth grade at Rogers Junior High, Peter became more serious, developing a sudden interest in money. He took on a paper route and a variety of other menial odd jobs. On the cerebral side, he was interested in how living things worked. Much of his hard-earned money went to magazines and books on biology. He read and reread them until the pages fell out, carefully marking selected topics with colored tabs.

Whenever possible, Peter would use one of his revered books or magazines as a blueprint while he carefully dissected some recent catch or kill.   Without a doubt, if all of his courses had been biological, he would have made straight A's.

* * *

During the summer between seventh and eight grade, Red Dickson's family arrived in Fort Lauderdale.   They moved into a home directly across the canal from Scott. By that time, both the Thompsons and the Smiths had upgraded to larger boats. Scott's family was a wide beamed, very seaworthy sixteen footer, the 5 TEES.   The Smiths ran an eighteen-foot tri-hull called MORE TROUBLE. Fishing trips became *big game* efforts. Dolphin, wahoo, even an occasional sailfish were their bluewater trophies, exciting fish to catch . . . until their first big shark.

Three of Scott's friends went fishing in Port Everglades Inlet at Lauderdale one night. They came back with a tale about an epic shark battle.   The huge shark got away, but, according to the disappointed fishermen, "was at least fifteen feet and a thousand pounds."

The following Friday night, in late August 1959, Peter, Scott, and the recently arrived Red, tied the 5 TEES to a cage marker on the inlet's north side.

"That's about far enough," Scott stated.   "Make sure the clicker's on." Checking the drag, he flipped the silver lever which put the 6/0 reel in freespool. "Both rods set? Hang on to your hats guys, we're shark fishing."

With darkness descending and the tide falling, two lines baited with bloody bonito fillets slipped beneath the blackening water. Three first-time shark fishermen settled down to wait, brimming with anticipation. That first half-hour flew by, a reel-melting strike only moments away. Then time began to drag.

"Shit man," Peter bitched. "Skeeter's startin' to come out." He splattered one of the fat insects that was feeding on his left leg. "Damn, must have sucked a pint of my blood," he estimated, observing the nickel-sized spot of red on a untanned leg. "Where's all the sharks, Thompson?"

"Give it time mosquito-bait. We just got started," Scott replied, adding, "The night's still young." But nothing happened, and three active young minds wandered in different directions before giving in to sleep.

The quite night was shattered by the screaming clicker on the starboard reel. *"Strike! We got a strike!"* Scott shouted as he awoke. His fishing reflexes were superior to his friends and he grabbed the rod before the others even moved.

"He's taking a lot of line Scott," Red said from beside him. "Should you go ahead and hit him?"

"Yeah, if he hasn't swallowed it by now, he ain't gonna," Scott agreed. The line had been disappearing off the reel at an alarming rate for almost ten seconds. Flipping the silver-lever on the black-faced Penn 6/0 reel forward, he locked it in gear, and reared back on the rod.

The tremendous pull he experienced was unbelievable. "Got him! Hot damn, look at him go!" Scott yelled excitedly as the white fiberglass rod bent in a pronounced "U" and eighty-pound Dacron line vanished into dark inlet waters. The fish was large and powerful and it took Scott the better part of an hour to wrestle it to the boat.

"How many jumps, Scott?" Red questioned. "I make it about twenty-five." Jumping acrobatically over twenty times, the pale moonlight reflected from its glistening sides and splashes of white water interrupted the calm inlet's monotonous blackness each time it crashed back into the sea.

"Least that many Red!" Scott yelled in response. "But I think it's a tarpon! Must be! Jumpin' too much for a shark!"

"Yeah man, sharks don't jump like *that*," Red stated with excitement. Without turning around, he asked their other companion, "How 'bout it Peter? You get a good look at it yet?"

Well into the battle, the three boys were sure it was a big tarpon. The large fish's effort was valiant, but after fifty back-breaking minutes on Scott's part, the swivel broke the water alongside the 5 TEES. With Peter between them holding the spotlight, a silvery shape emerged from the depths.

"It's a tarpon, has to be. Sharks don't jump like that." Looking up at the guy with the rod, Red made that final profound statement as he reached over the side for the leader.

The indistinct form materialized quickly as a glimmering aberration congealed into a well-defined shape. Exploding through the surface, a gaping mouth, filled with wickedly pointed and inwardly curved teeth, appeared two feet below Red's grinning face as his head turned back toward the rapidly tiring fish and he grabbed the heavy wire. All Red saw was teeth as the jaws snapped shut mere inches from his reaching fingers.

"Jesus Christ!" Red screeched, lurching backwards and

banging into Scott before landing on his butt. One startled young redneck's slide across the cockpit floor halted abruptly against the far side of the hull. *"It . . . it's a fuckin' shark! Almost ate my fuckin' face! Shit man!"*

As Red performed his acrobatic retreat, Peter and Scott came unglued. "Come on Red. Help me with this tarpon. Sharks don't jump like that," Scott roared. "Why'd a little ole tarpon make a big, brave redneck like you shit your pants? Damn it all, where's my camera when I need it?"

"It still on Scott?" the ever-serious Peter blurted as he clinched his sides with both hands. "Did that darned old tarpon have teeth? Must be a new species of silver-king? Come on Red, give a guy a hand."

"Screw you two and the horses ya'll rode in on," Red rebutted, before adding one more *"It almost ate my fuckin' face!"* Somehow the boys restrained their mirth and landed the fish.

"That's got it!   Make sure that noose is tight!" Peter commanded from a safe distance. "Don't let it get away! Tie it to that cleat."

Their first shark turned out to be a fair-sized sand shark. Tail roping the feisty fish, the fight was finally over once the nylon tether was snugged tightly around a stern cleat. A short time later the falling tide ebbed. All further attempts to put out bait proved ineffective and the boat was pushed into the cage-marker by a slight onshore breeze, previously offset by the strong outgoing current. The big chunks of bonito also began attracting crabs and catfish, which sporadically pulled out line, setting off false alarms and frustrating the trio. Forty minutes after bagging that first big shark, the boys went to the nearest dockside scale and weighed their fish.

"Reads 142 pounds, guys. Not bad for our first shark." Red acted as weightmaster, reading the long black pointer on the circular scale. "Let's get this verified so we can dump it overboard. It's starting to stink."

On the morning after, three cocky teenagers hauled the aromatic carcass onto the Lauderdale Marina dock just north of the 17th Street Causeway bridge and weighed it. The sand shark would earn Scott the first of many "City of Ft. Lauderdale Fishing Festival Citations."   Deftly wielding his razor-sharp knife, Peter quickly extracted their first shark trophy, a set of eight-inch wide jaws.

That sand shark ignited a fever within them. *Challenge the sea's fiercest creatures and prove their manhood.* This thought completely obsessed the trio of friends. During the following twelve months, almost every permissible night with the right wind and tide would find them parked in the inlet, always hoping for a bigger shark. Growing boys, hopelessly addicted to shark fishing

Chapter Four

SCOTT DAVID THOMPSON

Scott Thompson's childhood ended with that morning fishing trip and *monster sighting* in 1964. The University of Florida and *adulthood* lay ahead. Dreams of giant fish and vanishing boats would plague him occasionally and he sometimes recalled the letters *O-N-E-Y H-O*. Waking after each obscure episode with his bed sheets drenched by perspiration, Scott was often burdened by vague, uneasy feelings. His terrifying trips to the twilight zone started and would continue indefinitely.

Four years after that final excursion, Scott graduated from the U of F in Gainesville. Thirty pounds heavier than when he entered, his muscular 190 pounds was well distributed over a six-foot frame. Barely twenty-two years old and recipient of a B.S. Degree in Marine Engineering, the brown-haired, hazel-eyed young man joined the nation's work force.

Succumbing to a silver-tongued recruiter, he accepted a job with North American Oil Company in its Offshore District Office. Scott packed his bags and headed for south Louisiana. Naive about the oil business, he quickly learned Hollywood's silver screen depiction of the industry was grossly inaccurate. Never seeing the magnificent gushers he expected, Scott found out the *oil patchers* earned their *high-risk high-reward* money the good old-fashioned way; through sweat, blood, and tears.

Taking advantage of company training programs, his knowledge of the petroleum industry increased rapidly. For the first couple of years, Scott did everything, from drilling and production to geology and construction. Three years later, he was drawn back to the sea and offshore construction.

Scott became an expert in offshore platform design, fabrication, and installation. North American Oil was continually developing new gimmicks to get offshore oil and gas to market quicker and at less cost.

Spending lots of time on the water and really enjoying his work, Scott was determined not to end as some *vegetative desk jockey*. He craved additional knowledge and took night classes at the University of Southwestern Louisiana in his chosen home, Lafayette. At first he selected Petroleum Engineering courses, but the call of the sea was very strong. After a while, his interest shifted to graduate courses in Marine Biology. Then came love . . .

* * *

"Damn it!" Scott Thompson barked a reprimand at the unseen force behind him. "Can't you watch where you're going?" Brushing off his skinned knee and then wiping his hands on his jeans, he jumped to his feet before a Lafayette Mardi Gras crowd could trample him.

"Well excuse me very much, kind sir," came back an irritated female voice. "Pardon me for intruding on your precious space," the voice added facetiously.

Petite, brunette Louise Robinson was still sprawled perilously on the seat of her pants amongst the milling throng when Scott melted at the sound of her sweet, southern drawl. "My gosh, I'm sorry," he apologized. "I didn't know you were a girl. Can I . . . "Turning around, his perfunctory apology died beneath a furious glare from the most gorgeous brown eyes he'd ever seen. "Can I help you up?" Scott pleaded more than asked. The young engineer never had a chance.

". . . and I graduated from LSU in education two years ago." Louise paused, sipping Pepsi from a paper cup as the thousands of revelers struggled to depart from the parade route. "Plantation Elementary, that's where I'm teaching. The third grade," she continued. Her anger abated, a heavenly smile melted Scott even more. Through even, pearly-white teeth she asked, "How about you? What exactly do you do? That is when you're not knocking down defenseless girls?"

"Sorry," Scott replied humbly, "I really am. I, uh, I, ah, I . . . I work for an oil company, North American, here in Lafayette. Mostly offshore construction, building platforms, laying pipelines, stuff like that . . . anything to get away from the office. I'm from south Florida originally, Ft. Lauderdale," he added, desperately searching for anything to say to keep her there a little longer. After a prolonged silence, Scott blurted, "Where do you call home? Are you from Lafayette?"

Grinning at his obvious discomfort, Louise acknowledged, "No, I'm not from here." Those brown eyes continuing to bore unrelentingly into his susceptible heart. When she spoke, she seemed to purr, "Baton Rouge, that's where I was born, just off

Airline Highway. I've never gotten very far from home, really only been out of the state twice." Still smiling angelically, she glanced around and commented, "Looks like the crowd's finally thinning out. I've got to get going. Lesson plans for tomorrow you know."

"Not so fast, Louise," Scott almost begged, suddenly frightened that this *vision* was about to escape. "Can I have your phone number?" Stumbling over himself, he repeated the question. "I mean *may* I have your telephone number? You can't just come into my life like this and then vanish," he rambled on awkwardly. "Maybe we can go to dinner and . . . and then a movie. How 'bout it? You just gotta let me make up for knocking you down like that."

He'd blown it. He knew he'd blown it. Words he so desperately wanted to use failed him.

It's said that a man makes up his mind about a woman within twenty seconds of seeing her, but a woman takes much longer. Not here. It was love *fatal* within minutes for Scott Thompson *and* for Louise Robinson. Standing in front of this awkward, stammering, stuttering young man, Miss Robinson knew without question, that this man was to be her future husband. Men may THINK they are the ones who propose, but it's the woman who controls the situation and Louise Robinson was all woman.

"Dinner and a movie would be fine," Louise replied showing a comforting smile. "Saturday night okay?" Staring at the speechless man standing eighteen inches away, she volunteered her phone number. "I'm usually home by four."

During the weeks that followed, Scott couldn't stay away from the 5' 1" attractive young lady. A relationship developed that could only have one conclusion. Louise knew what it would be from that first meeting. It took Scott almost a month before *he* knew.

"Do you, Miss Louise Regine' Robinson, take this man, Mr. Scott David Thompson, to be your lawfully wedded husband? To have and to hold, for better or for worse . . . . "The likable pastor completed the marriage vows at Trinity Lutheran Church October 27th in 1969, less than a city block from Louise and Scott's impromptu meeting place.

Life and love blossomed for the young couple. Combining Louise's income with his salary increases from North American, they led a very comfortable life. It improved immeasurably on November 11, 1970.

"You have a fine, healthy boy, six pounds nine ounces," the rotund maternity nurse advised. "Your wife and son are waiting to see you."

Scott's chest puffed out and he stated proudly, "I'm a father! I've got me a son!"

Thomas David *Tommy* Thompson's arrival on schedule at Our Lady of Lourdes Hospital utterly domiciled Scott. He reveled in his young family. Investments were also prospering for the Thompson's.

Four months before Tommy was born, Scott looked up at his young wife in the living room and commented casually. "Hey honey, remember me telling you I'd bought some Premier Homes stock a while back? Well, I cashed in some of it and we didn't do half-bad."

Louise was ultra-conservative when it came to investments, being brainwashed by her parents into believing anything other than a savings account was far too speculative. Heaven forbid that someone would actually buy *stocks*. Scott's question took her by surprise.

"No Scott, I *don't remember* you telling me," Louise glared.

"Anyway, he continued, I margined 5,000 shares for $3,700 and I sold a little here and there and it's split a couple of times. We now own 12,000 shares and have $13,000 on deposit in our account."

From that day on, Louise Thompson's opinion of non-savings-account investments differed greatly and her opinion of her young husband's financial ability magnified. She knew she had chosen correctly. He was sweet, kind, caring *and* bright. She was happy with him and proud of him. Never again would she question him when he talked of buying stocks.

Scott also looked into other long-term investments. Convinced aquiculture and fish farming were industries of the future, Scott plowed proceeds from some of his Premier shares into 240 acres of supposedly worthless swamp land a few miles southwest of Lafayette. He leased the surface rights to a crawfish farmer and got duck lease commitments from three local hunters. Cash flow exceeded his note to the seller and spendable income increased.

Those transactions took place in early '71. With cash in the bank, shares of a growing company's stock, and a marvelous home life, Scott concentrated on becoming the best construction engineer in the oil patch. Things were going well, but fate generally interferes. On a balmy, mid-July afternoon in 1977, everything changed forever.

* * *

BOBBY CATCHMAN

In November of 1976, North American Oil began planning the abandonment and salvage of two platforms in the central Gulf of Mexico some seventy-five miles from shore in 160 feet of water. Scott was the Project Engineer with total responsibility. The project fell together perfectly and everything was going well. On July 14, 1977, the main support-barge was mobilized and the offshore work commenced. The final inspection dive to verify that the bottom was clear of debris was nearing completion and Scott was talking with the diver.

"Those pictures look okay?" the diver asked. "Water was real clear, even on bottom. How'd they look Scott?" Bobby Catchman, the diving supervisor questioned. Making that last dive, he was using an underwater.TV camera to video the bottom.

"Really looks good Bobby," Scott complimented him. "Turning out fine. You're doing one helluva job."

"Get his ass in gear," lead diver Sam Pitre suggested from his position near the gauges and controls at the diving panel. "Let's dispense with this idle bullshit so we can all go home. Sooner he gets up, sooner we go."

"Heard that, Pitre," Catchman replied, starting his ascent. "On my way. Let me know when I reach my stop."

"Hold it right there Bobby, forty feet on the nose." Pitre instructed. "You got twenty-one minutes to kill 'fore we bring you up to your next stop. Give me a Pneumo reading and blow them nitrogen bubbles boss-man."

Twenty minutes later Catchman was in the final minute of his first water-stop. Decompression allowed deadly nitrogen bubbles entrained in his body tissues and blood to slowly escape as he returned to atmospheric pressure and prevented a diver's most dreaded assailant, the bends.

"How much more time I got Sam?" Bobby asked. "Beginning to get a little chilly down here. Make sure they got some hot coffee in the decompression chamber." Hanging onto the bottom of the diver's stage, a type of underwater elevator, Bobby was babbling away with Sam Pitre. With Bobby in the water, Sam was controlling the dive from the deck of the derrick barge.

"No problem Bobby," Sam confirmed. "Coffee's already there. You got about another ninety seconds 'fore you move up to ten feet." Hanging off a stage can be lonely, so the lead diver kept up his chatter with Catchman. As Scott listened to the conversation, he was watching the TV monitor and admiring the abundance of marine life in the clear water around Bobby. The camera was hanging from the stage and rotating slowly from torque in its control cable. Every ten or fifteen seconds, the lens picked out the diver's flippers and legs about two feet away.

Having dropped below the stage for a closer look at a colorful tropical fish hovering beneath the lowest steel cross-member, Bobby continued his ceaseless barrage as Scott listened through a speaker on deck. "If I can get this cute little fellow on camera, think our amateur biologist can guess what it is?" Catchman asked. "What ya think Scott? Wanna see 'em? You up on local fishes? Ain't seen a dude like this in my fifteen years in the Gulf. Hold still little darlin', ain't gonna hurt ya."

"Try and get a shot of it, Bobby," Scott replied. "No sudden moves or you'll probably spook it." Scott glanced away from the monitor momentarily to check the VCR and make sure it was recording. The twin red lights over *play* and *record* switches were lit as the counter increased slowly. They were in business.

Returning his attention to the monitor, Scott's eyes bolted open and his lower jaw sagged uncontrollably. Mouth agape, the bitter taste of rising stomach bile burned his throat as terror consumed him. The engineer's breath quickened and it felt as if a bomb exploded in his head as the fourteen-inch color screen filled with a pointed snout, distended jaws and huge, terrifying, triangular teeth. The brutal scene was over in seconds, a swift and fatal assault which began and ended before Scott realized what was happening. But this time, the assailant was clearly visible.

Scott's nightmare returned with raw vengeance and he now knew, for the second time in his life, that he was witnessing a grizzly attack by white death. This thing happened years ago as Red and Peter slept. There *was* a shark attack back then and it *did* eat that boat.

This *must* be a dream . . . a . . . a *nightmare*. One minute Bobby Catchman was on a screen telling that fish, "Ain't gonna hurt you, just wanna make you famous, put you on TV." At the same time, Scott is listening to the rasping sound of air being sucked through the Kirby mask's demand-valve and the gurgling of bubbles being exhaled. Then, in the next breath, absolute silence and a TV screen filled with a snout, teeth, and gaping jaws. Scott heard Bobby exclaim, "What the hell . . .!" Then nothing. *Silence!*

Absolute silence.

"Christ Almighty! Bobby! *Bobby!*" Scott screamed as the color monitor's image jumped wildly. Then only empty water, a cloud of bubbles, and glimpses of the stage's steel components showed on the screen.

The camera had been dislodged and was hanging free with its powerful underwater light beaming out, but it was still working. For a desperately long and painful moment, the color monitor displayed a blood-red field, filled with giant teeth clamping down and then opening again and again. The jaws were so huge they seemed to move in slow motion. They closed with such force, the loud clapping noise they made sounded like a huge, heavy steel door closing.

Still kicking and squirming, diver Bobby Catchman was transformed into unrecognizable bits and pieces; a human body carved and chopped into a mass of descriptionless carnage, then devoured by a brutal, emotionless beast.

Captivated by the gruesome scene, tears flooded both eyes and Scott retched his guts out on the deck before him. He could not tear his eyes from the screen. For an instant, the Petroleum Engineer stepped back in time, witnessing a previous catastrophe. A gigantic apparition appeared and its indistinguishable shape exploded beneath the faint lights of a stationary boat. Blood and flesh were everywhere and the letters *O-N-E-Y H-O* flickered dimly. Then . . . Scott was again on the derrick barge, facing a more current atrocity.

"*Holy Shit!* What going on?" the diver-tender cried. "Someone give me a hand!" He reacted helplessly to the air hose being torn from neat figure-eight coils he'd made on the deck and racing into the water like a frightened snake. "Oh shit," he pleaded. "Somebody please help me!"

Not thinking clearly, he stomped his right foot down on the disappearing hose. A loop came tight around his ankle and he was jerked off his feet and over the barge's side. The tender's pathetic cry for *"Help!"* filled the stagnant, muggy air. Momentarily airborne, he plunged fourteen feet from the barge deck into the sea below.

"*Man overboard!*" Sam Pitre yelled, unsure of what was happening. "*Man overboard!*" he screamed one more time before roughly flicking down the black switch on the rectangular diver's communication box and demanding, "Bobby, what the hell's going on down there? Your Pneumo reading has you at seventy feet. Get your ass back up to your water stop. Bobby? Bobby, can you read me? *Come back, Bobby!*"

"*Mother of God, no . . .* " Scott muttered as he watched Catchman's mutilation. Using the back of one hand, he unconsciously wiped vomit from his mouth while staring hypnotically at the glowing screen. "Sam, get over here!" he shouted. "Look at that shark! Oh shit, Bobby!" By now Scott was screaming at the microphone and banging his fists against the inanimate object. Tears coursed down his cheeks, spittle and vomit residue filling the air with each comment as his body shook in fear and rage.

The video camera hung motionlessly from the diver's stage. Centered in the picture, not sixty feet from the camera, was a huge shark. As Sam reacted to Scott's statement, the shark turned and swam slowly toward the camera displaying its catch.

"Oh my God," dribbled from Sam's trembling lips. "Is that Bobby? *It can't be! Oh dear God.*"

Protruding from the creature's clenched jaws were Bobby Catchman's neoprene-covered legs. In apparent disdain, the massive pointed snout and head shook as the great fish worked its prize. Both men visualized the wicked teeth, their serrated edges rudely sawing through rubber, flesh, and bone. Brownish clouds appeared from the mouth of the almost-motionless creature. Jerking its head and opening those great jaws, death's chasm was presented to the camera lens for one last time. When they closed, Bobby Catchman was gone.

A single booted-flipper drifted downward through the picture carrying a foot and part of a leg, a whisper of brown trailing from it. Scott and Sam watched speechlessly as the severed end of the diver's air hose floated through the picture. The great shark turned and glided out of camera range.

"*Carcharodon Carcharias,*" Scott muttered in contemptible anger. "You no-good, rotten sonofabitch." In less than a minute, just one minute out of a fifteen-million-minute lifetime, sixty terrifying seconds ended the life of an oilfield diver.

The previously quiet deck now swarmed with people. All anyone other than Sam or Scott knew right then was that a tender had gone overboard and that Sam was trying to get the diver to answer him on the radio. Several hands were helping the frightened youngster out of the water, asking him what happened.

Scott and Sam simply stared at each other, neither speaking. Words were useless. Sixty feet below, the unattended camera's lens pointed into a now-empty sea. All signs of marine life vanished. The two red lights on the VCR continued glowing and numbers on the counter continued to increase. Only barren water was being recorded on the two-hour Memorex VHS tape.

* * *

That night while Scott reclined in the Company Representative cabin's lower bunk onboard the barge, his tortured mind relived it all. Insomnia assailed him as he tried unsuccessfully to get some sleep before flying back to shore the next morning. There was no mistaking the coal black, emotionless eyes set on either side of the broad pointed snout. He watched them roll back, protecting those eyes from external damage and indicating the instant the shark contacted its victim. The *Ampullae of Lorenzini* were there, freckle-like openings sprinkled over the shark's head and snout, which tie into its electromagnetic guidance and detection system. Bobby Catchman never had a chance.

"Christ, it has to be!" Scott screamed into the pitch black room as he burst awake. "It has to be! That monstrous shape! Those gigantic teeth!" Shutting out the nightmare was impossible. Awake or asleep, eyes opened or closed, alone or with others, its overbearing presence transcended all. The answer was right there in his biology studies. It was the only possibility. Scott stated a scientific name that would dictate the remainder of his days. "*Carcharodon Megalodon,* you bastard! You're *not* extinct. I saw you when I was a teenager. It *had* to be you. I didn't realize it at the time but it *was* you.

A CAREER CHANGE

Scott's wife of eight years was there when his helicopter flight landed at Lafayette Regional Airport the next day. His boss in North American Oil's District Office had called her the evening of the tragedy to let her know what happened but that her husband was safe. Gruesome thoughts that filled her mind while she imagined the worse gave way to relief as he entered the terminal and dispelled her fears. Going directly to her, he dropped his carry-on bag and briefcase to swoop her up in his arms.

They just clung to each other for several seconds. Finally

Louise spoke. "Honey, I'm so sorry," she sobbed as her voice cracked and the tears of relief came. " Let's go home now, the kids are worried about you."

That evening Louise provided consolation and relief as only her arms and body could. Her all-encompassing love and their love-making gave him temporary sanctuary from reality. Afterwards, she and Scott talked at length about what he must do with his career and of changes about to occur in their lives. Laying in each other's arms, the painful memories eased. Finally, he slept.

The next morning, Scott placed a long-distance call to Louisiana State University in Baton Rouge. He made the one hour drive across the Attchafalaya Swamp on I-10 to Baton Rouge where he kept his appointment. After the meeting he excitedly piled back into his car and reversed his morning trip. His mission was accomplished; he'd been accepted at LSU. He was now one step closer to his newly-chosen destiny; his *Quest for Megalodon!!!*

It was dinner time for the Thompson household when Scott burst through the kitchen door leading from the carport. Sweeping Louise off her feet and planting an almost vicious kiss on her lips, Scott was still excited and also very hungry.

"Who wants crawfish?" he asked happily. Three hands went up, though Kristine who'd turned three the previous February would have her usual hotdog. "Let's go then! We're going *out* for dinner tonight and time's a wastin'."

Rounding up the kids and buckling them into his white Chevy Impala, they took off to The Yellow Bowl, a nearby seafood restaurant where three Thompson's gorged themselves on boiled crawfish. Kristine ate her hotdog.

* * *

"Yes sir, it's my resignation," Scott informed the District Engineer. "I've enjoyed it here, but it's time to move on. There's something else I *have* to do." Scott's career with North American Oil was over.

The Thompson family moved fifty miles to the east, across the Mississippi River to Baton Rouge. Louise went to work for the East Baton Rouge Parish School Board and young Tommy Thompson entered a second grade class at his mom's new school. Pre-school aged Kristine was to be entertained lavishly and spoiled rotten by a doting baby sitter, who just happened to be Louise's mother. Yep, grandma's are allowed to spoil their grandkids.

Scott started classes at Louisiana State University in mid-September with an MS degree in Marine Biology as his immediate goal. Initial worries about his performance in a purely academic environment after nine years in the real world were totally unwarranted. University life and studying awakened a craving for knowledge, his mind becoming a porous sponge which absorbed mountains of information. All of his classes, core curriculum and electives alike, fascinated him. Enchantment with learning turned studying into recreation, not work.

Everything Scott learned throughout his college days would serve the purpose to build a foundation for his ultimate quest. His studies, his research, and his accumulated knowledge were simply tools which would help in the search for the gigantic, carnivorous beast he now knew existed.

The first year raced by. Every Marine Biology course he'd taken at USL transferred with full credit and the additional class work his degree required lay behind him after two semesters. Scott's Master's Thesis compiled and analyzed all available data on how sound, light, and temperature effected sharks' feeding behavior. He titled it <u>EXTRANEOUS INFLUENCES AFFECT ON THE CONSUMPTIVE DEMEANOR OF CARTILAGINOUS SPECIES</u>.

That meteoric year's activities included much more than class work and thesis preparation. A burning desire overwhelmed him, mandated by waking recollections of a huge creature with *larger-than-life* teeth. Amongst the carnage of his recurring dream, a craving demanded delegation of all possible time to shark-attack investigation. Using resources available through the university's library system plus contacts established within the marine biological community through his professors, avenues previously unavailable opened. In his *spare time*, Scott began compiling details of all marine catastrophes attributed to shark attacks.

He investigated hundreds of incidents and a thread of evidence emerged which linked several together. These reports were such that a normal scientist would probably have disregarded them. However, Scott's feeling he witnessed one incident and with certainty he'd witnessed a second, placed an entirely different perspective on otherwise implausible findings. The future direction of his blossoming research efforts became firmly established. Scott *had* to find an answer.

* * *

"You won't believe it. You just *won't* believe it." Scott said after hanging up the phone. Louise, noting her husband's apparent excitement, looked up from the kitchen table where she was busily grading papers. "Who was that on the phone, Scott?" she asked.

Scott, smiling from ear to ear, repeated. "You just won't believe it. Hell, I don't believe it."

"I don't have time for games," Louise forced a smile. "Who *was* that, Scott?"

"Take a guess," Scott replied, unable to wipe that ever-broadening smile from his face.

"*Scott David Thompson*," she demanded, "I am *not* in a mood to play games with you! Tell me who that was and what I won't believe and we'll just see if I *do* believe it and stop this nonsense. I have papers to grade."

Grabbing her shoulders, he jerked her to her feet and blurted out, *"Magnum Oil! That's who called!* The outfit *you* didn't want to lease our mineral rights to last January. Remember them?"

"Of course I remember them. What about them, Scott? *What about them*?"

Scott, enjoying her mounting excitement, hesitated more. Louise's brown eyes narrowed to wicked little slits. Scott, realizing he was now treading on precarious ground but still wanting to tease a bit longer, gave out bits of information. "You know they were drilling their first well? They got it down yesterday and logged it."

"I don't *care* about drilling or logging. Did they strike oil?" Still teasing, Scott continued deliberately, "Like I said, they finished the well, cut a gas sand. It isn't a bonanza, but we'll be getting some royalty money starting in July."

"How *much*?" Louise screamed. Ripping free from his grip, she clasped *her* hands on *his* shoulders and began shaking *him*.

"It's not the mother lode," her husband hinted, "but it'll do in a pinch. Looks like we'll only get . . . eleven or twelve thousand a month."

Disbelief flashed across Louise's face. "A *month!* Eleven or twelve *thousand* a month!" she babbled. "You mean *dollars*?"

Releasing his shoulders, she turned and walked in a daze to that comfortable recliner in their living room, and plopped down. Almost hyperventilating, she muttered repeatedly, "Eleven or twelve thousand *dollars* . . . a *month!*"

Louise sat rigidly, still talking to herself in disbelief. They were rich, *rich*! Tears streamed down her cheeks. She looked at Scott hovering over her. She jumped up and wrapped her slender arms around him. Their lives would change. They were going to live the good life. Hugging him with all her strength, she whispered seductively, "I love you."

* * *

"Yes sir, Dr. McMasters, I'm taking your offer. I'll be at Miami in the fall." As he hung up the phone, Scott added, "Thanks for your help."

Of all his newly-found contacts, the Chairman of the Department of Marine Biology at the University of Miami in Coral Gables was by far the most important. McMasters showed an exceptional interest in Scott's investigative research into shark attacks, an interest stemming from a family tragedy many years before.

An older brother of McMasters' wife, Harold *Fishy* Hawkins, disappeared out of Fort Lauderdale one night during a fishing trip. His boat, MONEY HOLE, simply vanished without a trace almost fourteen years earlier. They surmised it could have been the work of drug runners or smugglers. The case was never officially closed.

Charles McMasters had other ideas. The tragedy occurred early in his teaching career, but he always felt something other than man took his brother-in-law. The information Professor McMasters gathered over the years helped stoke the furnace of Scott Thompson's mind, bits of documentation that seemed to bond the department head and his soon-to-be protege.

Corresponding regularly, Dr. McMasters always furnished timely responses to Scott's requests. In April, he sent Scott some solicited information. With it went literature about the University of Miami and a suggestion Scott consider going there for a doctorate. Financial assistance was also offered. With Miami less than thirty miles from Fort Lauderdale, it appeared that Scott would be going home.

Scott completed his thesis at LSU in July, graduating with the summer class in August 1978. One week later, the family was on its way to Miami and an emotional homecoming. His widowed mother still lived in Fort Lauderdale, his father having died of lung cancer in 1975. Mary, his younger sister and her growing family resided in nearby Boca Raton.

Louise resumed full-time mother-and-wife duties, actively participating in local charitable efforts, and becoming an avid tennis player. The two kids were busy making new friends and starting school near their comfortable home in southwest Miami, about twenty minutes from the main campus. Scott plunged into a three-year PhD program in Marine Biology, emphasizing Ichthyology and the Cartilaginous Species.

* * *

Three years of study passed quickly and, on June 7, 1981, Scott Thompson graduated with honors. Field trips to many exotic ports were fringe benefits of his education. He related well with most of the students in his teaching classes and thoroughly enjoyed the teaching process. Teachings most exhilarating aspect was the spin-off learning effect of his instructional efforts. Questions, both simple and profound, forced additional thought and study. Those spawned a need for related research to adequately address the young, inquiring minds.   Questions bred answers which bred more questions which led to more answers. Always percolating to the top was just how little man really knew and how much there was to learn about this marvelous world. Learning was becoming his life and teaching was to be the nourishment required to sustain that life. Scott's *Quest for Megalodon* was to make learning a necessity.

Scott's research into cause-and-history of shark attacks continued unabated and the thread developed at LSU grew ever longer. Multiple files, based on probable type of shark and the location and month of attack were compiled. A subfile was created for Bobby Catchman's killer, the Great White Shark, Carcharodon Carcharias. Scott also established a file covering his nightmare creature, a fish of unknown size and shape which was the driving force in his unquenchable search for knowledge.

Although no real proof existed to support his conjecture, Scott formed some strong opinions of his mysterious creature. He would frequently discuss these ideas on an informal basis with select graduate students who showed an interest. One such session took place in April of 1983.

". . . and we can estimate its size by comparing fossilized teeth with those of Carcharias. Take a look at these photos," Scott paused in his lecture as he produced several black and white pictures. Continuing, "Based on the tooth size of a twenty-foot White and this eight-inch fossil tooth, the length of Megalodon could range from fifty to seventy feet. Much larger teeth may still be out there. Extrapolating weights, you all know how bulky the Great White is, a sixty-foot shark could weigh over fifty tons."

Pausing briefly, Scott thumbed through his notes and then just laid the entire package aside. Looking at each of his five student's interested faces, he said, "Just a couple of more comments and then we'll call it quits for the week. There is *no reason* to assume Megalodon is extinct. Nothing in the sea could kill it and other species of sharks have survived, relatively unchanged, for tens-of-millions of years. Assuming a small population and the large quantity and variety of potential prey, there is a strong possibility that it still exists. The other great predators were all air breathers; they had to come to the surface and expose themselves to all kinds of potentially deadly elements. A giant shark wouldn't need to. It could survive without ever entering shallow water. I believe it's still out there. I am convinced it can be found." Scott paused with a deep sigh. "Well class, that's enough for today, see you on Thursday."

Scott frequently recalled that September of '64 boat disappearance as a *giant shark attack* and often discussed his beliefs with students and colleagues. The certainty that his early morning sighting was real increased a thousand-fold during the third year of his PhD studies. While scanning microfilms from the Lauderdale Daily News, an article caught Scott's eye. It read in part:

"*. . . no report on the whereabouts of Joseph Mason and Harold 'Fishy' Hawkins. The men disappeared without a trace last week on September 4th during a night fishing trip in Hawkins' charter boat the MONEY HOLE. Coast Guard officials stated that weather was near perfect . . .*"

"*Jesus! September 4, 1964*," Scott blurted out loudly, incurring scathing glares from two elderly women sitting near him in the library. "Excuse me," he apologized before quietly adding, "That's the day before that last fishing trip, just before Peter, Red, and I took off for college. We saw that torn up cushion with the letters *O-N-E-Y H-O* on it. That fits in MONEY HOLE, the missing boat's name. And Fishy! Damn, that's the name of McMasters' brother-in-law who disappeared years ago." Scratching his head and rereading the article, Scott recalled his department head mentioning the incident in passing just after Scott had started his PhD studies. "Can't be that many Fishy's around. Can you believe it? I may have seen Charles McMasters' brother-in-law get killed by my bloody shark. Small fuckin' world!"

Scott now *knew* what he saw was real. Not even the hint of doubt remained in his mind, especially after McMasters confirmed the Harold *Fishy* Hawkins in the article was his brother-in-law. It prowled the ocean depths, that animal his contemporaries claimed was extinct. At the apex of the world's carnivores, invincible and eternal, *Carcharodon Megalodon was still out there!*

* * *

The Thompson family were going on vacation. Hopping a Continental flight to Los Angeles, they spent several days in Hollywood and southern California. Then United Air Lines carried them to beautiful Hawaii for three more weeks. Father and son went fishing while the girls enjoyed the hotel pool and white sand beaches that beckon so many vacationers to the island paradise. They toured all the islands, snorkeled in gin-clear water, and played tennis frequently. For those few short weeks, Scott forgot his quest, *almost*!

Money was still plentiful, thanks to his gas lease near Lafayette. Scott also signed a contract with McMasters before his vacation and was now an Associate Professor of Ichthyology which brought many perks with it, including authority to pursue the search for Megalodon.

Coincidentally, one of his two closest childhood friends was being forced to make a career change. Though it would take some time and effort, Scott was going to transfuse a considerable dose of overwhelming urge to one of them.

Chapter Five

WILLIAM PETER SMITH

Peter Smith's life was driven by an obsession too; one about how and why living things worked. Ardently pouring over anatomy books, biology articles, and National Geographic stories, his high school years were enjoyable. Loving music, Peter mastered the saxophone and joined the high school band. Scott and Red were his only real friends but Red was busy with athletics and Scott was busy with a variety of things, especially girls. Throughout high school, Peter lived from day-to-day, never finding any real direction. Actually, his entire pattern of life was shaped then but Peter didn't recognize it. Who does?

In the fall of '64, the trio took off on different paths. Scott enrolled at the University of Florida while Red accepted a University of Georgia baseball scholarship. Peter chose Tallahassee and attended Florida State University. As childhood friendships go, changing schools and especially going to different colleges, there was little contact among the three during the next several years.

Still unsure of his goals in life, Peter graduated in June of '68 with a B.A. Degree having taken every conceivable biology course, including marine biology and a few pre-med. In his junior year, he joined the U.S. Naval Reserve Unit in Tallahassee. After graduation Peter went to Officer Candidate School, enjoying the OCS program and its disciplined atmosphere. There, the inklings of a pending career emerged during first-aid training.

Ensign Peter Smith was assigned to the USS Saratoga, a nuclear-powered aircraft carrier. For junior officers, the opportunity for extra medical training was limited, but Peter lucked out when the Ship's Surgeon befriended him. The inquisitive young officer's knowledge of human anatomy impressed Dr. Howard Quail. During Peter's second year on the Saratoga, Quail pulled a few strings and enrolled him in advanced paramedic training. Then destiny intervened in Peter Smith's life.

* * *

It was a bleak and blustery November morning on a storm-tossed Mediterranean Sea when a seaman's carelessness during a drill detonated a live shell. The first explosion ignited other armaments and killed eleven sailors, including the unfortunate instigator, and one young ensign. Seven other enlisted men and Commander John Fuller were seriously injured. Fuller's wound was the most serious, a large piece of shrapnel entering his chest at the lower junction of his rib cage. Debris fell across his legs and pinned him to the deck, blocking all attempts to move him to the ship's hospital.

"In here! The screams are coming from in here!" Peter shouted above the ringing bells and continuing explosions. He was first on the scene. Responding to the alarm, he preceded Dr. Quail into an inferno, greeted by white-hot flames and choking smoke. Agonized cries of the injured filled the air and the dead and dying were strewn everywhere.

"Start over there, Peter! I'll check this one," Quail ordered, taking command of the emergency. "Get their pulses! Make sure they're alive before you spend any time on them."

"This one's dead," Peter moaned as he moved to the next sailor. "This one's alive, but barely. Dr. Quail, I think he's beyond help."

Rapidly checking pulses and performing superficial examinations, the extent of the injuries was determined and patients requiring the most urgent attention were identified. The two men battled lingering smoke and searing heat in their Herculean effort to save lives and limbs.

"I've got this one," Peter shouted, dropping beside yet another injured man. Several medics and other sailors were milling about, helping where they could. Peter was attending the officer and, recognizing the extent of the injuries, hollered, "Doctor, the Commander's in bad shape! Can you see to him next?"

"I'm here Peter," Dr. Quail said, placing a reassuring hand on Peter's shoulder. He'd left an unconscious petty officer with one of the medics. "God what a mess."

"This should stop the bleeding. I think this one's got a chance." Peter was applying a tourniquet to a seaman's badly lacerated right leg as the doctor knelt beside Fuller. The Commander's pulse was erratic and his breathing very shallow. His tan naval shirt was saturated with sticky blood. Six inches of jagged steel protruded from the center of his chest, surrounded by clammy, yellowish skin. The wound was already twenty minutes old. Something had to be done, quickly!

"Medic, tend to that man's leg." Dr. Quail ordered. "Peter, help me over here." The doctor recognized the determination and sensitivity in Peter's face. "This steel comes out now or he's dead. My bag quickly, then help me clear the wound."

"I've got it doctor," Peter said, turning his back momentarily as he reached for the surgeon's black medical bag. Behind him, Dr. Quail was leaning across the stricken officer, trying to remove pieces of debris.

The hiss of escaping gas was followed by a roaring bang and a blinding flash of light. *"God help me Peter! I'm on fire!"* the doctor shrieked pitifully.

"Jesus, Dr. Quail," Peter cried out, seeing the right hand and the sleeve of the doctor's white medical jacket engulfed in flames.

"Get it out! Get it out! Christ almighty, it burns!" Dr. Quail's screams continued. "Ow . . . God does it hurt!" With his left hand, the doctor was frantically trying to beat the fire off of his other arm.

"Look out Doc, I've got it!" Peter responded instinctively, throwing a wool blanket around the burning arm and cinching it tight to cut off oxygen to the flame. The doctor's knees buckled and he fell against Peter. The disgusting smell of newly singed flesh permeated the air.

"Corpsman, over here on the double! I need burn salve and gauze wrapping." Peter was in control, calmness epitomizing his every action. "That's it!" he instructed. "The blue jar!"

Quickly unwrapping the blanket, he saturated the doctor's burned hand and forearm with liquid antiseptic. He then carefully wrapped the burn with the special gauze before liberally applying more liquid. In seconds, the dressing's cooling affect diminished the pain to a tolerable level.

"You, help me with Dr. Quail," Peter ordered two nearby seamen. "Got to get him to the hospital now."

"Wait! We can't leave." The doctor's agony-distorted voice froze Peter and the seamen in their tracks. "That fragment has to come out now or this man is dead. Peter, my bag."

"Dr. Quail. Your hand, Sir," Peter stated. "You can't possibly operate, not with those hands."

"No Peter, I can't, but you can. *You must!* You'll be my

hands. You've got what it takes boy." Dr. Quail stared intensely through Peter's wire-rimmed glasses into sky-blue eyes, looking for any sign of fear or uneasiness. He was rewarded with only determination and confidence. "We have no choice. By the time another doctor gets here, the commander will be dead."

"Where do I start?" Peter slipped past the doctor, carefully opening the black bag containing a plethora of medical instruments. Confidently, he knelt over the badly injured man.

With his physician-mentor's guidance, Peter Smith performed his initial surgical procedure. All organs, arteries, and muscles were exactly where he knew they would be. He was talked through each step. First, Peter meticulously enlarged the opening. The large, fragmented piece of shell-casing was efficiently removed. Jagged steel actually touched the erratically beating heart of the injured officer. Miraculously, the vital organ was undamaged, but the air passage to the lungs was blocked.

"Okay Peter, that's good, very good. Take it out carefully," the surgeon cautioned. "Slowly now, slowly. That's got it. Good job." Incisions and handiwork flowed as if Peter had spent years in the operating room. "We need to close that artery now, and then remove the clamps," the doctor said, impressed with the young man's work.

Peter sewed shut a partially severed artery, carefully removed a pair of tiny clamps, and then closed the wound. The entire operation took just over thirty minutes.

As he finished, another doctor arrived on the scene, ferried across to the Saratoga from another ship in the fleet to assist Dr. Quail. Admiring the precise stitches in the center of the commander's chest, the new arrival complemented Peter on his handiwork, assuming he was a physician. The second doctor, assisted by several medics, continued tending to the less seriously injured while Peter directed rescue operations. Debris was removed from around Fuller's legs and the unconscious commander was moved by stretcher to the ship's hospital where other medical team members awaited the explosion's aftermath.

Dr. Quail's hand and arm healed quickly, due in part to Peter's rapid treatment of the burning flesh. Fuller recovered completely, with only a neat six-inch scar running diagonally across his upper abdomen. The surgeons onboard the Saratoga reopened the carefully closed wound to redo Peter's handiwork and to insure that the necessary disinfectants were applied. The sutures in the artery required no rework. The surgeon's report commented favorably on the obvious skill exhibited in inserting them. For the first time, Peter knew exactly what he wanted out of life. He found his calling.

DOC SMITTY

Completing his mandatory hitch, Lt. Commander Peter Smith retired from active duty. Armed with an eloquent letter of introduction to a medical school classmate of Dr. Howard Quail, he returned to college life in his native state. The classmate just happened to be Dean of the Medical School at the University of Florida. A more mature Peter Smith ventured onto the U of F's campus at Gainesville with definite short and long-term goals for his life.

As luck would have it, Commander Fuller was the eldest child of the honorable Albert Fuller. Mr. Fuller, recently reelected to a ninth term, was the influential senior United States Senator from South Carolina. Senator Fuller was most grateful to the young man who pulled his only son from the jaws-of-death. He also recognized extraordinary talent. His sincere appreciation and sponsorship served to expedite Peter's meteoric passage through formal medical training and the establishment of his subsequent practice.

Required pre-med courses behind him, Peter continued his medical education at Gainesville. Orthopedic surgery was especially appealing to the budding doctor. A strong interest developed in athletic-related injuries, due in part to his futile childhood attempts at sports participation.

Medical degree in hand and internship behind him, Dr. Peter Smith returned to hometown Fort Lauderdale. By Christmas of 1978, his South Florida practice was thriving. Aided immeasurably by Senator Fuller's referrals, his clientele included many well-known celebrities.

Although Peter benefitted from the outside help in obtaining his first patients, exceptional diagnostic and surgical skills along with a friendly bedside manner quickly escalated his demand. *Satisfied customers* spread the word. Professional relationships evolved, including consultation agreements with the Miami Dolphins and the Universities of Miami and Florida. The physical exams, surgical procedures, and rehabilitation responsibilities spawned from these organizations alone, could have kept him busy full-time. Peter blossomed under medicine's direction.

Active participation in local civic and cultural organizations became commonplace. Involvement would normally be restricted to worthy causes due to his grueling surgical schedule. His medical practice income alone quickly exceeded six figures and by the end of 1979, it was rapidly approaching the million-dollar mark.

Outside investments were needed to protect Peter's rapidly accumulating wealth and to shelter some of his income. Advice from two longtime friends familiar with South Florida's real estate market provided excellent returns. Investments in and improvements to depressed rental properties met with exceptional success. Not only was a significant portion of his medical income sheltered from the tax man, but property appreciation generated positive cash flows.

Peter was also sole heir to some very valuable property, acquired systematically by his parents during the late fifties and the early sixties. Peter's father had uncanny foresight about the growth-potential of Broward County. Bit-by-bit, he picked up parcels of unimproved land well outside the then-existing western limits of Fort Lauderdale, eventually controlling almost 1,500 acres in nine different sections. Seven of these sections, north of State Road 84 and west of University Avenue, were rapidly being surrounded by housing and commercial developments. Their value escalated into the millions.

Not yet thirty-five, Peter Smith was living the American dream. He lived in a comfortable waterfront home in Lauderdale Harbors and drove a candy-apple red Jaguar XJS, sporting the personalized license plate CUTTER. He also readily succumbed to his first true love, fishing. At least two months out of each year would be spent fishing for sailfish off Florida or Cozumel, blue marlin in Puerto Rico or the Virgin Islands, or bluefin tuna out of Nova Scotia. The location didn't matter, surgical schedule permitting, Peter made time to fish.

Striving to return something to his revered fishing, he became active in the IGFA. The International Game Fish Association was headquartered in Fort Lauderdale, at the eastern foot of Las Olas Boulevard's Intracoastal Waterway bridge. Peter was eventually elected to the Board of Directors of that organization, which governs, regulates, and supports true sportsfishing throughout the fishing world.

Certain tribulations accompanied Peter's success, such as the inability to establish lasting relationships with women. A workaholic, medicine and orthopedic surgery filled his life, except for fishing, and only twice would he come close to finding that special girl.

The first occurred during medical school at the University of Florida and included a formal engagement. It ended when she became almost intolerably possessive. Peter was saddened only briefly over this loss; he rather enjoyed single life.

Peter was of better-than-average looks, positive, had a pleasing personality, he was a professional man, and he was *rich*. Having overcome early introvertedness, he enjoyed other people's company. When you met him, you liked him and the more you got to know him, the better you liked him. But, he and the *right girl* apparently just never were in the same place at the same time.

Though maybe not marriage material, Peter's appreciation of beautiful women was apparent. He always had an attractive companion by his side, except for this one particular party when he first saw . . .

"Peter, this is Brenda James. Brenda, I'd like you to meet one of our most ardent supporters, Dr. Peter Smith." The unrequested introduction was made by the chairwoman of a South Florida charity at one of her *Christmas of 1980* fund raisers. Grabbing both parties by an elbow, the busybody, who fancied herself a matchmaker, flashed a sickly smile through far-too-much makeup. "Dr. Smith is an orthopedic surgeon and a Lauderdale native. He's also very single," she added with know-it-all confidence as she released them and started walking away. Before leaving the two, she winked signifying they owed her for her services, if not monetarily or with a favor, then certainly with a respect she would never deserve.

Brenda James was beautiful and seemed to exude a sense of *old money* and refinement. Born in Oklahoma, her daddy made his fortune in the days of the Texas panhandle oil boom. His only daughter attended the most elite schools and he spoiled her rotten, giving her everything money could buy.

Then Papa James went bust, leaving pampered Brenda with a meager income from a trust the creditors couldn't touch. She was *available* when Peter met her at that charity ball. Discovering that this unpretentious man was an extremely successful surgeon and loaded, she set her sights on him. Fancying life as a *Doctor's wife*, her game plan evolved. Peter almost never had a chance.

Brenda utilized that age old, but oh-so-effective tactic of playing hard to get. Convincing Peter she wasn't *that* interested in him, the bait was presented. Flaunting herself through minor acquaintances, she instilled the feeling that friendship, but nothing more, was possible. She advocated only a platonic relationship.

Peter, like a lamb to the slaughter, began a dedicated effort at bedding her. He liked the challenge. After several weeks of wooing, he began to feel that she was special. And Brenda, playing her game expertly, finally *gave in*. Then Peter, feeling a sense of accomplishment and even a tinge of guilt, began to have special feelings for this sweet, beautiful, intelligent, fun, not-so-easy-to-bed young woman. In September of 1981, after more than nine months of spending most of his off time with Brenda, he purchased a two-carat diamond for his proposal.

"Come on man, don't lose your cool." Peter tried to convince himself everything was under control as he stepped on the elevator. Making sure he had the ring, "Damn nice stone. I know she'll say yes. If she told him no, he'd never ever think of marriage again.

The elevator halted as the bright-green number "16" lit up and twin steel doors slid apart. "Here goes nothing," he said, stepping into the carpeted hallway.

It was early evening, somewhere around 7, and he usually called Brenda to set a time for when they would go out. And this was a usual work night when they never saw each other but Peter took this night off. This evening was special. Peter wanted to surprise her. He quietly let himself in with his key.

As he entered, Peter could hear raucous noises coming from the bedroom. "Brenda and her horrible taste in music. Sounds like a party going on," he said quietly to himself as he closed the door behind him. Must have that TV on the Playboy station. He called out a few times and the bedroom door, slightly ajar, opened and two naked bodies wandered out laughing, headed for the kitchen.

A large lump suddenly appeared in Peter's stomach. He squinted, shook his head and a million thoughts began racing through his mind. Unable to choose which to believe, he strode to the bedroom door and flung it open. His unsuspecting heart was shattered. There was sweet, hard-to-conquer Brenda, coupled on her king sized bed with a large, hairy, beast-of-a-man. The room reeked of marijuana, and dishes of deadly white powder, miscellaneous drug paraphernalia, and two more combinations of people were in the same bed. The apparently *high* attendees never even noticed Peter's brief appearance. Brenda did.

However out-of-it she might have been or how deeply engrossed she was in her sexual activity, her demeanor was that of sober shock. Their eyes met for one brief moment as Peter, steely eyed and stone faced, turned and fled the scene. They never saw each other again.

* * *

The crimson Jag sped across the 17th Street Causeway heading west. With no sense of direction, Peter found himself driving south on I-95, finally killing the high powered engine in front of the Thompson's house in South Miami. Why he would end up here was a mystery to Peter. He thought he might drive away and find the nearest bar to drown his disappointment in alcohol. But something seemed to draw him to this house of his childhood friend. Scott and Louise were always happy and smiling and Peter needed to be surrounded by, well . . . by happy and smiling people.

It was early evening and lights were on. Until recently, Peter had not seen Scott in almost eight years. Peter sat outside in his car for almost an hour, unable to believe what he had just witnessed. He shook his head in disbelief, looked at that two-carat bauble he almost became engaged with, then went to the door and rang the buzzer.

His unfailing friendship with Scott provided the outlet for Peter's emotions that night, and Scott's wife, Louise, proved a godsend. They sensed something was wrong with Peter no matter how carefully he tried to mask it. After several hours and as many drinks, Peter told them the Brenda James story from auspicious beginning to unsuspecting end. Louise and Scott listened intently and Louise, of course, gave her opinion. She helped Peter see the shallowness of his recent relationship and it became more obvious to Peter as he looked at it from a third party's point-of-view.

"We won't take no for an answer," Louise announced. "You are going to spend the night with us. And visit with Scott tomorrow. He has some things I feel will interest you and help clear your mind." Not one you turned down, Peter acceded to Louise's demands and called his answering service to cancel the following day's appointments.

He awoke early the next morning to a breakfast of homemade waffles smothered in real butter and Log Cabin syrup. Pleasant, but competitive banter of happy Thompson children filled the air around the breakfast table. By mid-morning, the Jag was en route across town and out the Rickenbacker Causeway. The two men were heading for the University of Miami's Research Facility near the famous Miami Seaquarium. There, they examined many of Scott's specimens and talked about a myriad of things and about nothing. The two friends ended the day laughing about it all.

* * *

"I can't thank you enough," Peter said to his hosts. "Don't know what I'd have done without you." He was past pain when he pointed his car north that afternoon. Strangely enough, there was no bitterness toward Miss James, only pity. Peter's eyes were opened in time and he came away a little wiser in the ways of the heart. After that, Peter's women *friends* were all inconsequential affairs. Each episode would conclude with a short term bed-and-breakfast encounter as he neatly sidestepped out of their lives. He learned how to hermetically seal his heart from any true emotion. Sometimes 60 or 70 percent of himself would succumb, but Peter was always able to control the small percentage remaining and avoid commitment. The only true affection he ever developed was for the gal Scott already had.

Chapter Six

"RED" DICKSON

On Wednesday morning, October 3rd, 1945, Mrs. Elaine Johnson Dickson presented her husband with a strapping baby boy. Their first of four children arrived before dawn at the County Hospital's two-room maternity ward in Macon, Georgia. William Alexander Dickson, Jr. entered the world as a 6-lb 8-oz screamer. His only distinguishing characteristic was a shock of blazing red hair. From the time his proud parents walked out the hospital's front door, he was Red.

William senior, a stock broker with a local three man firm, was reasonably successful. The family lived in a modest three bedroom home near the corner of Ash and 7th Street on the south side of Macon. In March of 1959, Red's father accepted a position with a major brokerage firm in Fort Lauderdale and started his new career on April 6th. When school let out at the end of May, Mrs. Dickson, Red, his brother, and two sisters watched their possessions loaded into an Allied moving van. The five then took off in the family's 1957 black and white Chevy station wagon to join William in Florida.

Mrs. Dickson and her four claustrophobic kids, crammed into an overloaded station wagon, pulled to a stop in front of their four bedroom waterfront home in Fort Lauderdale. Seemingly at once, the car's doors burst open and pent up energy in the form of four ex-Georgia kids exploded from within. The two girls, nine-year-old Suzanne and Mary, who was six, ran into and out of daddy's open arms, heading for the house and their new room. Red, with ten-year-old Bobby on his heels, was hell bent for the back yard to check out the canal their dad wrote to them about.

Clearing the corner at the rear of the stucco house and twenty-five feet from the seawall, Red's advance screeched to a halt at the sound of an unfamiliar voice. Young Bobby, close behind and unable to stop as quickly, ran into Red and both boys went sprawling in the thick St. Augustine grass.

Standing on the seawall, a lightweight spinning rod bent nearly double, was a youth of about Red's age, clad in ragged cutoff blue jeans. An incredulous grin threatened to rip Scott's tanned face wide open. Amazement at the flaming red hair adorning the older of the two boys prone in the tall grass behind him was obvious as well.

Witnessing this klutzy arrival, Scott Thompson stated the obvious. "You gotta be Red. Wanna catch a jack? Come on, grab this rod. Crank with your left hand. Come on man," he struggled to get out between laughs. "This fish ain't gonna wait all day."

Living across the canal about 120 feet from the Dickson's new home, Scott was a personable and friendly boy. He'd already met Red's dad when asking permission to fish from his seawall. Now Scott was trying to get the newly arrived Red to catch his first salt water fish.

Red caught that fish, a three-pound jack crevalle, with its greenish-silver back and golden-yellow belly. During that brief encounter, he also made his first and best friend in his new home town. For the remainder of that summer, Red Dickson and Scott, along with bespectacled Peter Smith, were inseparable. The trio of thirteen-year-olds fished or water-skied constantly. When not on the water, Red and Scott would play one-on-one basketball in Scott's driveway or join in pickup baseball games at Croissant Park, Southside, or Holiday Park, where Scott played Pony League ball.

In August they caught that first "*almost ate my fuckin' face off*" shark from the 5 TEES in Port Everglades inlet. Then came September and with it came school. They rode the same bus five miles every weekday to Rogers Junior High at the old Naval Air Station. Red's athletic career began on the Rogers' basketball and flag football teams. The following summer produced numerous bluewater gamefish and lots of sharks, including the 856-pound hammerhead. Though they went to different high schools, time was found to fish, play sports, lie about girls, and just enjoy growing up in South Florida.

Red's parents enrolled him at Pine Crest, a private school on Broward Boulevard in Fort Lauderdale. Elaine Dickson became acquainted with several members of the school's faculty who convinced her it offered a superior overall education to the public schools. An enrollment of 450 students was distributed among the seventh and twelfth grades. Over eighty percent of its students went on to graduate from college. That alone, swayed the Dickson's high school selection process and Red became a Pine Crester.

Studies generally played second-fiddle to other activities, but Red still managed decent grades during high school. However, athletics consistently bode well of his future career and provided a possible avenue to fame. He excelled as a three-year starter in the major sports. Quarterbacking the school to district titles in his junior and senior years, he also played forward on the basketball team, making All-County as a junior and All-State as a senior.

But baseball was the sport that eventually earned him a college degree. With no real supporting cast, Red made second team All-State as a sophomore and first team in both his junior and senior years. Parade Magazine accorded him High School All-American honors for his final season.

For the first time in the history of Florida high school baseball, the same player won the state batting crown three years running. Red also led all state high schoolers in homers and runs batted in during his final two years. A good student with unlimited baseball potential, colleges and the pro's alike began hounding him his senior year.

Red graduated from high school on June 9th, 1964 with a B+ average. At six-foot-two, 195 pounds, the eighteen-year-old boy was still growing. Professional baseball was out of the question for at least four years, and the University of Georgia had a leg up in the wooing of Red. There was no way his parents, or Red, would even consider another college. William Dickson, William's brother, and Red's grandfather all matriculated from the U of G in Athens.

Boasting an excellent College of Business with recognized computer science and biology departments, Georgia met the Dickson family's stringent academic requirements. Its strong baseball program also sported a head coach with a reputation for developing his players and making sure proper attention was paid to the books. On a crisp, dry Monday morning, September 7th, 1964, Red Dickson moved into the athletic dormitory on the Georgia campus carrying fifteen hours of classes.

* * *

Four years literally *flew* by, filled with fun, excitement, above average academic success, and a college athletic career that was outstanding. Red, recognizing the demands he'd face during the baseball season, intended to concentrate on the books that first semester. He was on a full baseball scholarship, but his intramural basketball performance, played *just to stay in shape*, caught the freshman basketball coach's eye. Surprisingly little persuasion was required to get him to join the team. Red limited his play to home and nearby road games. The now six-foot three-inch point guard was second on the team in scoring at 17 points a game, while dishing out 6.7 assists and ripping down 5 boards each night he played.

Since freshmen were ineligible to participate in NCAA Division I varsity sports, the varsity baseball coaches could only drool over this remarkable prospect and wait for next year. During a twenty-seven game freshman schedule, Red played left field and hit .494 with 11 homers and 43 RBI's.

In Red's sophomore year, Georgia won the Southeastern Conference title, but was beaten by a strong University of Miami team in Regional Playoffs. It was his leanest year and he batted "only" .392 with 9 homers and 45 RBI's during a 26-6 season. Red really blossomed as a junior, leading the Bulldogs to another SEC title and a trip to the College World Series in Omaha, Nebraska. At the *Big Dance*, they lost in the finals. Georgia's record that year was 31 and 4, led by Red's resounding .518 average, 13 homers and 52 RBI's.   Willpower tested, he spurned several lucrative bonus offers from the pros.

Red was the consummate team player. In his senior year winning the NCAA Division I National Championship became his number one priority with graduation in June close behind. The Bulldogs lost to the University of Florida in 13 innings, and one nonconference game that season. They swept through the College World Series in the winner's bracket and the University of Georgia, propelled by Red's exploits, had their national championship. As his team was banging out a 41 and 2 season, Red rewrote collegiate batting records, leading the nation with an inconceivable .632 average, 23 homeruns, and 86 runs batted in. As June rolled around, he completed his eighth semester with a 3.09 overall GPA, but lacked two courses, totaling seven credit hours, of being able to graduate.

Red Dickson's collegiate eligibility expired on May 30th. On the afternoon of June 1st, 1968, at the age of twenty-two and with Mom and Dad at his side, the 6'4", 210 pound athlete signed with the Atlanta Braves. It was the most lucrative professional baseball contract ever awarded an unproven player.

The agreement stipulated a $225,000 signing bonus and salary of $150,000 for the remainder of the 1968 season and $250,000 for the 1969 season. Including incentive bonuses, he could earn up to $315,000 during the second year. An education clause was also typed in. The Braves would allot time for Red to complete the two courses he needed to graduate with a degree in Business Management.

On June 8th, Red started in right field for Atlanta against the St. Louis Cardinals. Lining a double off the left field wall in his first professional at bat, he went 3 for 5 and the Braves won 4-2.

Playing in 92 games his first season, Red batted .287 in his initial look at major league pitching. With 18 homeruns and 71 RBI's, he was the runaway National League Rookie of the Year. It would be his only Major League season under .300. The Braves finished third in their Division.

Trading bats for books, Red returned to the Athens campus and completed those two missing courses. He received his Bachelor of Arts degree in February 1969.

For nine years, Red's baseball career exceeded all expectations. The Braves dominated the sport, winning six Division crowns and four National League titles. Their four trips to the World Series saw them come away victorious three times, losing only in a seven game thriller to the Boston Red Sox in '73. Red's individual statistics were Hall of Fame caliber. He never batted less than .328 nor pounded out less than 34 homeruns. Winning three National League batting titles and six homerun crowns, his ultimate pinnacle was his second triple crown in 1977. His .392 average, 46 homers, and 164 RBI's gave him tremendous negotiating power as his three -year contract ran out.

By then, Red was already wealthy, thanks to shrewd investment advice from his father, his rising salary, and outside endorsement contracts with companies like Rawlings and Pepsi Cola. To top that off, the Braves rewarded him with a *lifetime contract*, starting with the 1978 season. Red became baseball's first-million-dollar man.

On December 17th, 1977 Red was offered and signed a ten year contract calling for $1.1 million in 1978 and escalating fifteen percent each year until it reached $2.2 million in 1983. From 1983 through 1987, his salary would remain at the $2.2 million figure. In addition, an annuity was generated which would pay Red $450,000 per year from retirement through age sixty-five. The entire package was guaranteed through Lloyds of London Insurance Underwriters. If Red suffered a career-ending injury, he would be paid the stated amounts through the year 2010. If he should die, an amount equal to two-thirds of the contract dollars would be paid to his beneficiary or his estate. Red Dickson was set for life.

* * *

In the 1978 season's opening game, Tommy Johnson of the Los Angeles Dodgers tossed a six hitter, beating the Atlanta Braves 4-2. Red drove in both Brave runs with a bases empty, opposite field homer in the fourth inning and a single in the seventh. After that, they opened a series at Shea Stadium against the New York Mets riding a twenty-two game winning streak.

In spite of his huge contract, the Braves felt they were getting the bargain of the century. Red was having an unbelievable year. The baseball, screaming in at over ninety miles per hour, looked like a basketball to Red and he hit everything with authority. In spite of getting twenty-five bases on balls in the first twenty-three games, he had already connected for 10 homeruns and driven in 38 runs. His batting average was an astronomical .554 and he played errorless ball in the field. Compared to salary versus performance of many other major league players, Red was being underpaid. But . . .

"It's the top of the eighth gang. Looks like the Atlanta Braves phenomenal winning streak may just run out of steam this Friday evening." The Atlanta Braves Superstation TV announcer's familiar voice seemed to be preparing a national cable network audience for the inevitable. "With two out in the inning and trailing New York 6 to 3, we have men on first and second and Dickson coming to bat. Red launched his eleventh homerun of this young season in the first. A towering shot into the left-centerfield bleachers with two men on, it gave the Braves a 3-zip lead and their only runs. However, Ryan fanned him the next two times up, only the third and fourth time Red's gone down on strikes this year in almost 100 at bats. The count is one and two on the batter. Runners take their leads. Ryan stretches, checks the runner on second, here's the pitch. It's lined out toward right center field. It's in the gap, going to the wall at the 396-foot mark." Spreading his infectious excitement over the TV network, the announcer continued, "One run is in, Martin is rounding third. He'll score. Dickson's heading for third."

Frustrated by his two strikeouts, Red was concentrating on just meeting the ball and putting it in play. Jack Ryan, a lanky lefthander, threw him a sharp breaking curve ball which started well outside the strike zone and broke in toward the right-handed hitter. The ball would have cut the black on the outside edge of the plate at the knees for called strike three if Red let it go. He didn't.

As usual during the phenomenal streak he was enjoying, the ball simulated a slow-pitch softball as it spun toward home plate. Red could almost count the red stitches in the white cover and make out NL President Chub Feeney's signature as he initiated his swing. There was no perceptible movement to his head as his sparkling eyes fixed on the incoming sphere. The white ball flattened when the sweet part of the heat-forged-hickory-Adirondack bat connected. He hit the ball millimeters below its center, not enough lift to leave the park, but Red knew no one could catch it.

Leaving the batter's box, the play was in front of him. He saw the backs of two Met outfielders pursuing the ball toward that distant wall. Rounding first, he watched the ball take a crazy bounce off the padded brick facade almost 400 feet from home plate and kick past the right fielder. He knew he could stretch this one into a triple. Scoring from third base was so much easier than getting in from second, and he was the tying run.

Approaching third, he realized it was going to be close. The Met third baseman's stance awaiting the relay throw told him a fade-away hookslide to the outfield side of the bag would beat the tag. The third base coach was on his knees, palms flailing downward at the ground, signaling Red to slide. He hit the dirt, left leg pointed ahead and aimed for the right-hand edge of the white canvas bag. His right leg was on the ground, bent up under him and catching his weight like thousands of times before. Red's right toe reached the bag an instant before the ball smacked into the third baseman's mitt and the ensuing slap of the tag on his left arm. He was in. The last thing he remembered before the pain was the downward spread of the third base umpire's palms as he bellowed "Safeeee!"

"Dickson's in at third with the tying run and . . ." the TV announcer yelled enthusiastically as his play-by-play continued. Unexpectedly, concern took over his broadcast as his voice lowered and he babbled, "Oh my God! The bag came loose! Red's rolling on the ground! It look's like his leg! He's hurt his right leg! Can the commercial, Joe. We'll stay here. Let's hope it isn't serious. But Red Dickson is definitely hurt."

As Red slid into third base, the bag came loose and his spikes caught in the tie-down ring beneath it. His right leg, from the knee down, stopped abruptly while the rest of his body carried on past the bag. The knee literally snapped, severely tearing cartilage and ligaments in the joint. Red felt instantaneous, blinding pain and then nothing. Nothing that is, until he tried to move and the second wave of pain hit him. Mercifully, he passed out.

"Here's the story as we know it. Red Dickson has been carried from the field on a stretcher." The play-by-play description continued. "He appeared to be unconscious and the Braves' trainer, assisted by the Met's team physician, used an inflatable air bag to immobilize the leg. It looks like the right knee. Once again fans, superstar Red Dickson injured his right leg and is being taken to the hospital. We'll update you on Red's condition as soon as we hear anything. In the meantime, the score is now 6 to 5 Mets. The Braves have the tying run on third base in pinch runner . . ."

The Atlanta Braves stranded that tying run at third and lost the game. Their winning streak ended. Two hours after being carried from the field at Shea Stadium, Red was wheeled into the recovery room, still under the effects of the anesthesia. Renowned orthopedic surgeon, Dr. Horace Kelso, was in consultation with two other physicians who witnessed the exploratory effort. The right knee was locked in the bent position. The medial meniscus was torn loose and flipped over. The separated cartilage wedged itself in the joint, prohibiting straightening of the leg. The orientation of the joint was distorted to the extent that X-rays were inconclusive. An internal examination was required utilizing an arthroscope.

Initial hopes that the damage would be limited to torn cartilage proved to be unrealistic. The lateral meniscus was torn too. However, the major damage occurred to both the anterior and posterior cruciate ligaments. This was correctable, but the degree of recovery varied dramatically from case to case. Most disturbing to Kelso was apparent damage to the fibular collateral ligament and the neighboring tendon of Popliteus near their attachment to the base of the femur. The severity couldn't be determined until the knee was opened up. Repairs would have to made at that time. In any case, major surgery was mandatory within eighteen hours. At 1:30 PM on May 15, 1978, Dr. Kelso, assisted by two other prominent orthopedic surgeons, began a six-hour operation attempting to reconstruct William "Red" Dickson's right knee. Red's season was over.

Chapter Seven

I WANT PETER SMITH

Rehabilitation efforts proved fruitless. When the team physician recommended cutting on him again, Red opted for another opinion. He chose his boyhood chum, Peter Smith, now a highly regarded orthopedic surgeon. His future would rest with one of his two closest friends.

"I want Peter Smith for the second opinion," Red demanded. Christmas was only a week away and he was six months into an exhaustive rehabilitation program. His knee was being examined for what seemed like the zillionth time and Dr. Kelso was recommending additional surgery. "The knee just ain't respondin' like it should," the frustrated athlete continued, disappointment obvious in his voice. "God knows I've been bustin' my ass with your damn exercises. Cutting on it again may be needed, might even do some good, but before I go through all that again, I want someone else's advice. I've known Peter since I was thirteen and I want him to take a look at it. Anyway, since Lloyds pays the bill, the front office wants another opinion."

* * *

"Come on, Peter," Red drawled. "You know damn well this ole country boy don't understand that medical jargon. Give it to me in plain English. What's the damage? Will I ever play again?"

Arms crossed, Red sat across the desk from his friend in Peter's office. While waiting on a reply, the redhead glanced around the room and spotted a fading 8 x 10 glossy showing the smiling faces of three boys and the grotesque snout of a huge hammerhead shark. They relived catching the 856 pound fish then got down to business.

"Okay Red, I'll cut through the BS and lay it out for you. I've examined the X-rays Kelso sent and I also reviewed records of your treatment so far and your rehabilitation progress. Then I looked over the new X-rays we took yesterday." Peter held several of the new pictures and was skillfully glancing at them one-at-a-time until he found the one he wanted. "Take a look at this area . . ."

"Basically, I can't tell you anything without going inside for a closer look. We'll have to use an arthroscope on your knee. If it shows what I think it will, it'll be much less traumatic for you if I do a routine surgical procedure on your knee while you're still under the anesthetic."

"And exactly what do you call a routine procedure," Red asked. "Remember buddy, it's me you'll be cuttin' on."

Peter smiled reassuringly. "I've done it a hundred times. The major procedure involves removing small sections of ligament from the front of each hip. Those pieces will replace portions of one of the cruciate ligaments and the fibular collateral ligament in the knee. These ligaments haven't healed properly since the first operation. The connection points for the new ligaments must be sound. Only the arthroscope can tell us about their integrity. If the damage is irreparable," the doctor paused for a second before continuing, "well, then we don't go any further. I'll simply retract the arthroscope and close up the quarter-inch incisions with three small stitches." A touch of fear was hinted in Red's voice as he asked, "In that case, what about me playing ball again?"

"Can't tell at this juncture. Only time will answer that question. I do suggest we operate as soon as possible." Without hesitation, Peter confidently added, "But I honestly believe we'll be able to patch you up."

Leaning forward in the plush leather chair and looking optimistically into the eyes of his friend, Red agreed. "Okay Doc Smitty, let's go for it."

The following afternoon, Red went under the knife again. An arthroscopic examination of the fibular collateral ligament showed it wasn't healing properly and a section of the anterior cruciate ligament was not responding to treatment. However, all the connection points appeared to be sound and the extended procedure was warranted. Red, the Braves, Lloyds of London, and Dr. Kelso had reached a decision earlier. If the internal examination confirmed more surgery was necessary, Dr. Smith was to do the selected procedure immediately.

Peter closed up Red and, while watching the orderlies wheel him out of the operating theater en route to the recovery room stated, "Well gentlemen, we've done all we can. It's now up to Dickson and God, maybe not in that order."

* * *

"Welcome back slugger," Peter said. "We did good. I think you've got a hell of a chance." His words didn't mean much to Red as the peaceful bliss brought on by the anesthesia gradually wore off. "How you feeling? You want an update now or should I come back later?"

"Doc Smitty, that you?" Red replied incoherently. "Time to go fishing already? Can't be morning yet, huh?"

"Damn Red," Peter blurted. "You and your nicknames. How many fingers you see? What year is it?"

Red spent the next four days flat on his back in a private hospital room and two more weeks confined to his plush apartment. He then started on the long road back. His physical rehabilitation effort in attempting to restore his right knee to pre-injury condition was profound. Before the cast even came off, six weeks after the operation, he was spending time with his physical therapist, Michael Dennis. Exercising other parts of his body, they meticulously planned a program he would follow once his right leg was workable again. The physical exertion seemed to cleanse Red. He lost himself in a private world of athletic effort and its accompanying fatigue. During his workouts, it was just Red and the challenge of his weights and exercise machines.

The months following surgery Red chose to rehabilitate in his adopted hometown of Fort Lauderdale and old friendships from his teenage years were renewed. Several long-unheard-from school and neighborhood chums still resided there. But the most noteworthy friendships rekindled were with Peter Smith and Scott Thompson.

Scott had given up the oilfield construction work he was doing the last time they corresponded and subsequently earned a Master's Degree at LSU. He now lived in Miami with his wife and two children. Attending the University of Miami full time, Scott was working toward a PhD in Ichthyology. That friendship's revival would deeply affect and forever change Red's life. Before that happened however, Mr. Red Dickson was going to experience some dramatic changes to his life.

* * *

Fascinated by computers and exposed to the financial markets via his father's profession, Red developed new interests. He had utilized a great deal of the idle time during his previous rehabilitation to investigate the stock and futures markets. In the process, he formulated historically accurate price charting models for market indices and for a few select commodities, including the precious metals. Red committed to "beating the market" during the non-exercise periods of his recovery.

Mike Dennis let him use a small, but comfortable, room at the therapist's facility. Equipped with a powerful IBM personal computer and modem, it connected Red via telephone lines to stock prices available at his father's office. He put a similar hookup in his ninth floor apartment, overlooking the Atlantic Ocean.

Red's fortune was made from *inside information*. A friend in Dallas advised him that two brothers, having made their fortunes in oil and other ventures including a football team, intended to corner the silver market.

". . . and we're sure it's more than a rumor," the baritone voice on the phone assured. "Severe shortages in silver are coming up. The brothers have been picking it up a few hundred contracts at a time, but they're about to really get serious."

"What's the timing?" Red asked, his financial adrenaline beginning to flow. "How soon do I need to get in?"

"Better plan on starting today, tomorrow at the latest," the distant voice replied. "I've got it on good info that the big players are accelerating their programs this week."

"Where's it stand this morning?" Red queried, referring to the market price of silver contracts.

"I think it'll open about $5.65 to $5.75," came the reply. "That's up from $5.37 last Friday. It can only go higher. Start taking your position and fasten your seatbelt, gonna be one helluva ride." A chuckle resonated through the wire as the voice concluded, "You're gonna make a bundle good buddy. Gotta go."

"Thank is a lot. Be talking to ya," Red grinned as he hung up the receiver. He'd been expecting this news and was prepared to take immediate action. The recent $5 to $6 per ounce prices were destined to escalate ten fold or more. Already positioned in the market, the men in Dallas planned to initiate a substantial buying program. Prices could only go higher. If you could afford a modest degree of risk, the upside potential was virtually limitless. Intrigued by the prospect of making huge amounts of money in a short time, Red took the plunge.

Through his father's brokerage firm, he opened a commodity trading securities account with $350,000. On March 15th, Red placed his initial order. "That's right Dad, 100 contracts for December silver at the market. I'll be adding to it later. Give me a call when we fill it and let me know what we paid."

Picking up an additional 200 contracts over the next three months, Red eventually controlled 1.5 million ounces which escalated almost daily in value. As silver's phenomenal run continued, the value of his contracts appreciated by millions of dollars each month.

By mid-September the Exchange Commission, which controlled silver trading, had systematically increased margin requirements, originally $1,000 per contract, to $20,000 per contract, trying to force the larger, market-moving speculators into covering positions and start selling. When this happened Red sold fifty of those December contracts at a price of $15.75/oz. His account was credited with just under $4 million and he still controlled 250 contracts. With the price soaring, he started liquidating his position. Just before the Christmas holiday he sold the second fifty December contracts at $24/oz. On January 5th of the new decade he unloaded a third fifty contracts at $37/oz.

Skittishness increased with each passing day. Red's strenuous exercise program under Mike's guiding hand exorcised building emotional strain, but dejection increased over a slow rehabilitation progress. Even optimistic Doc Smitty felt Red's chances to play professional baseball again were less that even money. With that heavy burden, and a vast fortune residing in his commodity account, Red placed another call to his father's office. On January 21, 1980, Red instructed, "Okay Dad, time to get out. Lets dump the rest at market and count our money."

His father's voice on the phone confirmed in a very professional manner, "That's a sell order for fifty March silvers and 100 May silvers at the market. Current price is $45.45. I'll advise when the positions are covered. It may take a while. Congratulations son, you've really done well this time."

Effective sales prices ranged from $45.50 to $49/oz, with an average of $47/oz. Red was safely out of the silver market with *forty-and-a-half million dollars* in pretax profits.

The rise in silver prices continued past the $50/oz mark.

Staying in touch with his Dallas friend throughout the run, Red learned that the Texas brothers were having trouble covering margin requirements. The bubble was about to burst. On a gut feeling that *what goes up must come down*, Red called his father one more time with the instructions, "Place a sell-short-order for me for 200 July contracts at $45/oz."

As January ended, the demise began. Silver prices started downward, filling his order which sold contracts he'd have to buy later to cover, hopefully at a much lower price.

The decrease gained momentum and silver prices plummeted. In mid-March, Red exited the volatile precious metal market when he instructed Dickson, Sr. to cover his short position. Filling the order at an average price of $14/oz, his real profits amounted to an additional *thirty-one million.*

Taking advantage of capital gains on commodity gains and losses, Red settled his tax bill and paid all outstanding commissions and interest charges. After all expenses, Red Dickson was left with over *forty-nine million dollars* in the bank. Coupled with a previous net worth exceeding $5.5 million built up before the silver runs, and the megabucks salary and a guaranteed annuity through 2010, Red Dickson was a very wealthy man. It was now time to find out about his baseball future.

* * *

Although Peter told him he would never be able to play professional baseball again, Red had his own opinion. A short run up I-95 in his new silver Ferrari got him to the Atlanta Braves training camp at Palm Beach. After a pleasant reunion with old teammates and friends, everything seemed just like it did before that fateful Friday night in Shea Stadium. Early stretching and limbering up exercises were uneventful and the excellent condition of his body surprised even him. Then came the quick starts in the outfield chasing fly balls. He couldn't get his remembered jump on the ball and even his throwing suffered. No longer could he plant his right leg and throw against it. Pain wasn't the problem. Though there, it was tolerable. The knee's lack of strength and his diminished reactions were his downfall.

Maybe just hitting? Red thought. There was always the *other* league and if he could hit anywhere like before, just two seasons ago, he could be a designated hitter. The Braves could deal him to the American League. He saw the ball really well. His arms and upper body were stronger than ever before, thanks to his exercise program. His bat was quick, no problem there. The problem was Red's right leg. He couldn't hit off it; could hardly get out of the batter's box without falling down. Red realized it was over, that Peter Smith's opinion was accurate. He was through with baseball as an active player. Packing his bag and wishing them a successful season, he bid farewell to his teammates. Tossing his gear in the back of the sleek sportscar, Red headed south toward Fort Lauderdale and a new life.

Interstate 95 was crowded and at the second Pompano Beach exit, the powerful Ferrari came to a crawl when it encountered the usual Friday afternoon exodus from work. Red's mind strayed from his driving, consciously searching for new direction to his life. What was he to do without baseball? Money was no object. He need never work again. But he wanted a new challenge, something to keep from going crazy, to make his life worthwhile.

Chapter Eight

LIFE CONTINUES

It was difficult for Red to accept never playing baseball again. He thought about coaching or a front office job. No, he was a participant, not an observer. Being around the game would only remind him of his loss. What to do? He had all the money in the world and yet he was unhappy.

The fishing bug had bitten him again during his rehabilitation efforts. He made several trips with Doc, Scott, and Scott's son, Tommy. Since his heart was into baseball at the time, the fishing excursions were therapeutic but unfulfilling. With baseball out of the picture, he felt he really needed to get away, to cut the string to his professional past.

A couple of weeks after leaving the Braves' camp Red dropped the lease on his apartment. With his platinum American Express and gold Mastercard tucked safely in his wallet and $25,000 of travelers checks in his coat pocket, Red left town. Money and investments would be controlled jointly by his father and Charles Franklin, a friend and senior vice-president at Broward National Bank. He would keep in touch weekly by cable or phone.

* * *

Red's first destination was Europe. He divided his time equally between England, Paris and Rome for more than three months but the "country boy" in Red found little solace. He felt if he met people, stayed busy, lived the *wild life* for a while, that his loss of playing the game he loved would lessen.

People were naturally drawn to this big, extroverted, good looking, wealthy ex-athlete. Near royalty, heiresses, aspiring actresses, and just plain gold diggers, all exquisitely figured and beautiful, spent his money in the daytime and attempted to win his heart after dark. Screwing himself to death once seemed like a great way to go, but no longer. The time came to move on. Red wasn't certain what he was looking for but this wasn't it.

He then flew to Southeast Asia and spent a few more months wandering aimlessly through Tokyo, Hong Kong, a week or so in

Manilla and then on to Singapore where, while in a restaurant, he came across a travel brochure that intrigued him. Just after lunch his bags were packed and he was on his way to the land Down Under, to Sydney, Australia.

The down-to-earth attitude of the Australians was pleasing to the transplanted Georgian. He journeyed to various ports around the coast and spent time touring the Outback. Choosing to spend much time alone and having the rest of his life to spend, he began reading. What fascinated him most were various tales of the past.

An almost analytical investigation of local legends uncovered during these stops became his *modus operandi*. Libraries and the archives of old churches and townships became his habitual haunts. Just talking with natives about stories handed down from generation to generation was fun for him. He kept so busy and was so involved in this newfound avocation that his mind was beginning to accept the fact that baseball was his past.

While Red was globe trotting, his broker and his dad were taking excellent care of his assets. By Christmas of 1980, his investments were earning him an average of sixteen percent, over a half-million dollars a month. His financial fortune continued to grow. Even considering all his traveling, a couple years of living like this would cost less than two month's interest alone. Things were good, and about to get better.

* * *

After two weeks in New Zealand, Red was returning to Sydney from Auckland on the North Island where he heard a fascinating tale from a seventy-year-old shopkeeper in one of those dusty, little shops on the waterfront. The gaunt, grey-haired New Zealander spun a century-and-a-half old story about natives who had reportedly encountered a gigantic shark, a tale perpetuated in fireside legend. Descendants of those fishermen were the elderly man's sources. They believed the *God Shark*, as it was called, first appeared near some large islands almost three thousand miles to the north, now called New Caledonia.

Red was shown some old drawings and carvings depicting the incident. The shopkeeper then took him to an ancient monastery on the North Cape that had information about the occurrence. This information referred to a hand-written account of what happened, transcribed in English by a missionary who arrived on the island about 1830. It was rumored that the original document was in a church near the town of Noumea on the southern tip of New Caledonia. The encounter was described to the missionary by the only survivor, a young man who later became chief. A necklace, made from the *God Shark's* teeth and manifesting mystical powers, was presently in the possession of a descendant of that chief.

Armed with names and places and excited over this new discovery, Red boarded a Qantas flight to Sydney, planning a trip to New Caledonia as soon as possible. The Boeing 727 took off and climbed slowly above the Tasman Sea. Bearing just north of due west, the aircraft started its six-hour flight to Sydney. Settling back in his first-class window seat and stretching those long legs out in front of him, Red began reliving the past few days. His mind flashed back, comparing those stories to what Scott said he saw off Fort Lauderdale almost twenty years earlier.

"Coffee, tea, something to drink?" the Qantas flight attendant asked him. "Perhaps a snack? We won't be serving dinner until we reach our cruising altitude, another forty minutes."

"Thanks," Red replied without looking up. "A little scotch with some ginger ale would be fine. On the rocks, please. And maybe some peanuts or other munchies," he added as he felt an embarrassing growl rumble in his stomach.

Feeling the young lady's continued presence, he glanced up quickly and his mind went blank at the vision hovering in the aisle beside him. With that glance, Cupid's sneaky little arrow found its way to Red's heart.

Jane Kent was the senior stewardess on his flight and was probably the most beautiful woman Red had ever seen. After spending so much time with the wealthy and would-be-wealthy in Europe, he was attracted to the simple, straight-forwardness of this twenty-five-year-old woman. He asked her to have dinner with him that evening. She agreed.

The evening was a success. Jane told Red of her family's small sheep ranch in Brisbane and how she enjoyed the simple life. The pleasure of just being across the table from Jane Kent excited Red and her genuine appreciation for and enjoyment of life was contagious. Completely at ease with her, Red's spirits were raised to pre-accident levels.

For the following month, he and Jane Kent were virtually inseparable. Just holding her hand, being with her, listening to her talk, feeling the warmth of her body and being in love filled Red with unimaginable joy.

One day while Red and Jane were lounging during that marvelous "get-to-know each other" time, Red dusted off his notes and information from New Zealand. Jane was easily convinced to take a week's holiday and fly to New Caledonia with him. On Friday morning, February 6, 1981, the couple boarded a TWA jet. They departed from Brisbane where Red met her widowed mother and two younger brothers. Their destination was Noumea. Jane really enjoyed the *nonworking* flight.

A quaint, thatch-roofed bungalow housed them for five splendid days and nights. The first night, Red held Jane in his arms and was content to sleep next to her warm body listening to her breathe and feeling her gentle movements. That first morning they enjoyed a breakfast of tropical fruit and juices at a small table in the open-air porch adjoining their bungalow. As they looked at each other across that table over cups of hot tea, both realized how serious their feelings for each other were.

On the second night, they made love. Jane had never before *been with* a man. Red took her slowly, carefully, lovingly. Reaching the initial climax of her life simultaneously with him, life's most wondrous event transpired, although neither knew it at the time. Jane Kent, assisted by William *Red* Dickson, Jr. conceived. That fabulous evening of lovemaking was followed the next morning by a lobster and fish brunch washed down by exotic tropical fruit drinks. During the meal, Red Dickson proposed and Jane Kent accepted.

Red's excitement over his pending marriage was barely controllable. When coupled with the eventual discovery two months later that Jane was going to make him a father made everything perfect.

Then, another extraordinary event transpired. Red located the small framed church that was so well described by the monk on the North Cape.

GOD SHARK

Friar James was very helpful, diligently guiding Red's careful leafing through centuries-old records. Fragile page after fragile page was void of any mention of a *God Shark*. Frustration and disappointment mounting, Red was nearing the end of the final ancient book. With only four pages of aging parchment left to read, his eyes suddenly widened with excitement and riveted to the script before him. *"Hot damn!"* he shouted. *"Here it is!"* Even the friar's chastising scowl at Red's profanity didn't diminish the moment.

The story written on those pages was by Friar Andrew in 1845, who transcribed the tale sometime after arriving on the island. The encounter supposedly happened fourteen years earlier, during an unusual period of famine and drought. Carefully written in the Queen's English, the story was related to him by a twenty-eight-year-old native chief, named Jarak. The reigning heads of local native tribes were generally much older.

Accompanying his father and ten native warriors, the fifteen-year-old Jarak had ventured into the unknown to search for the elusive dorado. Their village's survival depended on this hunt. They found the dorado, but a gigantic fish attacked their canoe, killing everyone but Jarak. He drifted to an unknown island where he found food and fresh water. A week later, he set sail for home.

"I was awakened by the shaking of other island boys. Too exhausted to even weep, I told about the giant fish's attack and the terrible deaths of my father and the others. Though there was much sorrow over the loss of so many, my miraculous survival and safe return was cause for joy. The bird eggs and coconuts my canoe carried from the distant land fed many as hope overcame the grief. There was a place within reach with fresh water and food. And the golden dorado were back. We would survive.

"A meeting of the Great Council was held. They called this fish, the God Shark. It brought us food and the dorado. The next day, all our canoes set sail for that distant island which had granted me life. With great honor, I Jarak, guided the lead canoe. Flower wreaths were thrown on the blue sea's surface one day into the journey. Immediately, the clear water filled with dancing silvers, blues, and golds of the dorado. As many as there were stars in the dark night's sky. The God Shark had spoken again.

"My people crossed the sea of death in one less moon than I needed to get home. Fear was always with us. We believed the God Shark would return to take its fee, to eat some of our tribe. My people were willing to die if necessary to feed the rest of the tribe. It did not. Late on the second day we saw land." Jarak's story ended.

* * *

Friar Andrew wrote; *"It was on this supposedly new homeland that I heard the tale about a God Shark. I did not believe it, thinking of it as typical native superstition and folklore. I continued preaching, striving to bring salvation and our savior Jesus Christ to my new flock. 'Forget such foolishness and turn to the true God. Only He can save you from eternal damnation!'*

"Then, during a sermon, Jarak produced the tribe's magical necklace. The tribe believed this necklace prevented the God Shark from returning to wreak havoc on fishermen of the tribe. They also believed that this talisman would guarantee the continuing presence of the dorado.

The necklace was made from the tightly woven fiber of coconut palms, braided into a long, single cord. On it hung five gleaming white objects which measured almost twelve inches from the edges of the roughened flat tops to the needle sharp tips at the bottoms. They were concave with serrated edges as sharp as my straight razor. I held in my hands the teeth of the God Shark taken from the remains of the canoe that carried Jarak home."

So ended the narrative, with a few additional comments by Friar Andrew including a statement about the liberties he took in effecting the English translation. Red's questioning of the mission's current caretaker, Friar James, a Noumea resident for twenty-seven years, revealed he'd seen the sacred necklace four times. Red wanted to see the necklace but this was not possible at this time. The time wasn't right for the man who was in possession of the necklace. Red, undaunted, would return when the time *was* right.

* * *

Neither Jane nor her mom had any real idea of just how rich Red was, only that he was, apparently, a *well-off Yank*. Mrs. Kent, fifty-five, was a widow of seven years. She took an instant liking to Red and was ecstatic when told of her daughter's engagement. The two youngsters, as she called them, had set June 15th as the wedding date. That was Jane's parent's anniversary. In mid-April, Jane learned she was expecting, but there was no urgency to advance the wedding, then only two months off. Red did ask her to quit flying. Returning to Brisbane, she took an apartment near her mom's home. There, she and Mrs. Kent began meticulously planning the impending wedding and prepared for the blessed arrival in November.

Red leased a silver Porsche and the lovebirds relished racing across empty countryside and negotiating mountain roads in the sporty little car. Red had a three-day fishing trip scheduled to the Great Barrier Reef but Jane chose to stay home and visit some friends. She dropped him off at the Brisbane airport for his flight to Cairns. After receiving instructions on when he'd be back, Red told her not to be late picking him up. He wanted to see her and spend as much time with her as was possible. "I want to hold you in my arms the very second I land."

Jane paused to watch his plane rocket skyward and then headed for the home of a childhood friend to spend the evening looking at crystal and silver patterns; important details to any bride.

Glancing at the 200-year-old grandfather clock, Jane was shocked at the time. The two black hands in front of the carefully painted bird and flowers registered 10:33.

"Oh my gosh, Cindy, what's happened to the time? Mom'll be worried sick. Got to go." Jane Kent carefully placed the catalog of lace linens back on her friend's coffee table and stood up. "What's Red say? 'My how time flies when you're having fun.' Thanks love. I'll call you tomorrow morning." A quick smile at twenty-six-year-old Cindy Barker and Jane sifted through her purse for the car keys. Locating the distinctive Porsche logo, she headed for the front door.

At 10:40 P.M. that evening, Jane Kent left Cindy Barker's apartment radiating happiness and bubbling with life, her life and the marvelous creation growing within her. A long and fruitful existence lay ahead with the man she loved. Turning the ignition key, she couldn't suppress her joy. Stroking her still flat stomach, she offered a brief prayer to her maker. "Thank you God for William Dickson. Thank you for my life and for our child. Thank you for all my many blessings." With so much to be thankful for, Jane Kent backed out of her friend's driveway for the twenty minute drive to her apartment.

* * *

At noon the following day, the police, alerted by a passerby who noticed skid marks and a broken guard rail, found the wreck. Apparently, an empty lorry had been speeding and lost control rounding a hairpin curve. The investigating officer surmised that Jane had been at the peak of the curve when it happened. The larger vehicle had broadsided the Porsche, forcing it through the guardrail and off a 300-foot embankment. Both the lorry and the sportscar plummeted to the bottom of the ravine crushing Jane Kent and their unborn fetus. The lorry driver also died and flames consumed both vehicles and their occupants.

Richard Kent, Jane's nineteen-year-old brother, made the call to Red in Cairns. Mrs. Kent required sedation. On that stormy May afternoon in eastern Australia, less than a month away from being married, Red Dickson's world was again shattered.

The tragedy engulfed Red, inflicting him with a lingering, agonizing death of his own in the same flames that took the life of the women he loved so deeply. His broken heart crashed and burned under the searing pain. She was so beautiful, so vibrant, so very much alive. She was his world, his sole reason for living. With Jane gone, life had no meaning. Thoughts of suicide filled Red's waking hours. Why try to go on? Burdened by self-induced pressures to "end it all," his world collapsed for a second time. But this time was far more profound than the last. Yes, he had loved baseball, but Jane Kent had become his *entire life!*

* * *

Red spent the better part of thirteen months trying to restore his shattered life. Many times he contemplated suicide. There was three months straight of total seclusion and brooding followed by seven months of drinking and spending. No one could find him. He needed this alone time, this time for self-abuse, this time to reason. Being stronger than most Red knew he could not escape reality. He had to face up to this lousy hand life had dealt him and pull himself together.

His resurrection began with five days in a French jail for being drunk and disorderly. Direction was reborn through the local prison priest, a middle-aged man-of-the-cloth who'd lost his wife, two young children, and both of his legs in an automobile accident outside of Paris. From his wheelchair, and helped by the one true God, that priest somehow infused Red with strength and hope.

A different Red Dickson set foot in Florida for the first time in over two years. His previously vast fortune had ballooned, appreciating by many millions of dollars. His parents were older than he remembered them and his mother's health was rapidly failing. The *"Big C"* had found yet another victim. Checking in with Doc Smitty's office, he learned his friend and physician was off on a fishing jaunt to Costa Rica and would be home in about a week. The day after he deplaned from a National Airline DC-10 in Miami, Red Dickson dialed the telephone number of Scott and Louise.

"My dad's at the university," the sweet young voice on the phone said politely, "but my mom's here. I'll get her for you. May I say who's calling?"

"Tell her it's Red Dickson please," he replied. "Is this Kristine? You sound so grownup. Do you remember me?"

"Oh yes sir, yes sir!" the little girl squealed. Red smiled at her enthusiastic response. He could hear her hollering, "Mom, mom, phone! It's Uncle Red! Yes ma'am, he's on the phone!" And back into the phone, "Just a minute please, she's coming." And at her mother again, "Come on mom, hurry! It's Uncle Red! It's Uncle Red!"

"Hello, Red," Louise whispered in a low and caring voice. "Is that really you?" The warmth and emotion he was hearing reminded him so much of his dear, departed Jane.

"Hi Louise, how are you?" Red replied. "Got in last night. Wanted to know if I might come by and visit ya'll."

"You are always welcome and wanted here," Louise offered. "We were so worried about you. One other thing, Mr. William Dickson, Jr. You are *never* to go off like that again," Louise scolded Red. "Scott and I love you very much and when you have trouble, it's only fair to share it with us. Thanks for coming home safely."

Red came over that afternoon and Louise insisted that he bring clothes to stay at least the weekend. After all, there was two years of catching up to do.

Red was overwhelmed by the similarity between his beloved Jane and Louise Thompson. Jane's natural beauty was reflected in Louise, but their unrestrained caring for others and down-to-earth sincerity really stamped them from the same mold.

During several hours of conversation, Red purged two years of absence. He felt no shame in his unrestrained tears. Voice cracking, he spoke of the love affair, the wedding preparations, the expected child, and of Jane's accident. An overwhelming burden lessened more that night and the bonds of love and friendship grew even stronger between the Thompson's and Red.

The following day Scott shanghaied Red for a visit to the offices and laboratories on the University of Miami campus. Then, the two friends drove out to the expansive research station on the northern edge of Biscayne Bay. Later in the day, Louise and the two younger Thompson's joined them and the five spent Saturday afternoon at the Miami Seaquarium. That evening, after grilled sirloins on the charcoal pit had been washed down by red wine, fishing stories and shark tales flowed freely.

The ex-ballplayer's fate was sealed by eight-year-old Kristine crawling up into his lap, flashing her baby-green eyes at him, and stating, "Gosh Uncle Red, you sound just like my daddy. With all you know about fish and sharks, you oughta work for him at the school." Young Tommy added, "That'd be neat Uncle Red. Then we could do a lot more fishing." And turning to his smiling dad, who couldn't have orchestrated his two children's comments any better if he'd planned it, pleaded, "Couldn't he dad? I mean, isn't that just a super idea?"

Chapter Nine

FISHIN' BUDDIES AGAIN

The charter was confirmed eight months earlier, shortly after Peter returned from his second trip to the northeastern coast of Australia. However, they did not fulfill his quest for a *grander*. Like so many affluent sportsfishermen throughout the world, Peter Smith intended to fight and catch a marlin weighing over that magical 1,000 pounds.

Captain Jim Gaffney, though not yet thirty years of age, had gained quite a reputation among the fishing community. He was already a truly seasoned veteran of the marlin fishing wars as well as a renowned shark expert. Several of Peter's colleagues through the IGFA had fished with Gaffney and every single report was positive. Even knowledgeable members of the International Yachtsman's Association were aware of Captain Jim Gaffney's marlin and great white shark fishing exploits half-a-world away. Comments such as, "If you're going all the way to Australia to drag a bait, you damn sure better get the best skipper. That'd be Gaffney," convinced Doc he should do just that.

Peter cabled funds to Gaffney's agent in Cairns and instructed him to book a trip if an opening developed during a *prime marlin period*. A cancellation occurred and, in February 1983, Peter, young Tommy, and Scott Thompson flew into Sydney from Los Angeles and connected with a flight to Cairns.

* * *

The five-day trip was successful as Doc and Scott each tagged and released two huge black marlin, including one *grander* apiece. The younger Mr. Thompson conquered a 576-pound blue marlin, which did not survive the long battle, and the beauty eventually found a resting place on a wall in Scott's Miami home. The action was steady and they spread it around, bringing at least one billfish to boat each and every day. In addition to what they caught, one other very large marlin succeeded in fraying the 300-pound-test mono leader in two after a grueling six-hour-battle with

Doc on the second day. Three other marlin threw their hooks in acrobatic aerial displays. It was one fabulous fishing experience.

Enhancing this memorable fishing, a mutual admiration emerged between Scott, Doc and Captain Gaffney. Scott's scientific interests in great whites really drew him to Jim. Three still-young men, separated by about ten years in age and diverse rankings on life's social pyramid, hit it off immediately.

Throughout the trip, Gaffney and Scott spent most of their time on the flying bridge discussing sharks. Doc's hands were full trying to answer Tommy's incessant barrage of questions, suffering repeated corrections when the doctor's responses were the least bit inaccurate. By the end of the fifth day, Scott knew if the chance ever came to lead an expedition after *his shark*, one Captain James Gaffney would be included. It also established a lasting relationship among the three intrepid adventurers.

Doc assumed the standing charter for BILLFISHER PERSONIFIED II during that empty time slot and faithfully made the annual pilgrimage to Australia. Scott accompanied him only once, without son Tommy, and Red was able to go twice. On every trip they caught, tagged, and released black marlin up to 900 pounds. However, the 1986 trip was the classic when both Doc and Red boated *granders*.

The pair of fish attacked two twenty-five-pound kingfish baits simultaneously. The resulting hookups produced the only time in Captain Gaffney's career when a double-header of 1,000 pound marlin would be fought and boated. Their initial runs were in opposite directions and, shortly after the strikes, two giant fish cavorted across the ocean's surface a half-mile apart. Only Jim's skillful manipulation of his boat enabled the two anglers to hang onto both fish. The battles lasted over four hours and were recorded for posterity by a video camera mounted on the flying bridge.

Doc brought his fish to gaff in three-and-a-quarter hours, white water flying everywhere when the tempered steel hook was driven into the fish's broad back above its right pectoral fin. During the ruckus at the stern, Red's even larger fish was doggedly keeping its head down, a hundred feet below the surface and 300 yards out. A few choice obscenities, including guesses about Doc's parentage, would escape Red while he was drenched in sea water and temporarily inconvenienced by the first and second mates' efforts to subdue Smith's fish.

While the man straining over a doubled rod wondered whether

or not he would also conquer his adversary, almost fourteen feet of magnificent marlin was hauled aboard. Colors fading rapidly, the superb creature came out tail first straining the block and tackle atop the starboard ginpole.

Thirty-five minutes later, the frenzied scene around the stern of the sleek sportsfisherman was repeated. Exactly four hours and thirty-seven minutes after the initial strike, a second, even larger black hung from the port ginpole. The sheer mass of these incredible fish boggled the imagination.

Doc's fish weighed in at 1,239 pounds and measured 13 feet 10 3/4 inches from the tip of its shattered bill, broken off several inches from its original tip during a recent undersea battle, to its six-foot-wide tail. The marlin Red subdued tipped the scales at 1,527 pounds, just thirty-three pounds less than Alfred Glassell's world record, established off of Cabo Blanco, Peru in 1953. His fish, its bill intact, was 15 feet 5 inches long. Indeed, these fish were the epitome of big game angling.

The grander Doc caught eventually hung in his Fort Lauderdale office, the brittle looking end of its shattered bill extending upward from the brilliant, dark-blue, nearing black, head and shoulder mount. At the eastern end of Las Olas Boulevard, facing the Atlantic Ocean, in that same south Florida city, Red's huge fish can now be seen. The famous fish is displayed in a magnificent full-length mount outside the worldwide headquarters of the International Game Fish Association. The two fish live on forever in the two-hour classic video *Doubleheader Granders*, photographed and edited by Captain James Gaffney.

* * *

Doc made the annual trip in 1987 without either Red or Scott. A medical associate of Peter's and a semi-retired Wall Streeter made their initial fishing trips to the Great Barrier Reef. All three men caught marlin, but the rapport typical of Red and Scott was absent and the days on the water just weren't the same. Doc and Gaffney took advantage of slack periods in the action to discuss the upcoming University of Miami sponsored expedition in search of Megalodon. It seemed that Dr. Scott Thompson was organizing the effort for that summer and each of them was invited to come along. Jim's face-to-face meeting with a huge shark several years earlier caused Doc to give even more credibility to Scott's vision. He was extremely excited with the possibility that such a creature existed and might be confronted. Stomach knotting, there was the inherent thrill of danger in such an encounter.

Jim Gaffney wanted to make the trip along with Rachel, his new spouse who was a marine biologist to boot. Fortunately for his charter business, the time he would be away coincided with the slow season down-under in Australia. He would also have some refurbishing work done on BILLFISHER PERSONIFIED II during his absence.

Only a half-dozen parties would need to be canceled and none were regular customers. He was confident that arrangements for them to use other local boats could be made, if the dates couldn't be rescheduled. Yes, both men were looking forward to the following July and its promised excitement. Participation in an event that could be *a revolutionary scientific confirmation* was an exhilarating stimulant.

Chapter Ten

THE NECKLACE

". . . leading the National League in batting three times, in homeruns six times, and in runs batted in four times, this inductee culminated his spectacular, and much too brief career by winning his second triple crown in 1977. Twice National League Most Valuable Player and MVP of three World Series, he finished his tragically shortened career with 402 regular season homeruns, over 1200 RBI's, and a lifetime batting average of .349, in less than ten seasons. It is my great pleasure to present . . ."

The stoic Commissioner of Baseball introduced Red Dickson to that Cooperstown crowd attending the 1984 Baseball Hall of Fame Induction ceremonies. After a few brief remarks, expressing his thankfulness of having been able to play the game that he loved for as long as he did, Red quickly retired from the podium to the thunderous applause of several thousand appreciative fans.

Excited by his near unanimous selection to the Hall during his first year of eligibility, Red quickly recognized his induction as the closing chapter to his past. While the Commissioner was extolling his baseball accomplishments, Red's mind was wandering half-way around the world. Mentally, he visited that island a few thousand miles northeast of Brisbane for which he was destined in a couple of days, this time with Scott and Tommy Thompson in tow.

He had to catch up with that mystical shark-tooth necklace, but doing so would reopen shallowly sealed wounds of a brief but eternal love. But that was pain he would have to accept. Verifying the existence of the necklace, so precisely described in the handwriting of someone so ultra-special to his heart, was crucial to his new life. He could not, would not return without seeing it.

* * *

Scott's commitment to learning about sharks and shark behavior astounded Red at first. But, the *make me smarter* bug proved highly contagious. Soon, the quest for knowledge, nurtured by a previously suppressed joy of learning, engulfed him. There was no turning back. His friend's presence was always stimulating and enjoyable. He marveled at the man's way with students, how easily he turned the drudgery of education into an exciting challenge, like an exotic drug one just couldn't get enough of. Red envied how openly and thoroughly Scott dispensed his time and efforts on research, students, and profession. But the envy was constructive and healthful, indelibly carving permanent changes into Red Dickson's character. A researchaholic and a perpetual student was born.

Two years earlier, not long after that invigorating weekend with Scott and his family, Red followed the lead recommended by Kristine and Tommy and enrolled at the University of Miami. Fifteen months later he earned a Master of Science degree and started after a Doctorate, with Dr. Scott Thompson as his advisor. As if stepping back in time twenty years, temporarily laid aside childhood camaraderie re-emerged. The shattered life of an ex-baseball player forged back into high gear.

The circle of comradeship didn't close with Scott and Red. Swept up with this tornadic pursuit of a common belief, was that third Lauderdale youth from a friendship entering its fourth decade. Welcome aboard Dr. Peter Smith, or to the Thompson-Dickson combine, Doc Smitty. Fueled by the remarkable tale spun by a new friend in faraway Australia, Doc found much merit in the quest of the professor and his *older* student.

When Scott informed them of the tragedy Jim Gaffney encountered with a large shark, there was too much similarity to what was depicted in Scott's vision to be ignored. And Red was determined to substantiate his carefully copied narration about a century-old giant shark attack in the South Pacific near New Caledonia. Confirmation of the existence and approximate age of the *God Shark* necklace seemed eminent.

Each man became a significant character in the development of Red Dickson's doctoral thesis CARCHARODON MEGALODON, EXTINCT OR SURVIVING? Through his many friends and contacts in the IGFA, Doc opened doors and paved avenues spanning the globe, especially when it came to fish lore. His contacts had their own contacts, who had other contacts, and so on. Available to Doc, via letter, cable, phone, and in person, was a perpetual information machine which they tapped to its fullest. Rumors, stories, and legends flowed into Red's database in ever increasing volumes.

Exploiting his computer skills, the PhD candidate created

sophisticated software for storing, categorizing, sorting, and rating the wealth of information being deposited with, and compiled by, him. While most of the affluent fishing groups at first questioned this ridiculous interest in sharks and shark-related incidents, sources came forth with heretofore undisclosed reports of strange and unexplainable occurrences. Since the three South Florida personalities initiating the questions were all well respected, many sportsmen around the world began tendering their information accordingly.

"All work and no play would make Jack a dull boy," the oft-used trite saying goes. The older boys always made sure that adequate time was allotted to pursue their first love, fishing. Often, business and pleasure were combined. Fishing trips to prime locations generated more stories and reports of encounters. In a very few instances, actual sightings of larger-than-life sharks were being detailed. Timing, location, and circumstances surrounding a more than coincidental percentage of events formed a defendable pattern. Something was happening in the vast oceans that could not be explained away completely by accepted theories. Concrete proof, however, still avoided them.

Red's *God Shark* necklace, with its so carefully described giant teeth, could sway the issue. Unfortunately, the post-Cooperstown induction trip of 1984 did not provide the total answer. Jarak's *descendent* was again out of touch, the necklace's whereabouts unknown. However, Friar James gave Red and Scott six moderately sharp 35 mm color photographs of the necklace. In two of the photos it was being worn by an ancient native. The remaining four displayed it on a mat alongside a meter stick, included for dimensional reference. These teeth were *three times* larger than any great white shark tooth on record. And the teeth in the pictures were a brilliant white, not the dirty gray which typifies fossilized teeth. Although the photographs did not provide irrefutable proof, both men accepted their validity. The need to see and touch the real thing now became paramount.

In twelve months, almost to the day, a ritualistic celebration was planned in remembrance of the native tribe's dramatic salvation over 150 years before. The grandson of Jarak would lead the festivities. The great tooth necklace was to play a critical roll in the ceremony. Returning to Noumea at that time would assure a first hand look at the relic.

* * *

The following twelve months dragged by. Exactly one year later, Red and Scott were back in New Caledonia. On the predicted ritual's third day, the ancient native granted them an audience. Looking at least 120 on his shriveled frame, but acting like a healthy man half that age, he carefully escorted them to a wooden hut. The frail building was set off from the rest of the village where the frenzied dancing, chanting, and offerings were going on.

Opening the unlocked door, the two men entered a dimly lit room. Following their wrinkled host, they advanced to a corner table, the only piece of furniture in the hut. Between the flickering flames on two melted-down, yellow-wax candles sat a rusty metal box. A decrepit looking steel hasp, held closed with a slightly-bent rusty nail, secured the contents. Skeletal hands carefully removed the nail and lifted the hasp, which groaned from inactivity, then slowly raised the lid. Inside was a faded cloth sack cinched tight by a single nylon string. The aged man slowly lifted the sack and its unseen contents from the box and placed it on the table. Tension and excitement permeated the two visitors. Looking at each other, they both prayed and wondered, "Could this finally be it? After all this time?"

Momentarily screening the two men by his scrawny body, the old man fumbled with the string. Red and Scott stood apprehensively less than four feet away. Completing whatever he was doing, the old man's head seemed to swivel without moving his body. What Scott remembers seeing first that memorable day was a toothless, kind of shit-eating grin, planted on a dark, shriveled face with gaping wide eyes.

"*God Shark!* You like? Here!" Broken Queen's English sputtered from the old man's lips, droplets of spittle reaching the transfixed onlookers' faces. The body turned in an effort to catch up to its head. Two scrawny arms held out the long sought-after prize. His offering was directed toward the paralytic, transplanted Georgian.

Finally Red moved. Motor skills responding to temporarily stymied brain signals, he deliberately, and oh-so-carefully, accepted the offering. Weighing about ten pounds, what he suddenly supported was far more than he ever really expected. Until that very second, what was more a wish than the belief he proclaimed, became reality. There were no more doubts or questions, only *where* and *how* the originator of these could be found. Red Dickson held between clinched and suddenly spastic fists, five perfectly shaped teeth. These teeth might have come from any of the great white sharks he had seen, except for one difference; a factor of three. Each of those teeth was over *nine inches* long and weighed about *two pounds*. They were *three times bigger* than the largest great white tooth on record!

"I see them! *I see them!*" Scott stammered. "Well Red, here they are, but I just don't believe it. After all these years, to finally know I really saw it." He stared hypnotically at five almost identical objects reverently held between Red Dickson's trembling hands. Almost inaudibly, he added, "God help us. Do we really want to find what *those* came out of?"

Scores of measurements were taken and carefully recorded. Over two dozen photographs were taken of each tooth using different lenses, different items for size comparison, and differing color and texture backgrounds. Hardness tests were made confirming they weren't fossils. Weights were recorded, varying from just under 27 ounces to just over 33 ounces. Minute scrapings were obtained from three of the teeth for accurate age-dating at the laboratory in Miami.

The entire procedure was video taped, using a low-light, high-sensitivity VCR camera, an episode which, uncut and unedited, occupied three 2-hour VHS tapes. Bringing back the teeth themselves would have been the only step which could have improved the documentation effort that took place in a village seventy-five kilometers north of Noumea.

"Can you imagine it, Scott?" Red spit out in excitement during the ride back to Noumea. "What a mouth that must be! Just think about it! Six or seven backup rows of giant teeth coming forward like an escalator to replace any it loses." After a moment lost in his own thoughts, the southern drawl resumed, oblivious to anyone paying attention to him. "*Gees-us Kee-rist!* Think of the size of that mouth! Ten - fifteen feet wide! Maybe more! And how long would the motherfucker be? Seventy - eighty - a *hundred* feet? Hot damn we did it! We got the proof!"

"Take it easy Red." Scott emitted a calmness and control he struggled for. "We've seen 'em, but we still have to find a live shark. We've got to *find* Megalodon. But I really think we got McMasters now. He'll have to let us have our expedition."

Scott looked at his long-time friend in the seat next to him. Grinning like a Cheshire cat, Red bellowed, "Yeah buddy, we got ole

Charley McMasters by the balls now. And if *he* won't fund your trip, *I damn sure will!*" Red was *really* excited. "Do you think, Scott, that the old guy who showed us the teeth was actually Jarak?"

"That would make him about a bit over 150 years-old, Red, Scott chuckled. "Think he was frozen?"

Red smiled. "He was sure wrinkled though, wasn't he? I guess he was the grandson or great grandson like he said. Christ, man. I don't think I want to live past a hundred and *only* if I don't wrinkle like *that!* What a story! What an adventure! Boy, I can't wait to see Peter," Red finished.

The drive back was one of utter fulfillment. The proof was theirs. Carcharodon Megalodon was alive. At least it had been within the last 120 years. Subsequent age-testing in Miami irrefutably confirmed that fact. Only one thing was left to do: *Go and find it!*

Chapter Eleven

JAMES GAFFNEY

"Bloody hell, who can that be?" he mumbled, stirring from a comfortable slumber. Daylight filtered through the loosely drawn drapes in the living room of his small two-room apartment. Jim Gaffney glared angrily at the black telephone, ringing uncontrollably mere inches from his nose. He had to stop that infernal racket.

"Hello, this better be good. Do you have any idea what time it is?"

"Hey Jimmy," the voice boomed happily through the ear-piece, "it's Kenny! You got room for me mate?"

Ken Gaffney, Jim's younger brother by five years, was far too elated for the senior Gaffney that morning. But Jim's mood buoyed rapidly when his brother confirmed he was finally headed for Cairns. School had been completed three months earlier, but there were *things Kenny needed to do* before striking off to work with Jim. The *things* were behind him now and Kenny would arrive by train in two days.

Two expedient years after that early morning phone call announcing his coming, two excited brothers entered the bountiful waters off of Sydney. Giant marlin and huge sharks became commonplace for Jim Gaffney. But now, after a phone call from a Sydney official, *they were on to something big.*

Jim developed a remarkable clientele for such a young captain and the BILLFISHER PERSONIFIED was by far, the most successful fishing boat operating out of Cairns. The sleek vessel consistently came in with big marlin or monstrous sharks. Contractual agreements were drawn up at the insistence of the PERSONIFIED's owner. Jim had already earned fifty percent ownership in the beautiful boat and she would soon be all his. Kenny ran the thriving sport-diving business, jointly opened by the two brothers, and was having a ball.

Jim's reputation opened avenues to other sources of income. Television specials and movies which required fishing expertise searched him out. Sharks were often involved, and the twenty-five-year-old Gaffney was rapidly developing a network of contacts with university and governmental personalities. The public relations assistant to the mayor of Sydney was just such a contact. It was a phone call from him that brought BILLFISHER PERSONIFIED to the waters off of that major Australian city.

Rachel McDavid entered Jim's life eleven months after Kenny arrived at Cairns. She was a marine biology student and asked the captain for help in compiling information on the growth rate of the black marlin. Tall and slender at 5'7" and 123 pounds, Jim found her tomboyish manner and pert little face extremely attractive and readily agreed to her request. Rachel's infatuation with the well-known personality eventually grew from admiration to love. Jim responded likewise.

* * *

Racing southward, James Gaffney watched Kenny proudly as the younger man meticulously arranged the BILLFISHER PERSONIFIED's cockpit. "Looks about perfect Ken," he hollered through cupped hands. "Come on up and spell me for a while," Jim added, looking longingly at the lengthy padded bench seat next to his chair. "And bring me something cold to drink."

"Okay mate," Kenny yelled in reply without looking up.
"Just about got her where I want her," and he ducked into the cabin. Reappearing a couple minutes later, he had a wry smile on his face as he climbed the silver-railed ladder and handed Jim an ice-cold coke.

"Thank's Kenny," Jim said in appreciation as he relinquished command. Stretching out on the padded white cushion, he asked, "What's got you grinning like that?"

Ken grinned even more, but ignored his brother question. Instead, he took a bearing on the compass and checked the engine RPM's registering on twin dials above the steering wheel.

Jim forgot his query and, shutting his eyes, let his mind wander to Rachel and how difficult it was not to let her come on this trip. He recalled rationalizing his decision by stressing how dangerous the giant shark they would be trying to catch might be. Anyway, she was safe-and-sound back on the beach.

* * *

The Gaffney brothers were bored from a lack of action. Contemplating the reported size of the shark he was pursuing, Jim was almost relieved when nothing bothered their baits as the evening crawled by. Shutting his eyes, his thoughts strayed to the $10,000 bounty on a rogue great white shark blamed for eleven deaths in the preceding fortnight. One of those killed was onboard the charter boat JENNIFER'S JOY. Jim knew her skipper, old man Sharpney, but was unable to contact him before heading for Sydney. Now, Jim and Kenny were pursuing the sizable reward, plus a guaranteed $1,000-a-day and expenses the Sydney mayor's office contracted to pay for their services. Rachel wanted to come along, but Jim wouldn't hear of it. Drifting off into a light sleep Jim thought, "Yeah, it's best she didn't come along, but I sure do miss her."

Awakened by the feel of warm breath and something nibbling on the back of his neck, Jim's eyes sprang open and he bolted upright. "Hi love. Miss me?" greeted him in that voice he'd grown to love. Kenny was sitting opposite him, grinning from ear-to-ear.

"What the hell are you doing here?" was his instantaneous response. I thought I smelled something cooking in the galley but figured I was dreaming. Kenny, you knew about this! You know I didn't want Rach on this trip. You know I . . . He stopped his tirade and pulled Rachel to him. Smiling, he said, "Rachel, I'm glad you're here but it's a bit dangerous, lass. Damn it, how *did* you get aboard?" he barked.

Her immediate response was to ignore his comments and ask, "Who's ready to eat?"

Jim, certainly happy to have Rachel with him, had the initial impulse to abort the trip and take her back to shore. "I'm glad to have you along lass, but this is not a family fishing trip. There's danger involved."

"Aw Jimmy," she chided him. "What could possibly bother us in this fifty-four-foot battleship of yours? Anyway, I know you can't live without me for a whole night," she added in coquettish fashion, flicking her eyelids open and closed slowly. "With the captain's permission, maybe I can take your mind off your precious fish for a little while."

It was 03:00 A.M. when Rachel reluctantly rolled away from the love-of-her-life and fell asleep. A few minutes later, Jim eased his way out of the queen-sized bed in the owner's cabin and headed topside to relieve Kenny.

* * *

Their drift had started four hours out of Sydney Harbor. By daylight, a foul-smelling chum line extended several miles behind his boat, slicking the ocean. "What the hell was that?" Jim asked himself. "Guess I'm just seeing things." At 06:30 he thought he saw a large shadow gliding silently beneath the putrid slick just east of the drifting boat. However, the blinding glare of the rising sun prohibited confirmation. He diligently searched the calm surface before concluding, "Nothin' but wishful thinkin' I guess." Jim put his feet back on the padded bench seat opposite the post-mounted, swivel chair he was occupying and shut his eyes.

Less than five minutes later a screaming clicker jerked him awake. Kenny was already in the fighting chair manning the doubled-over rod as the powerful fish made a single long run before turning back toward the boat.

The twelve-foot white shark circled at the conclusion of its initial run and was twenty feet from the stern when . . . the ocean suddenly erupted as white death exploded into Jim's life!

Varied reports of the killer shark terrorizing Sydney waters had guessed its length from twenty-five to thirty-five feet. "Bullshit," was Jim's mental response. Sharks always appeared bigger than they turned out to be, especially being reported by people watching someone being eaten alive. The Gaffney's expected to catch maybe an eighteen footer, and they were correct. But, the thing that mauled the twelve-foot shark Kenny was fighting was as long as the BILLFISHER PERSONIFIED.

"Holy horse shit Kenny! Look at that fuckin' thing! It can't be that . . ." was all Jim got out before fifty feet of shark-like terror staved in the PERSONIFIED's transom as the rived head of a 1500 pound white pointer landed almost in their laps.

At that very instant, a teeth-rattling collision followed, throwing Jim cruelly against the stainless steel steering wheel on the bridge and bounced him viciously off the rear handrail. His left forearm was shattered on the metal-cased Loran C unit. It's useless flesh and bone now lay limply beneath him, impeding his efforts to claw his way to the edge of the bridge. Oblivion threatened with each movement as Jim tried to drag himself forward. He must find Kenny.

Reaching the back of the bridge, Jim got his first close look at the monster. The only description he could give it was *Satan's Spawn*. Grabbing his twisted arm, he shot looks of despair at the creature below and the destruction surrounding it. "My God! Look what it did to my boat!" And the shark suddenly slipped beneath the turbulent water.

Writhing in torment, Jim thought of his brother. "Oh shit! Kenny," he spat out hopelessly, "where the hell are you?" From a sprawled position on the PERSONIFIED's flying bridge, Jim could barely see into the cockpit below. His belly plastered to the deck, he cried pathetically while hanging onto the sternmost edge of the spacious bridge. "Kenny! Kenny! Where are you? K-e-n-n-y! he screamed" All the while, searing hot knives of pain lanced unmercifully through his shattered arm and shoulder.

"Here it comes again!" Kenny's panicked shriek greeted him. Further comment was cut short as the gigantic creature hit the boat another time. The impact threw Jim from the bridge and he crashed into the gunwale below, ricocheting into the cockpit instead of overboard where an incredibly large messenger of destruction awaited. His collision with the gunwale was cushioned by that impaired left arm, somewhere between the shoulder and elbow, and a distinct cracking sound like a rifle-shot hung in the fear-stenched air. Blackness threatened again as an intensified wave of pain swept through him. The boat's stern was awash, completely underwater, and the transom's starboard corner was strewn around Jim. He helplessly watched the joining of his ship and the sea.

"Jimmy, over here!" Kenny yelled, after he righted his body that was also slammed to the deck on that last attack. "Got me a bang-stick, Jimmy. I'll blow that sonofabitch to hell," Kenny announced as he confidently lifted the six-foot pole with its specially machined head capable of firing a 10-gauge shotgun shell. Casting a quick glance at his injured brother, dread and sympathy were apparent. "Damn Jimmy," he said, relief obvious in his voice, "thought you went overboard, flying off the bridge like that. Check on Rachel, will ya? What the hell happened to your arm?"

The Gaffney brothers, recently the hunters, were now the prey!

* * *

Minutes dragged by as Jim finally dragged himself to the stateroom door at the head of the cockpit. Rachel was somewhere below. Begging a reply, Jim barked, "Rachel honey, where are you? Come on honey, answer me!"

Jim felt like he was climbing a steep hill as the stern settled and the bow raised. The boat's aft-end was flooding. The sternmost of two buoyancy compartments had been breached. With Rachel not answering him, Jim hollered at his brother again. "Hang on

Kenny! I'm checkin' on Rachel. Get to the stairs! May be safe in the cabin!"

Just then he saw Rachel lying motionless between the galley and the entrance to the head. Cherry-red blood trickled along her right cheek between her nose and nonsmiling lips, but at least she was breathing. Jim started to inch his way down the short stairway leading to the lounge area, every movement bringing increased anguish. Behind him, the devastation was appalling. In minutes, that gaping set of jaws had destroyed the aft-end of BILLFISHER PERSONIFIED. Her transom was nothing but splintered wood and shattered fiberglass. Jim crawled through misery toward his unconscious girlfriend.

"Here it comes again!" Kenny screamed. "Come and get it you bastard! I'm waiting for you"

Endless jaws obscuring the horizon and uncountable ivory teeth flailing outward, this monstrosity was unlike any creature the Gaffney's had ever seen. Catfish-like barbels covered its snout, and the skin that was visible appeared leprous and rotted. The hideous creature's attack came in a flash, but seemed to play out in stop action, slow motion that featured every movement in exquisitely clear detail. Jim was both mesmerized and helpless, yards from this enormity from hell.

Kenny, raving like a lunatic, both hands gripping the shaft of the bang-stick, actually *charged* the shark and jammed the powerful 10-gauge business end in wicked, gnashing teeth. The roar of a shotgun shell detonating blended with Kenny's warlike yells as a loud boom sounded. "I got it, Jimmy. I shot the sonofabitch in the mouth," Kenny yelled in victory. At the same time, the void in those jaws vanished, crushing the transom's splintered remains. Those gargantuan jaws snapped shut within a mass of dangling feelers and grotesquely contoured skin as the stern of Jim Gaffney's treasured boat vanished as the shark eased back into its watery domain.

Then the *unimaginable* came again! Mouth spread wide, jaws distending, innumerable unforgiving teeth reflected the early morning sunlight. That *conqueror of time* exuded a prehistoric indestructibility. At that moment, Captain James Gaffney knew, "*It couldn't be stopped. Christ man, it couldn't even exist!*"

The stricken boat shook as a monster that couldn't possibly exist lifted it from the water, and both brothers slid toward an immense mouth with its endless picket fence of teeth. When the boat tilted, the scattered contents of her once organized cockpit slipped steadily toward that yawning chasm. Fishing tackle, so neatly stowed minutes before, slid toward the creature. The foul smelling, forty-two gallon drum of blood and whale oil bobbed seaward, its gory contents contaminating the infusing water while casting a deathly red veil. An engraved Penn International 80 wide was leading the race, with Kenny close behind, a second fully-charged bangstick in his hand.

Kenny wasn't going to be first, he knew, but he was definitely going. He wasn't going without a fight either as he slipped toward that uninviting abyss.

"No! No! Please God," Jim pleaded, watching Kenny sloshing around in the floating debris. Jim was too far away to do anything but watch. His good arm was wrapped around a railing and his bad arm hung limply, unable to do anything but dangle. The wicked jaws of the giant shark clashed repeatedly, each time coming closer to his brother.

"It just about got him that time," Jim thought. But it *did* get him! A part of Kenny's right leg was missing. Kenneth Gaffney screamed but was past feeling. Barely conscious now, he washed about in the cockpit's remains, and like the rest of the litter, floated toward a gruesome death. The last thing Jim Gaffney recalled was Kenny disappearing inside the giant mouth of their attacker and the muffled sound of a second bangstick detonating. The huge leviathan released the vessel and sank from sight.

* * *

The ensuing hours were fraught with emotion. Jim Gaffney would never know how long he lay there and reality only returned when the jolting movement of his wallowing craft resumed. Again, what remained of the BILLFISHER PERSONIFIED lurched unnaturally on the calm water. A sound similar to finger nails grating down a blackboard permeated the morning air.

"That murderous bastard is back and, like a cat, it's toying with its prize before . . . before what? Before finishing his boat? Before eating him? Before eating Rachel? *Rachel!* Christ, I forgot all about her." Stretching to look, he saw her laying motionless on her stomach a few feet behind him, her face away from his view. Paranoia gripped him. "Not Rachel too," he muttered through tearing eyes as all the worst thoughts racing through his ravished mind. He clamored to her side, ignoring his fractured left arm.

On his knees, Jim tried desperately to roll Rachel over, but his abused body wouldn't cooperate with his brain. Dried blood streaked her cheek and she was an inert mass as Jim struggled to move her. Defeat suffocating him, he was afraid he'd lost her too.

Subtle banging against the boat's hull by the creature outside resumed. Rolling unexpectedly, Rachel was suddenly laying in Jim's lap. Relief flooded Jim as he felt the warmth in her body and watched the methodical rise and fall of her chest. "Thank you God!" he gasped in relief. At least one of his prayers was being answered.

Two hours crept past, 07:15 marching forward to 09:30 according to the ship's clock securely attached to the wall between the barometer and the thermometer. The two survivors huddled in a corner of the floundering vessel and listened to and felt the huge shark banging into and physically moving the boat about. Only an occasional rapid shake indicated any violence; the prodigious killer seemed to be toying with the boat's remains.

But, the creature was surely there and the cloak of fear spreading from its proximity grew heavier and more oppressive. Only Rachel's sobs over learning of Kenny's death could be heard above the sloshing of waves as the remains of BILLFISHER PERSONIFIED hung on.

The boat's clock sounded, its rich chime indicating half past nine. All at once, as if fired from a cannon, the monster below went berserk, crashing into the doomed vessel's hull and hurling its remaining occupants to the far end of their haven. Smashing into the stanchion at the doorway to the cockpit, Jim's left arm flared and darkness prevailed. As light rapidly diffused from his mind, the boat shook more violently than ever before. Reality fading, he imagined hearing metal fatiguing, followed by the hiss of escaping gas.

Jim was awakened shortly by an hysterical Rachel as the sea closed in around them. BILLFISHER PERSONIFIED was going down. That final attack breached the forward flotation compartment and escaping air was the hissing sound Jim heard earlier. Nothing remained to keep his valiant lady afloat.

"Jim! We've got to get out!" Rachel's panicked cries revived him. "Here, slip this on." She offered the opening of an orange life vest to him, guiding his good right hand into it. A second vest was pinned between her right elbow and rib cage. With her careful assistance he was able to secure the vest. Rachel donned the second vest as they exited the rapidly-flooding cabin. Clinging to each other, they watched Jim's once beautiful fishing machine disappear into 5,000 feet of water in the Tasman Sea.

Miraculously, the six-man life raft came loose from PERSONIFIED's foredeck before she went under. Two devastated survivors reached it and struggled aboard where they waited for the deadly fish to return and finish the job. Their only protection was a rectangular, foam-filled buoyancy hull and the loosely woven rope net below their bodies. In fear and apprehension, anger and hopelessness, fatigue and pain, Jim Gaffney and Rachel McDavid waited and prayed.

The monster did not return. For some unimaginable reason the giant creature from eons before spared their lives. At 11:00 that morning a Coast Guard helicopter, sent to check on the BILLFISHER PERSONIFIED's status since communication had been cut off several hours earlier, arrived at the scene and hovered over their raft. Shortly after noon, feeling like survivors of the holocaust, Jim and Rachel were assisted aboard an Australian Coast Guard cutter and rushed to a hospital in Sydney.

Mercifully, Rachel remained unconscious throughout most of the ordeal. She would never see the monster, though she could hear something outside and feel the boat being banged around. She and Jim both saw the five, giant, white triangular shaped teeth embedded in the cockpit's remains, several times larger than any shark's tooth she had ever seen.

* * *

Sudden erratic behavior by the smaller shark he was following, along with intensified blood and whale oil scent, fully activated feeding instincts in the *centuries-old* creature as he severed the much smaller great white with a single bite. He then furiously attacked and crippled the boat which was emitting the odor he tracked. Much of what he swallowed proved inedible and was regurgitated except for one tasty morsel, Kenny Gaffney.

His malfunctioning brain created irrational behavior and kept him prodding the battered craft, mouthing what he could. Nothing else was edible. He instinctively tried to leave the area and return to the sanctuary of great depths and safety, but his brain's bad spot would not permit that.

The demise of nature's exquisite eating machine was due to the slender pole Kenny Gaffney fired as he was being eaten alive. It was extreme misfortune for the greatest-of-fish when the second high-explosive detonated, sending the heavy lead slug and its accompanying gases upward through ancient cartilage and flesh. Before exiting the great fish's head, the lethal object passed through a lobe of the brain and removed the malfunctioning matter.

Convulsing, the giant shark flung himself into the boat. Biting viciously, the hard skin yielded and a flood of bubbles surrounded his snout. Shaking spasmodically with every muscle in his superbly sculptured body, his instincts and drives evaporated. Smell, sound, and vibration sensations vanished. No light or image passed through the retinas of his eyes. No thought or instinctive action remained. The great jaws opened and, for the first time in several hundred years, the great tail hung motionless. Air bladderless, his vast weight was negative and he sank toward the distant bottom.

In total darkness a mile below the quiet surface of the Tasman Sea, just when the pair of survivors were being assisted aboard the Coast Guard cutter, sixty-four feet of Carcharodon Megalodon settled into the powdery sediment on the ocean's floor, there to be consumed, ever so slowly but thoroughly, by creatures much lower on the food chain than he. Only the teeth would remain, covered over, buried, fossilized, never again to feel the light of the sun.

* * *

Vicious attacks in the waters off of Sydney ceased. Kenny Gaffney, accepting his own gruesome fate, made a last ditch effort to save his brother's life. Grabbing that second bang-stick as he slipped into the deadly maw, Kenny jammed it into the same jaws that decapitated his mutilated body. The slender weapon dealt out its own capital punishment to a prehistoric beast.

Jim spent three days in the hospital. His airborne departure from the flying bridge resulted in a severe, but clean, fracture in the Humerus's Lower Extremity above his left elbow. The forearm suffered only a deep bruise and the accompanying contusions. Rachel spent one night in an adjoining room. Doctor Weldman was concerned about a possible concussion, SOP for persons suffering loss of consciousness from a head-blow. Tests proved negative and she was released the next day.

BILLFISHER PERSONIFIED was insured and a liability policy, taken out by the Mayor of Sydney before the shark hunt, contributed toward her replacement. Jim never considered giving up fishing, it was all he knew. The tragedy occurred in early April, and by

November, BILLFISHER PERSONIFIED II was patrolling the waters off Cairns in search of the giant black marlin.

The grief created by Kenny's passing dimmed with each passing day, but the emptiness remained. Rachel offered irreplaceable comfort, as a friend, companion, and lover. Jim's waking hours evaporated as he worked on and outfitted the new boat. Almost a father-son relationship with Kenny had grown into a brotherly-love and best-friend combination during their months in Cairns. His camaraderie, affection, and pride for his younger brother continued and it was almost impossible at times to accept the man-boy's absence. And what a man he proved himself to be. Yes, time heals, but it doesn't erase.

Five days after the Coast Guard vessel plucked Rachel and him from the quiet waters, Jim gave a deposition to joint representatives of the Sydney mayor's office, the Sydney police department, and the Australian Coast Guard. Painfully, the events of the night were carefully recreated. His description of the vicious attack and his fifty to sixty foot guess at the predator's length were met with skepticism. Since Rachel never *saw* the shark, she could not substantiate its enormous size during a separate deposition. Jim's description of his brother's death was painfully rehashed several times. He was the only witness and the case was suspended pending completion of an ongoing search for the body.

One month later, the case was officially closed. No further shark attacks took place and the mayor's office concluded the rogue shark had been killed during its attack on Gaffney's boat. The bounty was paid, which provided the money Jim needed for normal living expenses while his new boat was being completed.

Kenny's body was never found and he was officially termed deceased, *death by misadventure*. A policy on his life was honored after administrative delays with benefits going to his mother. Kenny was gone, but not forgotten.

Chapter Twelve

THE GRANDERS

"Okay, Tommy," Jim Gaffney hollered down from the flying bridge. "You ready to get some of that line back? I'm backing down on her. Keep reeling. Ready?" Squinting ineffectually through Polaroid sunglasses as he stared intently into the reflection of the late afternoon sun on that balmy summer day, Gaffney quietly issued instructions to his young angler.

Twelve-year-old Tommy Thompson had been strapped to a beautiful Pacific blue marlin for almost five hours. Jim knew the lad had to be tiring, but the marlin was too. It's last run took only thirty yards of precious line off the Penn International 50 wide reel, used especially for the smaller fisherman. Until now, all offers of aid had been rejected. But there wasn't much energy left in the small, bent over body. Gaffney knew that they must take the fish now.

Twin GM diesels laboring sweetly, white spray blew over the transom and into the young angler's face. Jim's mate Tad, Peter, and the lad's father watched anxiously. The charter's two sponsors shared a growing pride and admiration for young Thompson's dedicated effort. As the hand-crafted fiberglass rod bowed and dipped, bowed and dipped, Tommy religiously pumped the large fish toward the BILLFISHER PERSONIFIED II. The youngster was gaining line, grudgingly.

"Double-line, Tad," Jim advised as the Bimini knot atop the IGFA permitted length of double-line neared the surface. "Swivel. Damn nice fish," he added, "but she's belly up," alerting his mate to gaff the great marlin, not release it. Its valiant heart gave out during the struggle for freedom.

Tag stick down, the flying gaff replaced it across the stern. Tad carefully avoided touching the double-line, which would disqualify the fish from IGFA consideration as a legal catch, as Tommy continued to crank the large fish nearer to the boat. "Got the leader, Jim." Tad advised. "Kick 'er out of gear. She looks to be dead." The mate grabbed the 300-pound test monofilament leader. When the fading marlin broke the surface, he let go with his right hand. In a single efficient motion, he sank the stainless steel hook into the thick right shoulder of the vanquished fish. The large blue marlin never even quivered. The battle was over.

"G'day mate. Catch a wink?" Gaffney offered the query in his best Aussie accent as Tommy's head showed above the ladder. "You done a heck of a good job on that fish, lad. Reckon she'll go between 550 and 600."

The younger Thompson cratered after the long stint in the fighting chair, sleeping for almost two hours. Rejuvenated, the twelve-year-old now ate up the praise, searching for more. "I did do okay, huh? How long did I fight it? How many times did it jump? You sure it's only six hundred pounds? Looks like a *Grander* to me," he finished. Reverently, a small right hand extended and stroked the skin of the magnificent fish, hanging by its tail from the starboard ginpole. "Dad, we're gonna mount it, aren't we?"

Before Tommy's emergence on the flying bridge, Jim was having another *get-to-know-you chat* with Scott and Smitty who were fishing the BILLFISHER PERSONIFIED II for the first time. Gaffney felt they came off as down-to-earth chaps. His respect and liking for them broadened and deepened. Their rapport with Tad and himself, their obvious knowledge and understanding of the sea, its occupants, boats, and the love and attention given young Tommy, especially by his father, warmed Gaffney's heart. His comfort factor around the two Americans grew continuously. These were not a couple of stuffed-shirt, rich Yanks like so many he fished. *These two men were mates.*

"How many marlin have you caught?" Tommy's questioning continued. "What was your biggest fish? Do you ever catch any sharks? My dad's an expert on sharks; knows more about sharks than anyone else in the whole world." The boy's barrage of questions for Jim went on unabated and he never bothered to stop long enough to get any answers.

The two Americans had to chuckle. Finally, Scott was able to interrupt his son. "Slow down T. Give the man a chance to answer. Damn Doc, what do you think the sixteen-hour flight home on Saturday's going to be like if our fisherman here has this many questions already? I'd give anything for some of my students to be so inquisitive."

As if his father did not even exist, the verbal battering continued. "If this is the BILLFISHER PERSONIFIED II, was there a

ONE and what'd you do with it?" And for the first time, young Tommy Thompson's mouth stopped moving. Innocent, wide eyes stared expectantly into those of Jim Gaffney. The slight glistening in the young captain's eyes brought on by the question went unnoticed, except by Tommy, as Gaffney willed back potential tears. Silence, except for the well balanced throbbing of the matched diesels propelling the party homeward, hung momentarily over three men and a boy on the vessel's bridge. Then, for the first time in many months, Jim felt compelled to relive the tragic ending of his first boat and the death of his younger brother.

" . . . sort of wraps it up," Jim concluded. "Except that no one, not the cops, not the other skippers, not even my fiance believes how big that thing really was. Even I'm starting to question what I saw, it's gettin' vaguer all the time." There was a long moment of silence. Then, Scott spoke.

"You can believe it, " Scott chimed in solemnly. "I do. Sort of saw one myself. Spent a thousand nights dreaming about it since." Scott's cracking voice caught Gaffney completely off guard. "When I was a kid, a few years older than Tommy here, I saw something huge destroy a boat. We were less than a half-mile away at the time. Peter here was with me. So was another friend, Red Dickson, but they both slept through it. It all happened so fast. I've been dreaming about it ever since. And now, you witnessed Megalodon. There is no doubt in my mind that what I saw from a distance more than twenty years ago was the same thing."

Gaffney stared incredulously at the scientist standing next to him at the wheel. Dropping his eyes for a moment, Jim eventually looked up and said, "Tell me what you saw, Scott. What I went through was so horrible, with Kenny being eaten by that . . . that *thing,* that I don't know if it happened or not. If you saw what I did, tell me about it. It just save my sanity."

Dr. Scott Thompson relived his experience and nightmares for a new found friend, his childhood fishing buddy, and his son. The tale finished as BILLFISHER PERSONIFIED II throttled down to enter the small, neat harbor in Cairns. Meanwhile Peter, not having seen anything that day but wanting to believe his friend wasn't just hallucinating, now became a believer. He developed additional invaluable trust stemming from confirmation through a similar story by their boat captain. Three grown men seeded the roots of a friendship which was to flourish and strengthen for the rest of their lives. And a fascinated twelve-year-old listened silently to two stories about sharks too big for even his vivid, youthful imagination to comprehend.

* * *

"I now pronounce you husband and wife. You may kiss the bride." Rachel McDavid officially became Mrs. James Gaffney. A year-and-a-half of serious dating, another two spent living together, and on August 19th, 1983 in a quaint civil ceremony that took place on a breezy Friday afternoon, their union was certified. At the small municipal building in Cairns, both mothers cried, and Papa McDavid, during the small reception which followed, muttered something to the effect of *it's about bloody time* after his second toddy. Friday night through Sunday noon at a cozy Bed and Breakfast Inn in the country constituted the honeymoon and consummated their wedding vows. Then it was back to work.

Six months had passed since Tommy Thompson boated his 576-pound Pacific blue marlin. But these new friends kept in touch. Every three or four weeks, correspondence would crisscross the ocean, transferring information between the trio. Jim funneled any information he came across concerning significant shark catches and/or sightings to Scott at the University of Miami. Meanwhile, Scott kept him appraised of his ongoing plan to find Megalodon.

In the meantime, Red Dickson enrolled at the University of Miami in the fall of 1982. He intended to develop his doctorate dissertation around the possibility of such a prehistoric shark surviving in modern seas. In early 1983 Red was invited by his friend, Dr. Peter Smith, to accompany him on his annual fishing trip to The Great Barrier Reef. Jim Gaffney was enchanted by Red's story of his search for a sacred necklace of five giant teeth. The relic was supposedly secluded on an island a couple thousand miles to the east. Jim's memory did an instant replay of the giant teeth the monster shark left behind when it sank PERSONIFIED I. The gleaming white objects went down with his boat. Red's unpretentious manner gave Jim no inkling that the tall, lanky man with the deep southern drawl was a multi-millionaire several times over. However, Captain Gaffney did recognize his fishing skills. Red and Doc both caught large black marlin during that trip, but no *granders*.

* * *

Fishing prospered and married life agreed with the Gaffney's.

Continued success on the marlin and shark grounds proliferated Jim's demand as a technical expert and skipper with TV producers and film makers alike. It became almost commonplace for his face to pop-up in outdoorsman shows or marine documentaries watched by his friends on the opposite side of the globe. Scott's letters seldom excluded a paragraph on Tommy's bragging to his friends about fishing with Jim whenever one of the shows aired in Miami. He would always drag his buddies to the mounted marlin and his picture with Gaffney that hung beneath it. Filmings since their last trip became standard topics of conversation during Doc's annual excursions to Cairns every February.

BILLFISHER PERSONIFIED II's equipment complement expanded continually, especially her video capabilities. The additional cameras paid off handsomely in 1986 when Red and Doc boated their two *granders*. Considerable editing was required due to the proliferation of four-letter words during the time it took to conquer the magnificent creatures. Through the magic of video tape, that episode turned the threesome into household names among big game fishing enthusiasts worldwide. The action film would be run repeatedly by television stations and networks across the globe and eventually made James Gaffney over $75,000. The cameras were in the right place on that fishing trip.

* * *

Doc Smitty's February trip to Cairns in 1987 was his first without either Red or Scott. He enjoyed the trek although no marlin over 700 pounds was caught. Something special was lacking; neither of his two valued friends were along with him. Discussions got serious during four fishing days as Doc and Jim went over proposed details for Scott Thompson's impending expedition to find, identify, and prove conclusively the existence of Carcharodon Megalodon. The three south Florida friends were scheduled to make the one to two-month jaunt aboard the University of Miami's Research Vessel OCEAN EXPLORER less than five months hence, departing from Rio de Janeiro. Two Gaffney's were cordially invited to go along.

Captain James Gaffney would not miss that trip for the world. And, as far as he knew, Rachel Gaffney was not about to let him go without her.

Chapter Thirteen

GREEN LIGHT

The day was cool but sunny, with a stiff northeasterly breeze. Offshore, the seas were running six to nine feet, not very good for small boat fishing, but they weren't fishing that day. Scott Thompson and Red Dickson were making a formal presentation to a select group in a conference room adjoining the office of Professor Charles McMasters, Chairman of the University's Department of Marine Sciences.

McMasters' interest in Scott's hypotheses about the possible existence of a species of monstrous sea creatures dated back several years, well before the young man's arrival from LSU. The current Department Head had been a brand-new Associate Professor at U of M when his sister's husband, *Fishy* Hawkins, disappeared during a night fishing trip a few miles up the coast. No verdict was ever rendered as to what happened, but McMasters own gut feeling eventually spurred his interest in exactly what Dr. Thompson and his prize doctoral candidate, William *Red* Dickson may have turned up.

Scott cleared his throat, and continued. "It is my belief that the documented information presented today mandates approval and scheduling of this research effort. Our confirmation of this creature's existence will enhance the University of Miami's prestige and could also save innocent lives.

"Timing is critical, assuming William Dickson's Doctoral Thesis proves accurate and I assure you gentlemen, it is. Coincidentally, the present two year schedule for our primary research vessel is ideal for this expedition. The OCEAN EXPLORER will complete her current one-year excursion to the South Atlantic during late-May of next year. She should make port at Rio de Janeiro in mid-June before returning to Miami for her five-year ABS Inspection.

"Our studies indicate that Megalodon should approach the Brazilian coast in late June or early July. It should then proceed east of the Caribbean Islands and follow the Gulf Stream between Florida and the Bahama Islands. The OCEAN EXPLORER's return trip will almost coincide with its anticipated movements. Gentlemen, we are on the verge of this century's greatest biological discovery."

Carefully laying the seven-page document on the table while

glancing across at his boss, Scott addressed his closing statement to McMasters. "Thank you for your time. I trust you will give favorable consideration to my proposal. Lives will depend on it!" His part in the formality completed, Scott picked up his papers and quietly returned to the straight-back chair he recently occupied muttering to himself, "Well, the ball's in their court now. Let's see what happens."

Dr. Charles J. McMasters listened intently to his young professor's presentation. Age ringed his piercing, sky-blue eyes which cast their attention individually on each of the attendees in turn. Three of those present in the spacious, oak-paneled conference room adjoining McMasters' tastefully furnished office on the Coral Gables campus withered while under his gaze. McMasters attention eventually dropped to the small, shiny, apparatus on the table before him, much to his audience's relief.

He lifted the nearest stainless steel ball and released it, watching hypnotically as it struck the adjacent ball. Kinetic energy shot through five stationary balls and a seventh ball, at the opposite end of the hanging spheres, jumped away from its neighbor. Its return swing reversed the process as the five interior spheres remained motionless and the initial one rebounded back toward him. Diminishing metallic clicks echoed through the room as end balls continued leaping away from stationary ones, feigning perpetual energy. Watching intently for several seconds, McMasters leaned forward, adjusted his bifocals, and again, though less ominously, scanned the surrounding faces.

All eyes looked reverently back at his; all accept Scott's. Used to the *Old Man's* antics, his attention now focused on the group of distinguished individuals invited along with him to Dr. McMasters' inner sanctum.

Dr. Allen Franklin, Dean of the College of Science, was dozing. Prodded none to gently, his face flushed bright red as he snapped awake. "Just resting my eyes Charles. Excellent presentation Dr. Thompson. Very interesting indeed. Now where were we?" A bit *long-in-the-tooth* and, everyone well knew, just passing time until his retirement the following June, his presence was a mere formality.

On the other hand, Dr. Bob Rogers was a professor of Ichthyology with an excellent and well-deserved reputation on campus and off. His opinion could influence McMasters' decision. "Very interesting Scott," Rogers stated. "You and Red have done your homework." As an afterthought he added, "Good to be in the right place at the right time."

Harry Lauderville was responsible for scheduling and maintaining the marine fleet at the University, and had been for almost twenty years. He would comment on the availability and capabilities of this equipment. When McMasters' eyes paused on him, he confirmed, "Dr. Thompson is correct about the OCEAN EXPLORER's current schedule. The additional cost to supplement her return from Brazil with the requirements of the proposed expedition should be minimal."

Red and Scott were proposing a scientific expedition for the following summer. Red was completing his doctoral degree in marine biology under Thompson's guidance. Lounging in a cushioned chair away from the massive table the others occupied, he almost seemed disinterested. His friend knew better. As Scott's eyes hesitated on Red, a nervous grin etched across the pinkish-red complexion of a perennially sunburned face.

Last, but not least, was Helen Thiel, McMasters' private secretary. Graying head bent to the task, she diligently recorded the meeting minutes in her seemingly indecipherable shorthand. Nary a word would be omitted from her final meticulous transcript.

Finally, the very air in the room seemed reincarnated as McMasters spoke. "Thank you very much for a detailed and excellent presentation Dr. Thompson. I want to congratulate you and Mr. Dickson on the thoroughness of your effort. I know you will need to begin preparations as soon as possible, should the Department decide in favor of this scientific excursion of yours. I have been following your work and read all of your published articles. The information you presented today has forced me to seriously consider your hypothesis."

Looking up at the fourteen-foot ceiling, he seemed to orchestrate his words before continuing. "You have injected irrefutable evidence into what was, until a few hours ago, a fantasy in my opinion. We academicians seem to dream about discovering unknown phenomenon, only to stay in the safety of our hallowed halls and classrooms. You and Mr. Dickson have ventured into the real world, pursuing this undertaking. If you can confirm it, a dramatic impact on the biological sciences will result. I want to thank you for sharing your ideas with us. Now, if you and Mr. Dickson will excuse us, the Dean, Dr. Rogers, Harry, and myself will discuss your proposal in private. We should reach our decision in short order.

"It is now Thursday afternoon, and I have a commitment off

campus tomorrow. Please make an appointment with Helen to see me on Monday morning when your schedule permits. Now, would you three gentlemen be kind enough to join me in my office for some sherry before we put this matter to rest?" McMasters rose abruptly from his oversized chair, giving the steel ball one last swing. Turning to his right, he walked majestically through the side door leading to his office. Following obediently in single file were Messrs. Franklin, Rogers, and Lauderville.

Click . . . click . . . click . . . and receding footsteps.

* * *

"You heard me Dickson," Scott shouted into the mouthpiece, "you old redneck. We've been given the green light. We got everything we asked for. What you say to cutting your Doctoral Thesis Review 750 class today and celebrating? I'm gonna call Doc now and get him to join us. Where? Hell boy, your Lauderdale Yacht Club, where else? I can't afford to buy drinks on a professor's pay. Yeah, yeah, up your's too. See you there shortly. About 1500 hours will be fine. *Adios mi amigo.*"

The click in his earpiece and a subsequent dial tone did not subdue Scott's mounting ecstasy.

"Hot damn, we're really going. Get to show the whole world I'm not crazy, that my monster shark really is out there. A ballplayer, a surgeon, and the nutty professor going fishing again. Look out Megalodon, you sonuvabitch, here we come."

* * *

Scott arrived in Rio de Janeiro first, accompanied on a week-long holiday by his wife and daughter. During seven fun-filled days, Scott, Louise, and fourteen year old Kristine simply relished each other's company. His son Tommy didn't make the trip because of college demands. Now the week was over and the Thompson girls were about to return home.

Struggling to hold her composure, those same brown, caring eyes that first captivated Scott glistened from eminent tears. "God will look after you. He'll bring you back to us," Louise smiled. Pausing for a moment, she produced a kleenex and daintily blew her nose. "Now, why don't you just go and take care of your business, find that giant shark, and come home safely," she said with deep love and affection.

"No problem honey," Scott answered, his voice also cracking with emotion. "Megalodon is no match for my crew, and the OCEAN EXPLORER is darn near a battleship."

She reached out with both arms and embraced her husband, finishing with a long, loving kiss. He turned and scooped his daughter off her feet. Kissing her repeatedly on each cheek, Scott finally set her down saying, "Take care of your mom for me, Kitten. You know daddy loves you!" God how he loved them! God how he loved life!

* * *

Red and Doc Smitty were arriving on a flight from Caracas only two hours after Louise and Kristine's TWA flight for Miami took off. Scott elected to wait at Santos Dumont Airport, using the time to review plans for the impending voyage. That task proving difficult, he looked for another diversion. Salvation was sitting on the shelves of an airport bookstore. The crowded alcove housed a variety of items including paperback books. One he hadn't read in ten years caught his eye.

He poured through the novel of a Long Island town terrorized by a large fish. Peter Benchley's giant white shark didn't seem so monstrous anymore, not when compared to what they'd soon to be hunting. Finishing the book, Scott Thompson laid it aside and anxiously awaited his friends.

* * *

Peter slumped down in the Rio taxi's back seat, heading from Dumont Airport down Avenue Infante Dom Henrique toward Impanema Beach. Scott was leaning against the opposite door, and Red was in the front seat next to the driver. Peter and Red had stopped off en route to Rio de Janeiro for a fishing trip in LaGuaira, Venezuela, a quaint seaside resort near Caracas, often regarded as the *white marlin mecca of the world*. They'd stay at the Rio Sheraton until moving onto the boat. Red stretched his lanky 6'4" frame out, trying to work the kinks out of his bum right knee. Steering his '73 Caddy through the honking traffic, their talkative Brazilian cabby played tour guide, disregarding the near total absence of English in his boisterous vocabulary. Broken French, Portuguese, and occasional *American* filled the air around the three compatriots.

Attempting to ignore the incessant babble from the driver's seat, Scott paraphrased his earlier question. "Come on guys, how was LaGuaira? You do any good? What'd you catch?"

"Screw our trip, Scott," Red interrupted. "How 'bout our shark hunt? What's the boat's status?"

Peter also jumped in, "The crew arrived yet? You still think Red can get pictures of your big shark? What . . .?" Doc's excitement was contagious. The forty-two-year-old orthopedic surgeon turned question machine.

"Rein it in Doc," Scott laughed, "you inquisitive son-of-a bitch. You first! How 'bout LaGuaira? Bite-by-bite, or I won't tell you a damn thing till tomorrow." Looking at his watch and a street sign they were passing, he concluded, "We'll be another forty-five minutes reaching our hotel. Okay, one at a time, tell me everything."

Realizing Scott was serious, Doc and Red provided details of their side-trip marlin fishing in Venezuela, spiced up by some fun tales concerning senoritas. Their stories spent, Doc turned his attention to Scott. "Okay Thompson, let's get serious. Exactly where do we stand on our trip?"

"Yeah," Red demanded, "bring us up to date."

"You two nomads are just gonna have to wait a while longer for project details. Now, I have to check on my two grad students, Chad and Karen. They're down at the boat stowing our gear." Scott also advised them about the other members of their cast. "The Gaffney's will be flying in from Melbourne in about two hours. We'll meet in the Sheraton about eight for dinner. I'll fill you in on details then. Meanwhile, go check in. I've already confirmed your reservations."

The pungent smell of burning rubber accompanied squealing breaks. One dark green Caddy screeched to a halt, inches behind a stationary yellow cab of much more recent vintage. Separating his surprised face from the backside of the front seat, Scott gasped, "Guess we're here. Pay the man, Red." Alighting from their taxi, Doc asked in a more serious tone, "Everything is going according to plan, isn't it?"

Scott answered by saying, "Should clear port day after tomorrow around daybreak."

"Okay Scott," Red grudgingly agreed, his interest painfully tweaked, "but you can be a real asshole when you try."

Accepting their briefing delay, both Red and Doc turned

toward the lobby and headed for the main desk. A thought hit Doc and he halted momentarily. Looking over his shoulder, he asked, "Hey Scott, my air freight package get here okay?"

"Yeah, meant to ask about that," Scott replied. "Got excited when you arrived and it slipped my mind. A 150-pound crate came in two days ago via British Air out of Miami. As per your instructions, I didn't open it and it's down at the boat now. We'll check it out in the morning. What's in it? With what all I conned out of the University, I can't imagine what else we can use."

Doc grinned, "My secret. You're not telling us about the trip so I'm not filling you in on what's in my box. Gonna be surprised, but bet you'll like it." Turning, he hustled after his tall friend.

* * *

Their Brazilaire flight arrived at Santos Dumont Airport right on time and Jim and Rachel Gaffney were following the route taken by the three American friends four hours earlier. Sharing her feelings with her husband, Rachel spoke softly, "I'm excited about our trip, but I do have mixed emotions." Divesting some of her fear as she talked, Jim's presence created a warm feeling of safety. After a moments hesitation she added, "And I know you have a vested interest in finding that shark. But, for the past few weeks all I've been thinking about is what happened to us off Sydney. I'm scared, Jim," she confided to the man sitting next to her. "Do you really think *anything* is safe from one of those monsters? Are you absolutely certain this is right? Tell me. Reassure me." There was no hiding the deep-felt fear exposed by her trembling words.

For the moment, her husband didn't reply, just pulled her even closer. Squeezing her reassuringly, he brushed her forehead with his lips and tried to absorb the terror filling her thin body as if through osmosis. God how he loved the smell and feel of her, the absolute faith she seemed to place in his every judgment. Silently, he asked himself, "What if she's right?"

Giving her yet another comforting squeeze, Jim Gaffney gazed lovingly at his wife. "Take it easy *little Sheila*," he assured her. "There is no risk, none at all." If I felt there was the slightest chance of danger, I wouldn't want you along. The boat we're going on is built like an icebreaker. Nothin' short of a submarine could sink her."

Pausing briefly, he stared protectively into her trusting eyes while struggling to find just the right words. Justifying his decision,

Jim continued, "I probably know as much about that monster's closest living relative, Carcharodon Carcharias, as anyone on this bloody planet. And I saw it! I damn well know what I saw. Nobody really believes what happened to us that morning. Well, now we've got a real good chance to prove it. If Scott's theory is right, that certain noises attract those fish, we may stop some other people from antagonizing such an awesome creature and paying for it with their lives."

Repositioning himself in the cab's back seat, Jim could feel the deep-rooted horror slowly permeate from his wife's shivering body into his, where it became part of the controlled fear he too experiencing.

"Rachel, honey," he promised, "We've come this far. Let's hear the plan, take a look at the boat, then make up your mind. If you're the least bit uneasy, you can fly on up to Miami and wait for me at Peter's."

"No way! If you go, I go," Rachel stated flatly.

At that moment, the taxi slowed and pulled to the curb in front of the Rio Sheraton. "We're here love," Jim confirmed. He assisted his wife from the cab as a muscular, dark-skinned bellhop unloaded their luggage. Weaving through a maze of plants covering the hotel's entrance, Rachel glanced affectionately at her husband. Forcing a grin she purred, "I love you so much."

* * *

Karen and Chad were graduate students in Marine Biology at the University of Miami. Working on their Masters Degrees in Ichthyology, both were specializing in shark behavior. As part of its program, the school places graduate students in summer jobs complementing their class work. They earn eight credit hours, are exposed to real-life situations involving their chosen careers, and meet industry contacts.

Concerned about possible hazards and the students' safety, Scott initially objected to their inclusion. When it became clear that, for University funding to be granted, not to mention use of the OCEAN EXPLORER, two students must accompany the venture, Thompson reconsidered. After all, most of the potential dangers facing them would relate directly to their transport's seaworthiness, and the OCEAN EXPLORER was a stable, 135 foot vessel. Designed for Arctic duty, her steel hull simulated an icebreaker's and the chance of *any* creature sinking her was remote.

At first, Scott was opposed to the second student being a female, but after discussions with Professor McMasters, he condescended. Scott was living in a *man's world* and believed that women, while maybe not the weaker sex, needed to be protected by men. His dad had been that way with his mom and Scott was that way with Louise. Something inbred, that becomes habit, is difficult to change.

He didn't really want Chad there either. Despite being male, Chad Brown wasn't much more than a boy and Scott didn't want to feel responsible for any young life, male or female. Both students were twenty-one and would graduate one semester after the trip. Top notch in the classroom, they also proved to be tireless workers. The more Scott was around them, the more he appreciated their presence. After minimal directions, he left them to assist in outfitting the EXPLORER.

* * *

"I grew up just outside of Eskridge in northeast Kansas, 'bout halfway between Topeka and Junction City. We were thirty-two miles from Topeka and my folks owned a farm, just under 1,200 acres. We grew mostly wheat." Chad Brown raised his eyes to look at a gull dipping toward the mirrored water of the slip alongside OCEAN EXPLORER before resuming his life history for Capt. Hendrickson. "The only water I remember was in the Dragoon Creek, and that wasn't much. You could almost walk across it in the summer without gettin' your feet wet. We did catch a few trout now and then, mostly on handlines. Used worms or grasshoppers for bait."

The young man from Kansas stood up momentarily and stretched. "Cramp in my leg," he muttered before doing a couple of knee bends and sitting back down. Removing his Atlanta Braves baseball cap, he ran his fingers though a thick shock of coal black hair and then continued. "Guess I got interested in fish and the sea from watching those Cousteau specials on TV. Then, when I was thirteen, we took a family trip to Galveston. Never saw so much water as there was in the Gulf of Mexico. One afternoon, my oldest brother and me walked down to the fishing docks and saw a nine-foot shark. Found out later it was a tiger shark. From then on I was hooked. Never wanted to be nothin' but a marine biologist."

"You'll get to see all the water you can stand on this trip, Chad," Captain Hendrickson replied with a knowing smile. "How about you Karen? Where do you hail from and how'd you end up at Miami?" he asked, turning his attention to the attractive young lady sitting Indian style on the deck next to Chad.

"It was simple for me, Captain," she replied. "I was born and raised in Boynton Beach, Florida and have been in or on the water ever since I can remember. My mom, dad, and two older brothers were fishing and diving fanatics, so it just came natural to me. I guess I was sort of a tomboy; liked fish, crabs, and bait, things like that, more than dolls or pretty dresses." Chad made a face.

Smoothing out the few strands of natural blond hair which were being displaced by a gentle breeze blowing across the deck, Karen Korinski didn't fit the picture of any tomboy. A loosely fitting blouse couldn't hide her swimmer's shoulders and slim waist or the large, well proportioned cleavage of her chest. Navy blue short-shorts exposed her long, tanned legs. Her strong chin, dainty nose, and emerald eyes would have impressed any talent scout. And, beneath the gifted physical features was a genuinely nice person with a brilliant mind.

Scowling at her fellow student, Karen looked again at the boat captain. "I guess I did well enough on my college boards so the University of Miami offered me a scholarship and here I am. This trip is a dream come true. You should have seen how jealous my brothers were when they heard where I was going and what we were going to be doing. I didn't feel too sorry for them though, they always got to go on the best fishing trips with my dad, the ones they couldn't take little girls on. I guess life has a way of evening things up, huh Chad?"

Chapter Fourteen

TROUBLE AHEAD

At 6:35 PM, Jim and Rachel Gaffney were checking into the Rio Sheraton. Dr. Peter Smith and Red Dickson were each unwinding under steaming showers. A tan phone rang persistently in room 506. Dr. Scott Thompson hurried out of the bathroom, crossed the carpeted floor, and lifted the receiver on its seventh ring.

"Dr. Thompson?" Chad's troubled voice sprang from the earpiece. "Is that you?" He was calling from a pay phone near the OCEAN EXPLORER's berth. "This is Chad, Dr. Thompson. Big problem down here. Can you come over?"

"What's up Chad?" Scott replied, a cold sweat breaking out on his naked back and shoulders. "You and Karen okay?"

"Yes, we're both fine," Chad answered unconvincingly. "It's the boat. The port engine just cratered. Captain Hendrickson says the oil leaked out and the thing just blew. The oil level alarm and the high temperature gauge showed nothing wrong, nothing at all." The young man on the other end of the line was rapidly coming unglued but was able to add, "The Captain says it's torn up bad, threw a rod or something."

"Of all the luck," Scott groaned into the phone. "Chad, where's the Captain? Can he come to the phone or call me? And by the way, I'm expecting you and Karen here about eight. You can fill us in while we eat."

He heard Chad's distant reply, "I'll ask Captain Hendrickson to call you," followed by a noisy dial tone.

Hesitating momentarily, Scott replaced the receiver in its cradle. "What could have happened?" he muttered angrily under his breath. "What the *hell* went wrong? Those engines were running perfectly!" Scott glared into the full-length mirror and spat vehemently, "Christ man, it's impossible! Lauderville and Hendrickson really look after their boats. A couple of meticulous bastards, those two." Pausing, he turned toward the sliding glass doors mumbling, "We'll have to see how bad it really is and just what we can do about it."

After zipping up his shorts, he walked through the open glass doors and collapsed in a plastic chair on his balcony while gazing out over the busy street below. Beyond the moving traffic were the white sand beaches and the calm, blue waters of the South Atlantic, clearly visible from his perch five floors above the city. The water seemed to be never-ending, like staring into space. That gigantic beast he was hunting, the probable culprit in God-knows-how-many disappearances, was out there somewhere. It was his destiny to find that monstrous killing machine, to prove its existence. Maybe even kill it, if necessary, although he prayed it wouldn't come to that. Hell, he didn't even know if something that Promethean could be dispatched by something so insignificant as man.

For a while, Scott got lost in his thoughts. Dark was still two hours away, but he didn't notice the scantily clad girls soaking up afternoon rays on the beach. Without formal instruction from his brain, he subconsciously began going over what he'd just learned, cultivating responses and solutions. His thought process addressed the problem and, in computer-like fashion, asked questions, provided answers, cataloged, sorted, and stored responses.

Forty minutes later, the same tan phone again shattered the stillness. Rising abruptly, he glanced at the bedside clock with 7:35 showing on it in glowing green digits and strode toward the shrill instrument. Apprehensively lifting the receiver again, he answered instinctively, "Hello, Scott Thompson here."

* * *

Scott arranged for his group to eat dinner in a private room on the Rio Sheraton's second floor. Informal introductions followed by cocktails and hors d'oeuvres preceded a sumptuous main course, eaten heartily, in spite of the day's misfortune.

"Sure it's disappointing," Scott stated, "but let's not get discouraged, not yet anyway." Swirling the remains of his third rum and coke in a crystal glass, he concentrated on the tiny whirlpool whose vortex reached a red maraschino cherry. Continuing, "As I see it, we have three options. The first is chuck it and go home. I don't think any of us want to do that. Second, wait for Hendrickson to fix the OCEAN EXPLORER, but that's no good either. She'll be out of commission for six weeks minimum. By then, assuming Megalodon's migratory pattern is anywhere near what I think, we won't stand a chance of finding one and proving it exists this summer. Our third choice is to locate another vessel for our search.

If we get lucky, and if the university will pick up the tab, we can still have a go at it. Any other ideas?"

Red caught Scott's attention and asked, "Do you know for sure what the damage is? Maybe the engine ain't as bad off as we think." He was echoing his longtime friend's initial thought after Chad's call. But, the second call was from Captain Hendrickson and it confirmed the worst. The port engine was beyond repair. It also threw a cylinder which damaged injectors on the starboard engine. A new engine and the necessary parts were six weeks away in the States.

"No Red," Scott said grimly. "The Captain advised me it will take six weeks minimum, more likely longer."

"Okay Scott," Peter Smith interjected. "We all know what this means to you. If the school won't fund your junket, Red and I will. Neither of us came all the way down here to quit cause the boat broke." Doc glanced at Red, who winked an okay at his commitment of Red's money.

"The real problem is finding the right vessel," Doc stated. "What we need won't be easy to find around Rio. This isn't the ideal place to be looking for a work boat. She'll have to handle the open sea and carry enough fuel and other supplies to get us most of the way to Florida. For good measure, the fortunate lady may have to take on one of those God-awful creatures."

"What do you think Jim?" Scott shifted attention to the quieter side of the table and addressed the male Australian. "You've got more boat time than any of us and you know what we're up against. Do you think we can locate another boat around Rio? Even Caracas or Port of Spain are possibilities. It'll reduce our search area, but starting farther north is better than nothing."

Jim hesitated before replying, "There's not much chance of finding a boat like we need in this part of the world. My experience has been on sportsfishermen, the biggest was a sixty-foot Bertram. No way I'd chance going against what I saw in something that small." Pausing to let his comment sink in, James Gaffney put his arm around Rachel and continued his statement. "We'd need a special boat, like the ones they got in the oil patch. You know, off southeast Asia, in the Gulf of Mexico or the North Sea, the likes of that. They *are* doing some drilling in Brazilian waters, so there may be a little hope."

"Telephone call for Dr. Thompson." The assistant hotel manager courteously interrupted. He was standing stiffly by the table after silently appearing through a side door. "You can use the phone by the main door if you wish sir. It's a Captain Hendrickson. He says it's urgent."

"Thank you," Scott said politely, a glimmer of hope igniting. The captain had been going to the Harbor Master's to report the engine damage and arrange for an extension to the time OCEAN EXPLORER would be in port. He said he would check on vessel availability while there, promising to call Thompson immediately if any hot prospects turned up.

* * *

"Come on guys, Scott barked at the group while covering the mouthpiece with his right palm. "Keep it down, I can't hear the man speak." Moments later, he wrapped up the phone call saying, "You say she's due in about ten-hundred hours tomorrow? Yes sir. Thank you Captain. Thank you very much. We'll be at the boat at zero-eight-hundred. Thanks again. Good night."

Suspense saturated the enclosed room as everyone hovered around Scott. The phone left his ear and questions were flying.

"What is it Scott?" Red asked, "another boat?"

"How big?" pleaded Chad.

"Who's getting in at ten?" piped Doc, "and where?"

Scott turned around slowly, savoring the moment, and looked from face to anxious face. For several seconds he just grinned at them, taunting them with his lack of response.

"Come on goddamn it!" Red bellowed. "What the hell is it?"

"We just might have us a boat!" Scott finally replied, slapping his hands together. "Seems Providence may have answered. Anyway, Hendrickson's at the Harbor Masters right now and it just happens a vessel's due back in Rio tomorrow morning. And not just *any* vessel. The SEA NYMPH he called her. Was under charter to a bunch of Aggies who've been monitoring interactions between gators and dolphin in the Amazon River. Well, she came off charter three weeks ago and put in at Rio for a couple days. Seems the owner and his lady boarded her here and headed down the coast. That was ten days ago and, before she sailed, the SEA NYMPH's captain asked the Harbor Master to be lookin' out for traffic headed for the States. He was planning to deadhead back himself and wants to share the cost."

Finishing that dissemination of his newly acquired knowledge, Scott, still grinning from ear-to-ear, scanned the group crowding around him. Faces brightened quickly and the questions resumed.

"How big?" Chad asked again.

Jim's question was, "Any schedule problems with her and just when's she due in?"

"How about accommodations?" Karen asked.

The questions flew fast for several minutes and Scott even took time to answer a few. However, it was a final query from Rachel that brought him quickly down to earth. In all sincerity she asked, "What's an Aggie?"

For the first time since that initial phone call, Scott laughed. He couldn't help himself. It took him thirty seconds to control his guffaws before he could respond.

"Thank you very much Mrs. Gaffney," he chuckled, "and I'm not laughing at you, I'm laughing with you. Please excuse me, but one sometimes forgets what we take for granted may be plowing new ground for someone else." Fully regaining his composure he informed her, "Aggies are simply what we call students, graduates, or teachers of Texas A & M University, an interesting school in central Texas with a superb football team and a marine biology program that's somewhere between very good and world renowned."

That explanation behind him, Scott fielded some of the other questions. Between laughs he stated, "Now for some of your other questions. She's aluminum hulled, ninety-four feet long, and took care of eleven Aggies plus her crew so she can handle the seven of us. The Harbor Master didn't elaborate, but SEA NYMPH is well outfitted and suitable for the high seas. She'll be in about ten A.M. and I told Hendrickson we'd be at the OCEAN EXPLORER around eight."

Pandemonium reigned briefly until reality emerged in the guise of Red's melodic drawl. "Sure sounds great," he allowed, each word trickling off his lips. "Guess we're destined to make this trip after all. OCEAN EXPLORER craters an engine and our trip looks as if it's canceled. Then, a perfect replacement vessel shows up the very next day. Can't look a gift horse in the mouth," Red continued. "First, we have to be the *unluckiest* sonuvabitches around gettin' our boat all messed up like that. Then, outta' the blue, we're suddenly the *luckiest* bastards when another boat shows up here in the middle of nowhere! Imagine, another research vessel poppin' up in Rio this time of year to save our asses! Yeah, must be destiny."

Becoming more serious, Red rose slowly to his feet and raised his half-filled glass of scotch, offering a toast. "To destiny folks. To *our* destiny and to Megalodon. You big-toothed son-of-a-bitch. We're after your ass. And we're gonna get it! *Ladies and gentlemen, here's to our QUEST FOR MEGALODON.*"

"Red, you can't imagine how much I want this good fortune to be true," Scott stated in a less enthusiastic voice. "It just has to be. We have to leave as planned if we're going to have a snowball's chance in hell of finding Megalodon where I know he'll be and, well," he proceeded after a slight hesitation, "nothing's definite yet. We aren't even guaranteed this mystery boat will be suitable or even available." His penetrating gaze ricocheted from Red to the others and back before he continued. "Yeah, I'm afraid nothing's definite as yet, but we'll get to see for ourselves in a few hours. Well, tomorrow is another day and if SEA NYMPH looks okay, we'll try to cut a deal. Let's all get some shuteye."

It was getting late and everyone was tired as the group began to disperse. Scott grabbed Red and Doc by their arms and whispered, "Hang back a minute guys, we have to talk."

* * *

"Everything go all right? You did fix their boat, didn't you?" the short, stocky man asked. He was immaculately dressed in custom-tailored white slacks and a flowery silk sportshirt. Demanding answers, he slurred, "Nobody suspicious? Any problems I need to know about? Fuckin' university assholes."

This ninety-four-foot ocean going vessel, the MV SEA NYMPH, was all his. Questioning his *lieutenant* in the vessel's elegant salon, the sleek luxury boat was only ten hours south of Rio, heading back to that Brazilian port.

"Coded message came in twenty minutes ago," Tex answered. The tall angular man with olive skin and a fearful, gravelly voice advised. "Hit oil' boss. It's a producer. Everything's set." About his superior's age, both approaching forty, Tex was several inches taller and much leaner than his boss. Catlike movements exuded athletic grace and assurance. Eleven years in the organization and an ex-green beret, he was proficient in the necessary skills. "Also said 'Harbor Master expects arrival about 10:00 so the dumb-asses don't have no choice. They gotta book your boat."

"Very good Tex," the shorter man replied, a sallow grin darkening his evil face. "Very good indeed." His exquisite scheme was coming to fruition.

He was an imposing figure. He had a lantern jaw, concealed by a neatly cropped beard. His accent was Cajun, probably Terrebonne or Lafourche parish in South Louisiana. His unsolicited comments continued. "Once those educational dick-heads commit tomorrow, I can guess their ETA and finalize my distribution plans. Very good indeed. A quick sip to celebrate and then I'll pleasure the bitch downstairs one more time."

* * *

It all started for the unscrupulous owner with a single workboat during the oil boom. Driven by greed and the success of others, Mark *Bubba* Breaux bribed, bought, bullied, and coerced his way into a very successful boat company.

Bubba's financial breakthrough and slide from moral grace began with that first exposure to illicit cargo. Under cover of darkness, he received six bales of *grass* one moonless night offshore. Five hours later, the marijuana was delivered to a couple of waiting pickups at Cocodrie, Louisiana. Seven hours and a little diesel fuel pocketed him $5,000 in U.S. greenbacks. Easy money, and the hook was set.

With untaxed cash rolling in, the wily Cajun was well on his way to being rich. Through unscrupulous dealings, blackmail, brutality, and even murder, Bubba Breaux steadily increased his fleet and constructed a criminal empire. With more vessels, legitimate work rapidly became a secondary source of income. Undercutting competition, his share of the legitimate market escalated along with his drug running. Along the way, he promoted himself from delivery boy to purchaser and then to distributor. Cocaine replacing pot, his take skyrocketed and the more he got, the more he wanted. The pain and suffering he caused throughout Louisiana grew daily. So did the contents of his safety deposit boxes.

When the oil business crashed during the early 80's, most of his vessels were suddenly laid up. Oil company operations slowed offshore and the demand for legitimate vessel traffic plummeted. But that didn't deter Bubba's other efforts. At the same time, out-of-work *amateurs* were turning to drug running in search of a quick buck but they were no match for Bubba. Several met brutal and premature deaths. As law enforcement intensified, Bubba's main source of income had to be restrained but that didn't matter. His conniving mind never let the drug flow stop, and the Cajun just got smarter and smarter, staying one step ahead of the *Feds*. Local authorities were never a problem, as key politicians' pockets were frequently filled from the fruits of his labor.

SEA NYMPH was Cajun Bubba's greatest endeavor. Conceived in 1978 at the oil boom's peak, no expense was spared. With accommodations for fifteen passengers in five luxurious three-man staterooms plus a crew of four, all she lacked was speed. Her top end was fifteen knots running and eleven cruising and her range exceeded 4,000 miles. She could also hold thirty days provisions. A wide beam plus greater-than-average freeboard made her an exquisitely seaworthy vessel.

Using her for special runs and select clientele, the corrupt owner relished *his baby*. When oil prices crashed, Bubba drydocked her and made several discrete modifications. SEA NYMPH's effective length shrank by eight feet as two false bulkheads were added, creating storage vaults four feet long in her fore and aft sections. These air tight compartments were inaccessible; perfect for cocaine trafficking.

Such a shipment was now securely stowed below deck as both compartments were filled with carefully wrapped parcels of white powder. Eight inches of Brazilian coffee lined each hold, emitting a strong aroma that would prevent drug dogs from detecting the primary cargo.

The loading was accomplished during a five day period when his unsuspecting charterers were off the boat. The Aggie students and professors had taken small canoes up a narrowing tributary to observe some native rituals involving crocodiles. Over 4,500 keys of pure Colombian cocaine arrived on two Widgeon seaplanes, along with a resupply of food and other staples. The five tons of cocaine was transferred to the SEA NYMPH, openings burned in the two decks, and the drugs stored securely below. Both openings were covered, seal welded shut, and the decks repainted.

As a final precaution, the boat crew on board at the time were paid off handsomely and relieved when the vessel arrived in Rio. Each departing crew member knew his life would be over if he crossed Bubba Breaux. Those manning her now, from captain to cook, were unaware of the hidden compartments or what was secreted beneath her deck. With a street value exceeding $75 million, this shipment would propel Bubba Breaux into crime's upper echelon. With absolutely no concern for what his secret stash would do to the junkies and kids it was destined for, Breaux was proud of himself. The wicked Cajun had everything mapped out to perfection.

* * *

"Have your drink ready in a second, boss," Tex offered while pouring four ounces of Chivas Regal into a crystal tumbler. The tall enforcer then added two clear ice cubes from an automatic icemaker fed with bottled water. Subserviently, the dealer-in-death handed his boss the drink.

"Thank you Tex," the shorter man acknowledged without emotion. "Get one for yourself."

"Sure thing boss. Think I'll have me another bourbon." Quickly fixing himself a Jim Beam, straight up, Tex joined Bubba in staring quietly at the moonlit ocean. The dark and forbidding coastline of South America slid by silently off the port side of SEA NYMPH. "Got to hand it to you boss. This has got to be the world's slickest deal. Bitchin' man, bitchin'."

"Quite right my good fellow," Bubba Breaux responded insolently, a false British twang replacing his regressing Cajun accent. "Once we get that boat load of scientists off on their fool fish hunt, nothing can interfere. When they hit Miami customs, they won't even get a once-over. The boat is clean, been doing scientific research." Shit, he grinned in an evil smirk, "I've thought of everything. With my planning, her clearance will be a paperwork formality. Then we'll run her around Key West and back home to bayou country. A night in my shipyard and it's easy street."

Rolling his eyes and sporting a wide, satisfied grin, Tex momentarily resembled a kid in a candy store. The hardness quickly returned. Soldier-like, he replied, "Amen boss. Great. Fuckin' great. But," he added, still catering to the shorter man, "it's only the beginning. Like you said boss, we charter her to some scientific eggheads, so long as they're goin' near our suppliers. Let the dumb shits bring in our stuff. Who's gonna worry about a stinkin' *research* vessel?"

Tex had no future. His selfish boss was not about to share this take. An *accident* was awaiting the taller man. Getting to his feet, Breaux glared smugly at Tex who snapped to attention without a second's hesitation. "Well Tex, enough gentlemen's talk," the conceited owner said. "Time to head below decks and thrill that lucky bitch before I call it a day. The girl don't know how good she's got it, sleeping with me. Oh well, duty calls." Indignantly he concluded, "Yes, my good man, it's been an excellent day. Close up shop will you." His parting statement was in no way a request.

"Oh boss, almost forgot. That sound gadget you ordered was in Rio when we arrived. The captain installed it before his relief came onboard. Said it's working fine. Put it in on the Q.T. so no one knows it's there. That contraption can track SEA NYMPH from Rio to Louisiana. Only a thousand miles or so when she'll be out of shore station range. Thought you'd want to know. Night boss. Have fun."

"Thank you Tex. Good evening." Rudely adjusting the front of his slacks, Breaux headed below.

Chapter Fifteen

THE SEA NYMPH

"Jim, you, Rachel, and the two 'old guys' take that cab," Scott instructed, renewed enthusiasm tempered by nagging apprehension. "The kids and I will be right behind you." He'd lined up transportation the night before and now the crew divided up, climbing into their respective vehicles. "Don't get lost Mr. PhD," Peter hollered over his shoulder to Scott as he shut his door in the lead car.

Moments later, a pair of oversized taxis labored valiantly as the hopeful crew headed to the harbor. At the previous night's private meeting, the three longtime friends agreed to divvy up the trip's cost above what the University covered.

At the dock entrance, ineptly secured by a rusting chain link gate, the uniformed guard made a phone call which cleared their party. Looking hopefully at the second cab's passengers, who were just arriving, Red Dickson commented, "Let's go see what we got. Our magical savior vessel should be arriving shortly."

Turning as the others caught up with him, Red and the group strode purposefully toward the wharf. Three hundred yards later, seven wishful souls stepped lightly aboard the OCEAN EXPLORER.

"Would you look at that?" Chad blurted. "Shit man, it's worse than I remember from yesterday." Disbelief spread over the young Kansan's face as he surveyed the damage around him.

"Christ, what a mess. There's bits and pieces everywhere," Doc observed. "It's a bloody war zone."

Everyone's mood sombered as they walked around the open hatches over the engine room. Carefully stepping over bits of jagged metal, seven would-be shark hunters avoided the profusion of debris strewn randomly about. Leaving the depressing scene behind them as they neared the door at the cabin's entrance, they all hurried inside.

"Something to eat or drink?" Captain Hendrickson asked hospitably, smiling at his new arrivals as they entered the salon. "We have a choice of coffee or fruit juice. Steward, please tend to our guests."

Waiting courteously until their orders were filled, Hendrickson recapped the situation. "Based on the Harbor Master's description, if she's at all like he says, the boat will be a viable solution to your predicament. We can probably transfer most of the OCEAN EXPLORER's electronic gear to her to assist with Dr. Thompson's search."

* * *

"Damn," Doc declared, staring in awe at the incoming craft. "That is one fine looking vessel." It was 9:55 A.M. when the SEA NYMPH glided gracefully into the slip astern the damaged boat. Doc was very appreciative of beautiful women and good boats, the latter inspiring his comment. "Look at all the antenna and radar equipment, he added. "She's as well outfitted as us. Hope we can afford her," Doc smiled.

"No time like the present to find out," Scott asserted, and started across the deck, closely followed by the other three men. Crossing to the wharf, they headed toward the second vessel's landing plank being lowered from her starboard gunwale. Rachel and the two students remained onboard the OCEAN EXPLORER. Transfixed by the gorgeous craft before him, Scott stated, "Hendrickson said they'd be expecting us. We should just go aboard and announce ourselves." His right foot stepped on the gang plank.

"Welcome aboard gentlemen," an authoritative voice said quietly. "Can I offer you something to drink? Coffee, a cold beer, or maybe a soft drink? I'm Captain Mason. The ship's owner, Mr. Breaux, was awakened when we entered the harbor. He will join us shortly."

"Good morning Captain. I'm Scott Thompson and this is Jim Gaffney, Red Dickson, and Dr. Peter Smith." Introductions completed, Red and Doc accepted beers while Scott had a coke and Jim abstained. "Thank you, sir," Scott offered graciously and took a quick swig from the red can with its well-known logo before resuming. "Captain Mason, I don't believe you're aware of our problem but . . ."

Mason interrupted. "Excuse me Dr. Thompson. The Harbor Master informed me of your unfortunate problem last night when we called to notify him of our ETA. A life-long seaman myself, I was distressed to hear about your engine's failure. I immediately advised Mr. Breaux and he instructed me to do whatever we could to assist. I am at liberty to show you around my vessel. If she meets your requirements and you elect to use her, we can discuss rates. I can promise you, the owner will not take advantage of your situation."

"Here it comes," Scott whispered to Red as his attention wavered. "Doesn't wish to take advantage my ass. Kick 'em while they're down I bet." Waiting to be screwed, he couldn't help but admire the well-equipped salon as cool air from an almost silent air conditioning system caressed his neck. Mumbling to Dickson under his breath, he added, "Even in hard times, this little lady would run upwards of 3 grand a day, plus the fuel." After some quick mental math, Scott concluded, "Shit, even if it only takes six weeks to find that monster, we'll be lookin' at 180 to 200 grand."

"Captain, would you excuse us for a couple of minutes?" Red asked politely. Mason nodded and disappeared into the wheel house while Red, smiling, turned to the others. "Professor, we're gonna book this boat regardless of the cost. And it's all on me! Scott I know you can't afford even a third over what this craft will probably cost, and Doc, your money ain't no good either."

Scott and Doc looked at each other, but before either could speak, Red's tirade continued. "I've been lucky guys. I couldn't spend all the bucks I've got if I lived to be 200. Because of you two, my life has some meaning and we even got us a mission. I was busted up pretty bad when baseball was over for me. Then I found Jane she and my baby were taken from me. Shit man, I didn't really want to live, but I didn't have the balls to do away with myself. Now I've got you and we got MEGALODON! So understand, I'm payin' for the damn boat and that's that! No more comments or you'll just piss me off."

There was no comment from Red's audience. They knew his way and to argue was futile. Noting the momentary silence, Captain Mason came back in and continued his conversation. "Mr. Breaux is striving to establish a warm relationship with the academic community. With this goal in mind, Mr. Breaux does not require charges typical for such an exceptional vessel."

Mason's eyes lifted imperceptibly, glancing at something behind his guests. Returning his stare to Red and then to Scott, he continued, "For example, she has just completed an eight-week trip. Took a group from Texas A&M up the Amazon River, a voyage I unfortunately did not get to make. We charged $1,200 a day plus fuel. Room and board was another $26 per person. You will have to agree that such rates are more than reasonable."

Before Scott could reply, Red leaned forward, first commenting and then asking, "That's reasonable indeed captain. I'm sure it doesn't even cover your cost. What exactly did your Mr. Breaux have in mind for us, if we decide to charter the SEA NYMPH?"

"I'll want $500 a day and $20 a man subsistence." The callous response came from directly behind them. A short, stocky man in tailored casual wear stood at the head of the stairs, leading down to staterooms below. The practiced British accent was obviously false, attempting to hide the Cajun drawl. How long he had been standing there, Scott could only guess. However, the generosity of the proposal flabbergasted him. "I am many things, and one of them is a realist. There is a remote chance of locating a charter in Rio at this time of year and my boat must be back in the States in three months for certain modifications."

Striding confidently toward Scott, smiling widely, he continued, "I am also endeavoring to work with universities and scientists, sort of a *Jacques Cousteau* type thing. I will do anything within reason to accommodate you."

Stopping between Scott and Red, he continued, "The ship's crew consists of Captain Mason here, a mate, a cook, and the ship's engineer. The cost quoted will cover roughly half my out-of-pocket expenses. Your use of my vessel should gain SEA NYMPH valuable exposure. Since I must run the boat home in any case we will also split fuel costs. What do you say gentlemen? Can the good Captain show you around my gracious lady?"

* * *

"Yes sir, Dr. McMasters, that's what the owner said, $500 a day. She is a viable replacement for the EXPLORER, only a little shorter." Scott cradled the phone between his ear and shoulder while Red crossed his fingers in support. "Yes sir, Hendrickson is checking some of his contacts and they've all been most favorable."

"What the hell, Thompson," the commanding voice rang, demanding respect from several thousand miles away. "You've sold me. The university will cover your excursion, up to six weeks that is." Since his earlier call from Captain Hendrickson, Dr. Charles McMasters had learned repairing OCEAN EXPLORER's engines would be fully covered by a maintenance agreement. Thompson caught him in an agreeable mood and the use of the SEA NYMPH was officially blessed. "Have Hendrickson double-check their papers and insurance. If everything's in order, we've got a deal."

The ensuing four days evaporated in whirlwind fashion. Captain Mason's enlightening tour of the SEA NYMPH convinced Scott of her suitability. Her forty-foot decrease in length from the OCEAN EXPLORER was conveniently ignored.

A single phone call appraised his departmental chairman in Miami of their situation and options. McMasters affirmed Scott's faith in mankind with his approval. Red's offer to finance the trip wasn't mentioned. That would be a surprise for Dr. McMasters and he could use the money to fund another trip with other lucky adventurers.

As instructed, Hendrickson reviewed the replacement vessel's documents and found everything in order with adequate insurance in force. Needless to say, the terms were accepted and the hasty provisioning of the SEA NYMPH began. Any additional equipment which might come in handy was transferred aboard as well.

The replacement vessel was admirably outfitted with electronic gear. All the additional items were really just icing on the cake. The first two major pieces were a backup LORAN unit, for accurate positioning at sea, and a high-resolution, color sonar device that permitted identification of underwater objects. Number three was a wide-range sound-impulse-generation and frequency-modulation package complete with its own diesel driven power supply. Scott and a couple of electronic and acoustical whiz kids at the university developed it and he believed its output would draw that ferocious, prehistoric atrocity to his ship.

The collection also included a Remote Controlled Vehicle or RCV which is a tethered device that carries an underwater video camera and other equipment. It is controlled from the surface and can be *flown* to depths of 1,000 feet. Visual inspection of something the sonar might detect could be accomplished without endangering divers.

A full complement of diving equipment, supplies, and even a shark cage were also placed onboard. Courtesy of Red, eight Penn International big game fishing outfits were added to their cache, along with necessary terminal tackle, rigs, lures, and two portable fighting chairs. Red Dickson never went anywhere unprepared.

"That takes care of everything I can think of," Hendrickson

commented as the final boxes of stores were transferred aboard. "Captain Mason topped her off with fuel and potable water, so you're ready to sail. According to the itinerary you discussed with me Dr. Thompson, you should get to Miami about the time we start home with the OCEAN EXPLORER. As far as Captain Mason is concerned, I've spoken with a couple of friends who know him, and he has a good reputation. Scuttle butt is he's very capable.

I also received some information on Mr. Breaux. Fancies himself a lady-killer and is rich. Also, he seems reasonable on the outside but we understand he's one tough SOB to deal with unless things go his way. He's into lots of different things, and talk has it he will do anything to make a buck. He's the kind who'll kick you when you're down. Why he gave you people this sweetheart deal doesn't fit," the captain of the non-running OCEAN EXPLORER continued. "Regardless, he's already headed back home so he will be out of your hair. All you gents care about is getting his boat anyway, right?"

* * *

"Scott, isn't there something we've neglected to do?" Doc interrupted, having come up on the afterdeck of the university's vessel looking for Thompson.

"Yeah, what's that?" Scott retorted. "Didn't pack enough hot and cold running women for you and Red?"

"Nope," Doc replied, shaking his head. With a sparkle in his eye, he said, "I think it's time we open up that box I sent down. Let's see if you can use what's in it."

"Damnation!" Scott cursed. He'd forgotten about Doc's air shipment in the hustle and bustle of changing out vessels. "Where's the crate? What goodies did you bring?"

"Chad and the mate hoisted it aboard the SEA NYMPH a few minutes ago," Doc informed him. "Let's go see what Santa sent."

Transferring to the SEA NYMPH was an easy operation. After topping her off, Captain Mason had laid her alongside the OCEAN EXPLORER. Three large, blimp shaped, foam filled, rubber fenders nestled between the two vessels, keeping them apart. Doc and Scott just stepped off one boat, onto the word SEAWARD stenciled on the sternmost fender, and then onto the second boat.

Jim Gaffney was alone with Chad, the SEA NYMPH's mate having gone below to assist the engineer with the predeparture check list. A crowbar was being used to pull the final nail out of the crate's lid. Sliding off the top, it took Scott a moment to recognize the equipment within.

"Doc, that's a pretty fancy video system," Scott commented, recognizing part of the crate's contents. "What's so special 'bout it? We've already got color TV on board." Feigning disinterest to irritate Doc, he lifted out a weather proof video camera. Beneath it rested a bright orange, rectangular, fiberglass box. Neatly coiled beside it was 120 feet of coaxial control cable for the system. Two other boxes of electronic gear were also fit snugly into the crate, but didn't appear to go with the TV equipment.

"What we have here Thompson, is a state-of-the-art remote video monitoring and recording system designed for use in a marine environment." Doc elaborated enthusiastically about his high-tech paraphernalia. "The color camera is equipped with mounting attachments that permit 320 degree panning. It's driven by an electric motor that's powered by batteries which are continuously charged by the ship's engines. The control cable runs from the camera to this high-visibility, orange box. I had your name plus the University's address and phone number stenciled on it."

"Just what we need," Scott interrupted, gigging his friend. "Another camera, complete with its own brightly-colored, self-addressed, unstamped, mailing envelope."

"Quiet please and let me finish Thompson," Doc snapped back. "You'll like this baby. The box is equipped with a dual recording system, each accommodating an eight-hour, high-resolution tape. When one tape finishes, the system automatically shuttles to the other recorder. There's a ten minute overlap when both recorders operate simultaneously. It will insure no break in whatever you record. An ultra-sensitive, directional-boom microphone will pick up any sounds coming from the direction where the camera is pointing, so don't even fart in front of it, okay? You can store thirty-six tapes in the box, plus the two in the recorders. That gives you over twelve days of records in one safe, secure place."

Doc rambled on for ten more minutes, showing his smiling friend how the contraption works. "Finally, the fiberglass case is self-contained and water-tight, except for the leads to the camera and power supply which are self-sealing. If you keep the box closed and latched, except to erase, edit, or change out the tapes, we will have an audio-visual record of everything that happens on this vessel. Should the box be lost overboard, there is even a seawater-activated homing beacon that will emit the international tracking frequency for up to six days. Pretty slick, huh, Thompson? Tell me you're impressed?"

Doc's toy *was* impressive. "That is one sweet setup Doc. I think we'll mount it to the top of that masthead over the bridge and aim it toward the stern. Most of the action should take place back there. Our only blind spot'll be directly ahead of us plus a few points to either beam. Great man, thanks a lot. Okay now, what are the other two items? Not more video gear?"

"That my dear friend, is our *piece de resistance*," beamed Doc. "What's been scaring you?" he asked excitedly before answering his own question. "That some *high-tech* outfit in Silicone Valley is going to market acoustical location devices transmitting in the sound-frequency ranges you believe will excite our big fish, right?"

"You weren't able to get one, were you?" Scott blurted out involuntarily. Those bastards have ignored all my requests for additional data. They keep telling me it's still developmental, won't be available for some time."

Doc, smilingly replied. "The answer is yes. I happen to know a San Diego surgeon, who got hold of some prototypes. The gizmos were sent on a test run between California and Hawaii late last year. We were discussing a mutual case back in March and I told him about your escapade. Well, seems he and a couple of friends sailed off on a cross Pacific junket. They'd been approached by the manufacturer to use a newfangled tracking device on their sailboats' hulls."

"Oh no, they didn't, did they?" Scott barked sharply, breaking in again as icy fear tore at his innards. "Come on Doc, did they do it? What the hell happened?"

Doc confirmed Scott's worst fear. "Thirteen yachts left San Diego Harbor, three equipped with prototype devices. One week out, one of the vessels foundered."

"Damn, I read about that," Jim Gaffney interrupted excitedly. "Few months ago in the Sydney Yacht Club Newsletter." He and Red had rejoined the three men at the crate. "But the article didn't mention any tracking devices. Just said that one boat was lost without a trace."

"That's right," Doc confirmed. "As I told Red here on the flight to Caracas, one night this boat was there, the next morning she's gone. No big ships in the area to ram her, no bad weather to sink her, no distress call to indicate trouble, no nothing. She just disappeared sometime after dark without a trace. Crew of five went down with her."

"Damn!" Sympathy was overshadowed by fear and rising anger. Scott spit out the questions. "You mean not a trace? No debris? No life cushions. Nothing? But what happened to the other two boats with devices? Were they okay?"

"Yes Scott," Peter Smith stated in absolute fact. "Nothing happened to any of the other twelve sailboats. Just the one, a forty-two footer with a fancy name a mile long. She simply vanished during the night."

Staring at Scott and ignoring the others who were also listening to his tale, Doc's eyes seemed to burn holes into his longtime friend. Deliberately, he added, "According to my friend, the other two gadgets didn't work. Only *one boat* had an operational transponder. And *she* disappeared."

Too much to be a coincidence, the sinking had to be significant. At that instant, Scott Thompson's worst fears were confirmed. He asked the obvious question. "But why the hell didn't that fact get reported anywhere? Surely it must have come up in the investigation afterwards. No company has the resources to cover up something like that. Not nowadays."

"Scott, my friend stated that when those sailboats reached Honolulu, you'd have thought it was the 7th of December in '41 and they were Japs. Navy brass and security out the gazoo. When those folks left their sailboats, the tracking devices were never mentioned again." Serious as hell, Doc grimaced with his final statement. "The bloody United States Navy is in this, up to its eyeballs. They're ramrodding the development of these tracking devices and they covered up the incident."

Gaffney and Chad were on identical wavelengths. In unison they asked, "How did you get hold of two of them then, if that's what these are?"

"Mums the word boys," Doc answered in a lighter tone. "What you don't know hopefully ain't gonna hurt you. Needless to say, I've got a couple of old navy buddies in high places. They confirmed, on the Q.T., what happened; that the development of the low-frequency tracking system is a pet project of a big brass's department." Smiling sarcastically, Doc added, "Seems that certain other folks in the pentagon are also wondering why only the sailboat carrying the working device disappeared. I happened to let something about

Scott's theory slip in the right ears. Don't you just love it? Seems someone thought the navy could use some help on this one. These two widgets simply showed up at my office one Friday afternoon, in a plain unmarked box via UPS. Dr. Thompson, I am pleased, I think, to present you with two operating LRLFTD's. Long-Range, Low-Frequency, Tracking Device units. Use them in good health. If what you believe is true, may God help us."

* * *

The next ten days slipped by quickly. The new camera was mounted and a simple mechanism for deploying the LRLFTD's was built. Thirty days supplies were laid in which would easily get them to Port of Spain, Trinidad. Final checks were run on all equipment. Everything shipshape, SEA NYMPH was ready to sail and Scott gave everyone the evening off. It was their last night in port and he felt his crew needed a final shore bash.

"Everyone have a good time," Scott advised, "and stay out of trouble," he added in parting, "but be back on board by midnight. We're out of here by daylight. It'll take several days to reach our optimal search area and I want to get an early start. Remember, no stragglers!"

"Yes sir, Skipper. Anything you say, Boss-man," Peter and Red joked with the professor before jumping ship. "Come on gang, let's do what the man says."

Four consenting adults and two college students stepped off the SEA NYMPH. Scott remained behind with Captain Mason to finalize his plans. The seven of them and the four crew members were going to spend the next six weeks in very close proximity.

* * *

The ship and her crew cleared the jetties at 05:00 the following morning. Nine uneventful days followed. They passed time by dragging high-speed fishing lures. Averaging ten knots, they were frequently throttling back to battle fish they hooked.

"What's that?" Red asked. "Number eleven?" His query was directed toward Scott as another thirty-pound wahoo hit the deck. Vivid blue and silver stripes glowed radiantly in contrast to the crimson pouring from its gaff wound.

"Watch it's teeth Chad," Scott reminded as the fifty-inch fish quivered in its death throes.

"Damn, he got me! Those teeth *are* sharp," Chad grimaced, jerking his hand away from the arrival's snapping jaws. "Jesus, look at the blood!" Chad added. "Hurts some too. Thought I was a safe distance from the damn fish."   At that instant, the young male student became the cruise's first casualty, carelessly forgetting to avoid the fish's sharp teeth. "Anyone got a Band-Aid?"

"Let me have a look," Peter said, ambling up to the young man with blood streaming down his right wrist and forearm. "May need to sew a little on this one," he diagnosed, looking over the nasty gash on the pinkie side of Chad's palm. "Let's go below for a minute and tend to it. Come on Chad."

Down below, Peter pulled out his black bag and fiddled efficiently through its contents. A quick injection of novocaine followed by a single running suture and Chad was patched up. Returning to the deck, pain evidently gone and all smiles, Chad didn't miss a lick.

Joining the wahoo were several good sized dolphin, fish not mammals. Their white meat matched the wahoo's darker flesh as a delicious addition to the shipboard contingent's diet. Brilliant blues and greens of these trophy fish, radiating in life-like fluorescent lights, faded dramatically in death to dull and lifeless off-yellows and browns. Both fish were culinary delights. Fillets were fried, broiled, and even barbecued on the charcoal grill, providing a welcome supplement to the meat and poultry in the galley freezer.

"Look at that sucker go!" Chad Brown screamed in delight, a white gauze bandage covering Peter's handiwork. "Christ, he's stayin' in the air!" Young Chad was beaming with excitement as 250 pounds of blue marlin cavorted over a slick calm sea. "What a fish! Come on Karen, slow it down!" Karen fought and landed her first big game fish, in spite of Chad's ravings. Two days later, the young male student followed suit. After being brought to the boat, both fish were photographed, tagged, and released. The tags were small darts with stainless steel number plates and short streamers, supplied by the International Game Fish Association. Gratifying was an understatement as all onboard watched the magnificent fish swim defiantly into the dark blue water of the equatorial Atlantic Ocean.

Two fantastic shows with wild aerial displays were permanently recorded by Doc's video camera. Mounted strategically above the afterdeck, it didn't miss a jump. While replaying Karen's fish on the TV in the salon, the young lady flushed frequently as she listened to expletives depart her normally ladylike lips during the heat of battle.

* * *

"Come on Doc, quit your bitching and help me fill her up again," Scott badgered, stretching his aching back. He'd hung onto the straining rod for eighteen minutes as some unstoppable and very large fish was streaking toward its escape. "Bluefin tuna, never felt anything so strong. Just kept going. Never even slowed it down."

"Could've been a marlin," Doc countered. "I've had those big blacks make that kind of run down at Cairns. Well, lets get on with refilling that reel. It'll take a while and I want to get my beauty rest."

Darkness had just descended on the sixth day when that unidentified fish hit and sounded in the bottomless depths. Over 900 yards of eighty-pound line disappeared into the briny-deep. Doc and the professor refilled the oversized reel from spare spools of line and Doc eventually got his sleep. Scott's back continued to ache for several days.

The early stages of the voyage were very pleasant. SEA NYMPH sailed at 0500 hours on July 11th and, at her most fuel-efficient cruising speed of ten knots, they covered roughly 225 nautical miles each day. Toward dark on the sixth day, the night that mysterious fish smoked a reel, they came even with the eastern-most extension of land in South America. SEA NYMPH rounded Point Calcanhar and, now heading west-northwest, began running a course offshore of parallel to the northeastern coast of Brazil. Thirty-six hours later, on July 18th, at almost noon local time, they slipped over the equator and into the North Atlantic. At the time, they were roughly 300 miles east of the Amazon River's mouth.

July 19, 1987, Scott's log:

"The size of this fish is so awesome that SEA NYMPH may not be able to withstand an attack if one comes. I'm haunted by a twenty-year-old ghost that replaces probable reality with potential horror."

Scott shuddered apprehensively and paused from his writing. He concentrated on the soothing throb of powerful diesels and his vessel's peaceful heaving motion. Again, words formed effortlessly and his transcription resumed.

"We will maintain our WNW heading for two more days. Our destination is a spot in the open ocean 600 miles east of Paramaribo, Brazil at latitude six degrees north and longitude forty-five degrees west. In this area, the west running North Equatorial Current converges with the north running Antilles Current. I believe that Carcharodon Megalodon utilizes the major ocean currents in its perpetual migrations. The North Atlantic population should be following these currents about this time of year. Sometime late tomorrow, SEA NYMPH will be on location.

"Once there, we will begin baiting our quarry. Unconventionally, our bait will not consist of typical flesh and blood, or even the newfangled artificial lures, but electronically generated sound. I am certain my hypothesis is valid and that these giant sharks are attracted by certain sound frequencies. I also believe that these frequencies turn Megalodon into enraged killers. The sailboat's disappearance in the Pacific Doc told us about erased all my lingering doubts. Tomorrow afternoon the real work starts and with it, the inherent danger. I hope all of us will live to share our findings of the next few weeks with the rest of the world. I can't shake the premonition that this may be asking too much. Our real adventure is about to begin."

Scott was incorrect by thinking that the real work would not start until the next afternoon. Unknown to those onboard the SEA NYMPH, Bubba Breaux's hidden transponder was already pulsing its obscene invitation into the water.

Chapter Sixteen

HOMING IN

Many miles away, two huge shapes sped through the blackness two-thousand feet beneath the surface, prehistoric creatures being summoned by low-frequency sound waves emanating from a graceful ship's forward hull.

Great teeth meshed angrily and numerous hideous barbels continued to stiffen, then relax, then stiffen again as the monstrous creature propelled his Gargantuan body through his frigid kingdom. Unequaled senses plucked electrical and pressure impulses from the surrounding water while the inner lining of that tooth-encrusted mouth searched for the slightest hint of odor or taste. Only the twinkling glimmers of biological or chemical lights pierced the eternal blackness and this massive apparition took on an ethereal appearance in his travels.

Almost two weeks had passed since copulation, and hunger no longer drove this great fish since acres of squid were providing the high protein diet his massive body demanded. Energy levels were finally recovering from the cyclic low of his mating-induced fast. His bulging, over-filled belly occasionally emitted clouds of residue and the crystal clear water he traversed should have billowed a dirty gray as his droppings gradually diluted to nothing. However, light never reached the great depths of his domain and the billowing gray remained invisible, lost in a sightless sanctuary, robed in perpetual darkness.

For two full days, a persistent but faraway sound governed his every movement. It was an alien tone so faint that only the most sophisticated sonar could have detected it. He was equipped with the best. The source was still several hundred miles away, but its remoteness shrank with each stroke of his powerful tail. A distant, disturbing hum controlled his direction. He fed often to stoke the gluttonous engine which was his body but the origin of that sound alone governed his movements.

The North Equatorial Current was carrying him steadily westward toward its confluence with the Antilles Current. At first the irritating sound forced him on a more westerly course, negating the effectiveness of his hitchhiking efforts. The strokes by his perfectly designed tail increased steadily, compensating for the current's decreased assistance and placating the incessant vibration from afar. Accelerating gradually, the separation shrank.   As separation diminished, the aggravation from that all-consuming noise increased. Responding to its fervent command, the seven-foot tail beat ever faster.   Less time was spent feeding, modulated sound was amplified, and sixty feet of ageless shark drove his *forty-seven tons* into the darkness of the surrounding sea.

Two hundred miles north-northeast of the male, a second immense denizen was also being influenced by the same pulsating addition to her watery realm. Nature instinctively separated this huge female from her recent mate when the act mandated for species' survival was complete. Without feeding, she drove herself northward for forty-eight hours while he was retreating to the southwest. The expanse separating them eventually screened their presence from each other.   Due to their voracity, any non-procreation period encounter would probably instigate aggression and the demise of one of the two, probably the smaller male. Nature prevented such inopportune meetings through a combination of small numbers of the creatures and by scattering them throughout the vastness of the world's oceans. Nature's efforts were usually met with excellent success.

Although farther away than the male, her finely tuned receptors detected the low-frequency emissions within a few hours of her counterpart. Her due-westerly movement altered to the north, continually adjusting as the sound source also moved northerly. Her more powerful body and amazing senses gradually increased her speed as she likewise homed in on the remote antagonist. She was acutely aware of similar concentrations of three-foot-long squid and required more frequent feeding than her recent mate. Her body spanned almost a *hundred feet* and she weighed over *sixty tons!*

Several days of relentless tracking narrowed the distance separating both huge fish from the disquieting source, and from each other.   The female was within 100 miles of the much more audible source, less than seven hours away at her current pace and almost 2,000 feet beneath the surface. Her recent partner was much closer to the quarry. Dramatic increases in the irritating sound's intensity controlled his every action.

Now less than three miles away, the source had slowed its northward movement during the preceding two days, greatly increasing his closure speed.   Dim light now filtered through the reduced water column and the great carnivore slashed angrily at the hoards of blue-green fish he surprised. The eternal blackness of his normal world dissipated when he reached the shallower 600-foot depth now being crossed. His acute vision finally came into play, hypersensitive lateral lines, barbel antenna array, and Ampule of Lorenzini zeroing in more precisely on the slowly-moving source than any man-made sonar device. Prehistoric instincts, fine tuned over millions of years, peaked. He hurled himself onward and upward toward his destination.

The much larger female also ascended gradually, her arsenal of senses drawing her steadily toward the same intensifying source. Adequate distance still existed to prevent the low-frequency noise from jamming all other reception. She clearly detected the male as he closed relentlessly on their common target. A much lower frequency also reached her, one emitted by some large creature on the surface. The huge female could even decipher the large creature's proximity to the thing spewing out the intolerable noise. It seemed to be mating with her target and several other similar large sources of low pulsating noise dotted the surface. None interested her, only the creeping beast and its unbearable sound.

The male rocketed his almost fifty tons past the point of no return. Charging ahead, he focused on the object he had been pursuing these many days. The female was also accelerating, decreasing her arrival time by several hours. Two specimens of abject horror and ferocity from the ocean's protective depths converged on an unsuspecting vessel and its crew, needing to silence its disquieting hum. Neither creature could understand, that *they* were the entity of their prey's quest.

THURSDAY, JULY 23RD, 18:30 HOURS

"Can you fix it Bill? Guess we screwed up royally, banging the housing against the transom like we did, sticking it in the water." Scott Thompson scratched his head in concern. The underwater video camera carried by the RCV gave him a way to get underwater pictures of Megalodon without using divers. They could get pictures *if* it really existed, *if* the crazy low-frequency sounds attracted it, and *if* one of the gigantic *son of a bitches* came close enough to hear them. Lots and lots of "*if's.*"

"Not this one," Bill Parsons muttered in frustration. "Not this one either." The ship's engineer gazed intently at the motionless needle mounted in his magic black box. Switching settings and moving the alligator clips expediently around the camera's open housing, the expedition's leader was being ignored. Suddenly he barked, "Hot damn! That's the culprit!" The skinny needle on the Continuity Tester pegged in its clockwise rotation. "Piece of cake, Scott," he added quickly. Carefully lifting parallel black and yellow wires with his index finger, Bill commented confidently, "We got a short in this wire to the interlock switch. May take a while, but I'll have it up and running sometime tomorrow morning."

"Not before then?" Scott asked, feeling naked without the underwater TV camera.

"Sorry Scott," the ship's engineer advised, "I've got a higher priority right now. The automatic alarm that tells us when another ship gets within a mile of us went *kaput* this morning. Gotta get that equipment going pronto. We're chugging along in the middle of the north-bound shipping lanes. Those big tankers ride the same currents you're guessing your giant sharks like. Sure don't fancy letting one of those babies get too close. I'll get to the RCV quick as I can, that's a promise. But first things first."

"Thanks Bill," Scott conceded, "that's all I can ask." Quickly scanning the horizon, Scott counted three supertankers within ten or twelve miles of them, all headed in the same northerly direction as his craft. A small, but exceedingly real, knot tightened in his belly. Gut instincts were telling him their quest was not about to disappoint them. That *Prehistoric Fish* was real. *Megalodon was out there, somewhere!* Scott knew it was just a matter of time. But it would take time. The sound transmitter had only been spewing forth its beckoning message for thirty-six hours and an expansive ocean surrounded them. *It would surely take time.*

"Well, let's see 'bout the Automatic Alarm," Parsons mumbled, picking up his plastic tool box and heading for the bridge. Thinking about his wife and twin daughters, he skipped enthusiastically over the plated deck.

Scott turned to watch him for a second then meandered slowly toward two fishermen battling aqua-blue and green dolphin from the diving platform on the stern. Thoughts of huge sharks and nearby ships slipped conveniently from his mind. "Hey Doc, Red, my turn," he hollered, picking up his pace. "All work and no play makes Scott a dull boy."

FRIDAY, JULY 24TH, 03:30 HOURS

"What the hell!" Scott exclaimed. Awakened from a deep sleep, he found himself plastered painfully against the bunk opposite his. The impact had thrown him from his own sweat-drenched bed and interrupted a terrifying nightmare. Dazed and disoriented as he came back to life, his unpleasant dream vanished compassionately. "Oh my God! It's that *monster,*" he screamed, his knowing fear saturating the confining blackness of the bunk room. *"FUCKIN' MEGALODON!"*

As wakefulness restored his self-control, Scott remembered he wasn't alone in the room and barked an order into the night. "Chad, Chad, wake your ass up! You okay? Come on son, we got problems outside." Chad didn't respond.

As his eyes gradually adjusted to the darkness, Scott searched the opposite bunk for his young student. He could feel SEA NYMPH trembling like a flu-sickened child and his ears rebelled against the horrifying squeal of metal dragging across metal. All around him, the sounds of confusion and fright filled the early morning darkness aboard the small vessel as the plague of panic exploded within the air-conditioned spaces below her decks.

"What the hell's goin' on?" Red's slow southern drawl breached the night. "You all right, Doc?"

"Yeah Red, something clobbered us," Smitty replied in another cabin. "Think it's that shark? Let's get up on deck, see what the hell happened." Doc was all right. Scott heard the door to their adjoining stateroom slam against its rubber tipped stop.

Getting accustomed to the dimness, Scott could finally see Chad's shape sputtering to life in the lower bunk opposite his. "Professor Thompson, what is it?" His bunk was on the vessel's side which had apparently just been struck by *something*. The collision's force piled him into the exterior wall of the hull beneath a closed, oval porthole, restricting his travel to less than two feet. Covering both ears with his hands, the youngster pleaded, "What's making that noise? Christ it's bad!" and then added, "are we sinking?"

The piercing squeal and terrifying vibration continued unabated as Scott struggled to his feet. Pain knifed through his left side when he lifted that arm. A deep bruise would soon form below his left shoulder blade where he struck a large brass handle on one of the slide-out drawers beneath Chad's bunk. "I don't know Chad," he replied. "Come on, let's get out of here. We'll see if everyone's okay. What the damage is."

Numbing quiet and penetrating stillness grabbed them instantly as the grating noise ceased. It was replaced by the throb and churning noise of some giant machine passing close by. For a second or two, the sound seemed to enter the cabin and Scott was afraid they would be pulverized. Then their vessel's shaking subsided and the pulsating machinery receded. Chad, wearing multicolored boxer shorts, was pulled to his feet by his professor. Scott followed his student out the door and into a dimly lit passageway.

Rachel, clad in a thigh-length tee shirt, emerged from across the hall with husband Jim in tow. En masse, the four of them stumbled toward the open hatchway at the base of the stairs leading up to the salon. From somewhere on those stairs, Red's comments, directed to no one in particular, filtered down to the group below. Rachel and Jim, then Chad, and finally Scott cleared the hatchway and charged up the narrow steps.

Less than fifty yards in front of them, hulking black and ominous at this close range, was the stern of a medium sized tanker. Her enormous prop, throwing frothy, white water everywhere, laboriously pushed its loadless hulk northward. The empty ship rode high in the water with less than half of her rotating brass wheel beneath the surface. She sported some indecipherable Arabic symbols across the stern and never changed direction, never even slowed down. As the lethal vessel distanced herself, Captain Mason materialized alongside Scott and took charge.

"*May Day! May Day!* This is Whiskey Victor Charlie 6647, the SEA NYMPH. We have been struck by an unidentified vessel. Extent of damage unknown. Our location is . . ." Mason repeated the call for several minutes, giving Loran coordinates each time. Three vessels replied, identifying themselves and advising that their situation would be reported to the Brazilian authorities and other ships in the area. Mason sent Bill Parsons on a damage survey and all of them waited impatiently for his return. The injured vessel idled slowly on the calm sea, diesels humming almost noiselessly beneath their feet. An orange-crimson ring singed the horizon, heralding a new day.

"Captain, this is crazy," a flustered Parsons explained while the rest listened intently. "She's taking on water somewhere, our gauges have us riding eight inches lower than when I checked yesterday, but it's not showing anywhere. No extra water in the bilge and I don't see any unusual amounts in the forward holds. Our trim indicator has us bow heavy by three or four degrees, but nothing seems to be causing it. We got a hole, but I can't find it."

"Okay, Bill," Mason replied to his engineer. "Go below and keep an eye on things, especially forward. That's where the SOB hit us. Damn raghead captains, don't watch where they're going and don't give a shit either." Purple veins rippled in the captain's neck and cheeks as he envisioned the big tanker running northward on autopilot, its helm unattended for hours at a stretch. Looking toward the east, he commented, "It's getting light now. Won't be long till we'll be able to see just what the external damage is. For now, we watch and wait."

"Is that all we can do, Captain?" Scott asked. "Seems like we should be doing something."

"There is one thing Scott," Mason answered. "One of your folks can make sure Cookie gets breakfast made. I don't want to leave the bridge. Ask him to make coffee, plenty of it, good and dark. I want my spoon to stand up in it. These next few days will probably be long ones."

"Sure skipper," Scott replied, relaying the request. "Karen, would you go down to the galley and pass along the captain's instructions? Anyway, the shock of that collision is wearing off," he added, looking at his digital Omega which read 4:47:32, "and I'm suddenly hungry."

"Yes sir," the young girl replied, nodding her head in the affirmative, "I'm on my way." Looking pretty in her pink Adidas warmup suit, she turned and started down the steep stairs.

"Captain Mason, how bad is it?" Doc queried.

The seasoned skipper was cool under fire and was handling this trying situation professionally. "Both engines seem to be running fine," he advised. "Parsons couldn't find any damage in the rear section and we seem to be stable now. She's floating acceptably for the time being. My best guess is the hull wasn't breached and we can continue our excursion. But I can't commit until we know what the hull looks like. Give me a couple of hours, then I'll tell you."

"Scott, do you know if Bill got the RCV working last night?" Red asked, rekindling Scott's concern about that piece of underwater equipment. The problem was conveniently pushed aside the day before to catch a few fish.

"I know he intended to work on it after he fixed the radar alarm," Scott said pensively. "Since it didn't go off, I'd guess he didn't get around to it." Realizing that Bill had left the bridge according to Captain Mason's instructions, Scott mentally kicked himself for not asking that question sooner.

"We didn't work on it last night," Chad chipped in, entering the conversation for the first time. "Bill fussed around with the radar unit awhile and I tried to give him a hand. Never got it going. I turned in about 1 A.M. Karen stayed up with Bill for the graveyard shift on the bridge. I'm sure he didn't have time to fool with the RCV."

About then, cool air from below carried the savory aroma of frying bacon and fresh coffee to those on the bridge. "That sure smells inviting" Red muttered, not quite covering the growl of his always-hungry stomach. "What you say we go feed our faces and figure out who gets to make the early morning dive if we have to get wet."

Red, Doc, Chad, Karen, and Scott were finishing their first helpings when the Gaffney's arrived in the galley. Rachel had changed into her nondescript Levi cutoffs and a cotton top. "Daylight coming up fast outside," Jim stated. "Got to get topside and check our options." An experienced boat operator, James Gaffney placed the knowledge of his vessel's condition far above any stomach cravings. Quickly filling a styrofoam cup with steaming coffee, he added three heaping spoonfuls of granulated sugar. After a moments deliberation, a fourth spoonful followed. Grabbing a fistful of well-done bacon and a piece of buttered toast, he bolted out of the galley.

* * *

"What in the Sam-hill is that?" Mason said to himself. Some thirty feet back from the bow, he was leaning over the starboard side and staring down into the water of the Antilles Current. What should have been crystal-clear, dark-blue water was instead a dusky gray cloud, barely visible in the early morning light. As Jim and Scott approached, the captain looked quizzically along the side of the boat and continued speaking to no one in particular. "Got a rip in her that should sink a battleship, but we're not taking on any water. What the hell is going on here?"

"What's that white stuff, skipper?" Jim asked as they reached the captain's side. For the moment, that was a question no one could answer. Scott realized that, for probably the first time since they left port, Captain Mason was out on deck without the navy blue

Captain's Cap covering his brilliant gray pate.

The sacred cap was gripped tightly in his left hand as it rested on his hip. The darkly-tanned fingers of his right hand were absentmindedly scratching a bald spot on his head and the weathered brown face registered concern. Backing away from the rail, he crossed to the port side, stopping twice and kneeling. There were two almost invisible three-by-four-foot rectangles outlined by ground-down welds and painted over. Each was spaced about one third of the way across the boat's twenty-six foot beam. Rubbing his fingers along the perfect welds, Mason recovered his brow with the blue cap and strolled back to where the others stood before grunting in subtle admiration. "Well lads, me thinks there's a fox in this here hen house."

FRIDAY, JULY 24TH, 05:52 HOURS

Scott's Omega read 5:52:08 and the seconds changed quickly to 09 and then 10 before he looked back up. One-hundred-forty minutes had passed since that wicked collision flung him from his cozy bunk. The sun was well above the horizon and the dazzling day was heating up rapidly. No clouds marred the perfect blue sky and there was a notable absence of wind. Surrounding their boat was cobalt blue water, glinting and shining in the brilliant light of morning, except for the almost snow white cloud which seemed to support the SEA NYMPH.

The cloud was densest at the mouth of the four-inch wide gash extending from the slowly moving water line upward some four-and-a-half feet. The ominous opening also clawed its way downward below the water line, but disappeared into the obscuring whiteness a few inches beneath the surface. That cloud trailed their vessel for a quarter mile, tracing their slow path while fanning out negligibly to either side. By the time it reached the stern, about sixty-five feet from the breached hull, it was already turning gray. The slick it created gradually changed color, becoming powder-blue several hundred feet behind the boat. If Mason's theory was correct, the SEA NYMPH was leaving one very expensive trail.

Poor, greedy Bubba Breaux, had no way of knowing that his elaborate plan had backfired. Safely tucked away in south Louisiana, smiling from morning to night, he awaited his fortune with no inkling it would never arrive.

* * *

Scott, we got it all on video tape," Doc stated excitedly. He was the first to check the recording made by the camera mounted on the masthead.   "The bastard's name is in Arabic, but the characters are clearly distinguishable. And she was flying Libyan colors. Saw enough of those in the Mediterranean to know that flag." Catching his breath, he almost snarled before continuing, "Damn thing came down on us like she was *trying* to hit us. Never even attempted to swerve. Got it all on tape. The picture really jumped when we got clobbered, but it kept on recording. Showed two men standing along the rail of the ship. One, smiling through large teeth with separations, even flipped his cigarette at us, and spit at us."

"What'd you do with the tapes, Smitty?" Scott asked. "Maybe we can get some satisfaction out of the bastards when we get home?"

"I put 'em in the orange box where they'll be safe," Doc replied. "Also reset everything, so we'll record the next sixteen hours too. Damn, that system works great."

* * *

"Professor, I'm ready to go take a look now," Chad stated, having slipped up behind Scott. Attired in the sleeveless neoprene jacket of his wet suit, his diving knife was strapped to his right calf, and five one-pound lead weights were belted around his midsection. Looking over the edge of the boat at the milky water, the young man advised, "Karen and Bill have the compressor going and communications are operating fine." The marine biology student was burdened by guilt for not getting the RCV repaired and insisted on making the inspection dive. It made no difference that the RCV's camera would have been useless in the discolored water around the crack. Scott agreed to let Chad make the jump. What could go wrong? This was a routine dive.

"Okay, Chad," the captain instructed, "when we get the cord tied off with the knot at the waterline, feel your way along the crack in the hull until it ends and tie another knot there." Continuing his explanation of what he wanted done, Mason ordered, "Give us a guesstimate of how wide the crack is and what it feels like about every two feet or so. No rush, you've got all the time in the world.

We'll keep asking questions, just to make sure that stuff in the water isn't affecting you. When I say out, you're outta' there. Right? Come out quick, or we'll drag you back to the surface. Got that?"

"Yes sir, captain," the youngster replied confidently. "No problem, sir." Chad was an excellent diver and self-confidence was generally a plus around the water.

"Okay, kill both engines. Starboard first," Mason instructed the mate as he pressed the talk button on his hand-held radio.

"Starboard engine down," crackled over the radio, followed immediately by, "port engine off too."

As quiet settled over the SEA NYMPH, Chad quickly stepped to the dive station, buckled up the crotch strap of his wet suit jacket and pulled on his fins and Kirby mask. "All ready, here I go," boomed out of the diver's intercom at the dive control console. With a split-step, he left the side and plunged into the water, disappearing beneath the gray cloud they were all convinced was cocaine.

Every eye was intent forward. The young diver rapidly traced the aluminum hull to that angry looking, snaggle-toothed tear near the bow. Concentrating on his bubbles burping up through the milky surface, no one onboard the vessel noticed the gray, triangular object slicing erratically through the powder-blue trail behind the drifting vessel. Knife-like as it cut cleanly through the glass calm interface, the fin's tip cleared the water by at least four feet. Exposed for nearly a minute while zig-zagging toward SEA NYMPH, it suddenly submerged. By then, Chad had been in the water for almost six minutes.

"Okay Scott," Chad advised, "the crack's about two inches wide here and narrowing fast. Now we're down to about an inch. Over." His calm voice cracked through the diver's intercom as he asked, "You getting this? Over."

"Got it, Chad," Scott replied, before questioning him on the denseness of the cloud beneath the center of the boat. "Still zero visibility down there? Over."

"That's a Roger, skipper," came out of the intercom. "Can't see my hand in front of my mask. Shid man, dis water sure tastes funny." His voice slurred, a definite giggle accompanying the reply.

"Hey Chad, it's about time to call it quits," Scott said, obviously concerned. "Can you tie the knot at the end of the crack and come on up?" He was afraid the young student was feeling some ill effect from his short swim in the milky soup.

Chad's voice was cleared dramatically, "All right, Scott, I'm tying the knot at the end of the crack. Can't feel nothing past this point. Guess this is as far as it goes. Let me see. Shit, can't quite reach the keel. Crack stops six or seven feet from the hull's center. Okay, the knot's tied, pull away."

"Thanks, Chad. This exercise'll get you a couple extra credit points this summer." Scott was anxious to get Chad out before his head got totally screwed up by the drugs around him. "Come on up now. Red's pulling in your slack. Damn! Hose is hung up on something. Follow your hose back. See if you can find what it's snagged on."

"It's hung tight, Scott," Red confirmed, taking a strain on the topside end of the air hose. He couldn't retrieve any more. "He's gonna have to free it or someone else'll have to get wet. Jim's ready to go in."

"How you coming, Chad?" Scott questioned. "Find where it's stuck yet?" There was no response and everyone's apprehension jumped a notch. Just some shallow breaths belched over the intercom. Scott was worried. "Come back, Chad. Are you okay?" he barked into the transmitter. "*Over!*"

"That's got it," came the reply from down below. "Damn thing was wrapped round the starboard wheel but it's loose now. Hang tight for a second and get a Pneumo reading on me. I'm gonna drop down an' see how deep this shit goes."

Before Scott could countermand his suggestion, the black needle on the circular gauge at the dive station indicating the diver's depth began moving clockwise. As the depth increased, a definitely slurred statement floated out of the intercom. "Damn Prof, dis stuff sure dastes funny." Silence followed.

"*Cut it out, Chad!*" Scott yelled much too loudly. "We're bringing you up. Make sure you're exhaling." Fear gripped him, right down to his jockey underwear. Something was terribly wrong down there. "Get him up, Red!" he commanded, losing control of his normally calm emotions. "Now! Jim, give him a hand. *Hurry man, hurry!* I don't like the way he sounds."

As the needle indicated Chad's depth, thirty-six feet, they heard him say, "God, id's beaudiful. So clean and clear. I'm under de shid. Id's really nead." The young man was fast becoming incoherent.

"Pull you guys! He's in trouble!" Scott was yelling now. Fear in his voice provided added adrenaline for the two makeshift tenders. The needle halted, then slowly swung back to its left.

"Hey man, who's duggin on me up der?" the slurred voice demanded. "Cud id oud." Then Chad stated, "Hey man, der's a fuggin' whale coming oud of da shid. Here whaley. Here whaley. Whad da fug . . ."

Then nothing. No voice, no static, *nothing*. Absolute silence from the diver's intercom.

"Holy shit! What the hell did that?" Jim's startled query that coincided with the sudden silence from below flagged Scott's attention. "Goddamned rope burn! Something jerked the fuckin' hose out of my hands! Pulled a bunch of coils overboard. Christ, was that ever weird."

"Pull up on his hose guys," Scott shouted. "I've lost contact with him." A cloud of apprehension and rising fear shrouded Scott as he loudly demanded a reply that never came. "Chad, can you read me? Over! Come back Chad! Over!"

"Scott, he's gone!" Red stated excitedly. There was no resistance as he and Jim manhandled 100 or so feet of limp diver's hose. Scott watched as the end snaked over the side, cleanly severed. Reinforced rubber air hose, communication's cable, and quarter-inch nylon safety rope hung limply over the handrail. Expanding air still hissed from the open end of the air hose, the bundle's tip dancing like a cobra. Only the air compressor's distant chug and the generators below deck accompanied the deadly hiss.

"My God! What happened? Where's Chad?" The questions slipped from Scott's lips. Deep down inside, he already knew. Scott knew, but didn't want to believe. Not Yet! On a hope and a prayer, he pleaded, "Check both sides of the boat. Maybe the wheel cut the bundle. See if he's on the surface anywhere. For God's sake, look!"

Chapter Seventeen

MEGALODON CONFIRMED

Almost fifty tons of prehistoric shark rushed ahead, closing on the pulsating, infuriating sound. All his extraordinary senses peaked as he sucked in the wealth of information flooding the surrounding water. A creature of the deep, his eyes were slow to adjust to the intense light at the surface, and initial attempts to utilize vision induced mild pain. His olfactory senses detected the minute, but rapidly increasing, concentrations of an unfamiliar substance in the water. Smell supplemented his unaccustomed sight as the clear surface-water gradually clouded. A new sensation overcame the great fish, caused by concentrations of something being released at the source of the sound he was so arduously tracking. Certain senses increased in vitality while others retarded as exposure to the alien substance expanded. Still, driven by unalterable instinct, the ferocious male closed on a once-distant prey.

Several hundred yards from the source of the undeniable sound, he surfaced. Confused by new, drug-affected signals emanating from his central control system, the huge shark's dorsal fin sliced through the air/water interface. Tacking through the milky substance, he steadily closed on his quarry.

For almost a minute he went undetected, unnoticed by human eyes, but clearly outlined within the unforgetting lens of a single camera mounted high onboard. The camera continuously fed its visual data to an electronic recorder, forever preserving the image of an incomprehensible denizen of the deep on a VHS format tape.

Within a hundred yards of the vessel, two six-foot-long pectoral fins dipped and, powerful strokes by its awesome tail drove forty-seven tons of prehistoric shark silently downward through the discolored water.

The throbbing sound became much less predatory as the shark's exposure to the surrounding substance continued. Forty feet below, the milkiness diminished and the beast's sight was restored. Within three body lengths of its arrow-like snout and unforgiving jaws hovered something foreign. Dark like the sea lions he occasionally slaughtered, four light colored appendages extended outward, two ending in black flipper-like growths. A single, long, black antennae extended upward into the milky cloud. The motions beckoned the massive beast and, instinct *older than the ages* took control as the sixty-foot creature launched itself at the helpless man.

In a heartbeat, a yawning chasm, lined with knife-like, seven-inch teeth formed within the massive jaws to engulf the unfortunate Chad Brown. Slamming shut, uncountable deadly fangs carved through flesh and bone like it wasn't there, producing indescribable pain. A crimson cloud spread across the hideous ivory grin as the diver vanished behind a veil of white. The huge shark didn't feel the token resistance of the rubbery antennae before the teeth severed it.

Shaking its prodigious head and snapping those never-ending jaws, MEGALODON mutilated its meager meal, amplifying the dying man's anguish with fiery digestive-juices from its gullet. Meshing the great teeth again and again, a single small piece of its prey slipped from the cavernous maw and went tumbling into the dark abyss below.

Behind the Kirby mask's cracked face-plate, Chad Brown's sightless eyes stared vacantly into ever darkening water. His head started an oscillating journey to the seafloor, 16,000 feet below, trailed by a hint of reddish-brown.

The great fish circled erratically as the punch slowly dissipated from the once predominating sound. Primordial instincts were being obscured by the milky foreign substance through which he swam. His recent meal went unnoticed and confrontation with the object above him was inevitable. Its time would soon come.

For now, a prehistoric remnant cruised beneath its victim and waited. For reasons unknown, the great beast bided his time, circling methodically for over two hours. Only when the drug effects subsided and the thing above him came to life, did the monstrosity react.

FRIDAY, JULY 24TH, 06:45 HOURS

The search turned up nothing. There was no trace of Chad. A placid ocean looked peaceful and undisturbed. Inspection revealed a cleanly cut air hose and communication's cable. The quarter-inch nylon safety line was frayed, nylon strands dangling almost twelve inches from where it parted. The rope had apparently been shredded between sharp surfaces. *Something* had grabbed the bundle and torn it in two.

"Dr. Thompson, come see!" the excited girl yelled. "You're not going to believe this." Karen Korinski was glued to the TV monitor and the VCR setup. Chad had just disappeared and she was not aware of the accident. The four men raced to her side.

"What you got, Karen?" Scott asked, anger and despair obvious in his question. Red, Doc, and Jim were right behind him, staring over his right shoulder at the color monitor.

Karen pushed a silver button on the face of the VCR, activating the reverse search mode. "Right there, Dr. Thompson!" she exclaimed, pointing at the screen. "The camera was aimed behind us while Chad was down." Looking around and noticing Chad's absence, she asked innocently, "Where is he anyway?"

Four men towered speechlessly over the young female student. Ignoring Karen's question, all were mesmerized by the scene on the thirteen-inch color monitor, each realizing what he was observing. Red broke the silence. "That's a shark fin! A fifty-foot shark's fin!"

"It is!" Doc replied excitedly, "and it belongs to the world's biggest great white. It's gotta be three or four feet out of the water. Look at its wake."

"Right and wrong guys," commented Jim Gaffney. "What we've just recorded on film is Dr. Scott Thompson's creature. White pointers don't get anywhere near that big." He swallowed hard before adding, "We also know what happened to Chad." Glancing at the date and time imprinted on the tape and then at his watch, Jim concluded, "That fin goes under just before we lost Chad."

"*Lost Chad?* What do you mean? What's happened to Chad?" Karen shrieked, jerking around to face Gaffney, her eyes widening as alarm raised in her voice.

"Something happened to Chad a couple of minutes ago," Scott acknowledged. Tearing his eyes from the screen, he placed both hands on her shoulders and monitored the emotions playing across the attractive young face. Then he attempted to clarify the situation. "I lost communications with Chad and, at almost the same time, something pulled the dive hose out of Jim's hands and cut it. The last thing Chad said was something about a whale." The fallen look on Scott's face and his drooping shoulders expressed his guilt and frustration. With his voice cracking under the strain, Scott could only whisper, "After looking at that tape, I'm afraid the giant shark we're searching for is already here. I also think it just killed Chad."

Karen's composure held for a few seconds, then collapsed.

Scott wrapped his arms around her compassionately and pressed her gently to him. The emotional sobs shaking her delicate body were partially absorbed by his. As their intensity slowly moderated, Karen's face, buried against his chest, became a waterflood of gut-wrenching tears. Looking at the younger man standing next to him, Scott asked, "Jim, will you take Karen below? Ask Rachel to look after her." Caringly divorcing himself from his student, he added, "Go on Karen, honey, Jim'll help you get below. As the young girl left under Gaffney's attention, Scott addressed Jim saying, "Meet us on the bridge afterwards. We'll get with Mason and figure out just where we go from here."

Scott hit the recorder's off-button, removed the tape, and replaced it with a fresh eight-hour cassette. "Whatever happens during the next sixteen hours will be saved for posterity," he added as he punched the play and record buttons, reactivating the video machine.

Jim neared the salon's stairway with Karen as Scott spoke to Doc and Red. "Come on you two, let's find Mason and formulate a game plan. No doubt that big sonuvabitch will be back. Chad wasn't why it came here." Momentarily lagging behind, he double-checked the video system, then followed his friends.

"That bastard! That dirty Cajun bastard! Setting me up like this to smuggle his fucking cocaine." Captain Mason vented his emotion as the three men, along with Bill Parsons and first mate Mark Boudreau, discussed their predicament on the bridge. "Stashed away like that, no one on board had any idea it was there. Some devious but brilliant plan that coonass had," Mason continued angrily, several thick veins bulging in his neck. "I'd like to get my hands on him right now. But we've got bigger problems, don't we? Where do we go from here?"

"That depends on our vessel's condition Captain," Scott replied. "Do we have any immediate options? Doc told you about the fin the VCR recorded, didn't he? There seems to be one gigantic shark hanging around."

Mason grimaced as he nodded in agreement. Glancing at his mate he suggested, "Mark, why don't you give them a rundown on what we were discussing before they joined us on the bridge."

"Okay," Mark Boudreau began, his baritone voice oozing seriousness. "The three of us looked over the damage we can see and sketched out Chad's information. The SEA NYMPH seems to be in pretty bad shape. Before we can be sure, we're gonna have to burn off one of those covers on the deck and look inside. She's cracked more than a third of the way around already. I think it's several inches longer on deck than it was before daylight."

Captain Mason interrupted. "Bill, get out the cutting gear and open up that port-side hatch."

"Yes sir," Parsons replied, then quickly slipped away and headed for the locker where the cutting gear was stored.

"Like I was saying, Boudreau continued, "we're cracked about a third of the way around and the bloody thing's been growing while we've just been sitting still. We run at any speed, hit even moderate seas, this baby'll break in two. That happens and we drop the front thirty feet of the bow and what's left of her gets stern heavy. She'll upright like a pendulum and the aft end'll go under cause all the weight'll be in the stern. She'll flood and head straight for the bottom. That is, if she don't play iceberg, a couple feet of her above water. It'll depend on how good those internal bulkheads were welded when they rigged her up for smuggling. That's about it, Cap!"

"Very good Mark," Mason complemented his mate and added, "but, we may have a solution. I think we can get *inside* that hold and weld some internal supports across the crack. That could beef it up enough to stand the run back to Brazil. At five or six knots, we should make it to shore in a week or so, if she stays together. Any other suggestions?"

Doc Smitty piped in, "Captain, shouldn't we move any gear or cargo up closer to the crack? That'd shift the stern section's center of buoyancy forward, maybe lessen the probability of her sinking. We could also dump some of the weight near the stern. Where are the fresh water and fuel tanks? Anything toward the stern we can empty should help keep her afloat."

"Good thinking, Doc," Mason replied. "We can use the *stiff leg* to get gear out of the stern holds and move it as far forward as possible. The two auxiliary fuel tanks and a backup potable water tank are near the stern. I'll get Mark to transfer their contents to the forward tanks and dump whatever's left." Glancing toward the bow, Mason turned back, "Red, Bill's up on deck now. Will you give him a hand. I'll be up there to help as soon as I call the Brazilian authorities. Maybe I can reach the U.S. Coast Guard and Navy too. Let them know our location and what's going down. I also want to report the damned drugs." With a deep sigh, Captain Mason shook his head as the others scurried off on their assignments.

Jim joined the group early in the discussion, after telling Rachel about Chad's disappearance and leaving Karen with her in the galley. Grabbing Red's shoulder, Gaffney offered, "I'll go with you. I've done lots of work on my boats. Even burned some aluminum welding rods. It'll keep me busy. The sooner we get this craft bandaged up, the better I'll like it. You can bet that big sonofabitch is still around and it'll be back," he said with frightened eyes.

FRIDAY, JULY 24TH, 08:50 HOURS

Winds were deathly calm. Not a ripple marred the mirror finish on the endless waters around SEA NYMPH. The two closest vessels, a pair of heavily laden supertankers carrying crude from the rich Brazilian oil ports to refineries in the USA, were over forty miles away. Captain Mason's radio plea reached three north-bound tankers and the Brazilian Navy. The language barrier separating his limited Portuguese and a Brazilian naval officer's retarded English on the other end of the air waves left Mason concerned about the dialogue's success. In any case, no aircraft could provide assistance until they were within 300 miles of the coast and the nearest naval vessel was a distant sixty hours away. Satellite telephone enabled him to reach the U.S. Coast Guard station in Puerto Rico, but they couldn't help either. Mason furnished a statement about the illicit drugs on board, particulars of Chad Brown's death, vessel ownership, including more that a few expletives concerning Mr. Breaux, and information on the ten people sharing a common fate. Communications not withstanding, the SEA NYMPH's party was all alone. *And they would remain alone.*

* * *

Ninety minutes after the meeting on the bridge, Bill had successfully removed one of the cover plates on the hidden hold. They took out bag after bag of pure white powder and several sacks of coffee which were carefully layered around the stash. Doc Smitty confirmed it was cocaine and even suggested each person be given a little pop. "Just in case things worsen. May relieve some of our pain and suffering at the end." Forcing a smile in response to Scott's menacing glare, he hastily added, "Just kidding."

At the same time, Mark and Jim were busy moving materials

from the stern to forward locations on the crippled vessel. Eventually, almost 1,600 gallons of diesel and 1,200 gallons of potable water were relocated, leaving the stern tanks dry. Mark was down below in the hull insuring all vents in the tanks were sealed off and water tight. Buoyancy from those tanks could prove critical. Jim went forward for a few minutes to be with Rachel and Karen, while Cookie was giving Mark a hand with the tanks.

"Damn, sure can't get no hotter'n this!" Mark Boudreau spit as he and the cook, stripped to their shorts, suffered in stifling heat and humidity below deck.

"Shit gives ya the red-ass too," Cookie piped in as diesel fuel and sludge oil residues in the bilge created noxious fumes and clung unforgivingly to bare skin. Each fuel tank was equipped with a single vent-line that had to be removed from threaded connections and male plugs installed. Each water tank had two similar ports and a two-inch inlet fill-connection and a one-inch outlet to the main water tank plus six connections that required plugs to keep air in or water out. At 09:00 A.M., two sweating bodies completed number three and started working diligently on the water inlet at the very rear of the vessel.

Rachel Gaffney and Karen Korinski were making their way to the wheelhouse from the galley bringing cokes and pastries for those on deck. Karen had regained her composure and both young women wanted to help. Halfway up the stairs, the wall clock on the SEA NYMPH's bridge bonged for the ninth time and, except for its monotonous ticking, all was quiet.

Captain Mason was on the bridge and had the twin diesel engines idling quietly. Having just gotten off the two-way radio with his engineer in the *illicit drug storage locker,* the vessel master was heading his boat to the west-southwest and proceeding with utmost care toward the nearest land.

* * *

Parsons forced thoughts of his fifteen-month-old twin daughters from his mind and squatted down on soggy bags of cocaine. He knew it was expensive, but had no idea that seventy-five million dollars worth of drugs surrounded him. Wearing insulated rubber gloves on both his hands and a welding shield over his perspiration-laden face, he struck the first arc and a brilliant white light burst forth. Temporary repairs to strengthen the ailing vesse were underway.   The first eighteen-by-six by half-inch piece of aluminum plate crossed the treacherous gash inches above the lapping salt water. Their forward motion raised the bow slightly, letting that first metal piece be positioned as far down the crack as possible.   Bill would keep his skipper appraised of the crack's behavior via the radio which crackled with static beside him.

On the deck above him stood Jim Gaffney, assisting with the welding leads and monitoring the end of the crack for any propagation.   Facing forward, the light breeze generated by the vessel's movement brought welcome relief to the equatorial heat of the early day. Glancing up, Jim could see Red and Scott pulling life jackets and other items from the bow storage locker. A rectangular six-foot by four-foot life raft, made from a hard, foam-filled orange shell, was tethered to the deck near the forward-most hatch. It had a rope-net bottom covered by a watertight material, and rested to the rear of the crack next to a second, similar raft.

Red and Scott were hurriedly transferring C-rations, water, flares, and life vests to the other side of that ominous damage where it might be of value if the boat decided to break apart. Feeling an uneasy vibration as the boat got underway, Scott quickened his pace. In the distance, the eighth and ninth chimes from the clock on the bridge were faintly heard. Then, the first crackle and pop of the welding rod filtered up from the *dope room.*   Jim acknowledged Scott's forced grin, an uneasy attempt at reassurance, with a token nod of his head then returned his attention to the man laboring below him.

Attached to the hull's plating ahead of the crack and on the port side of the keel, nestled a small transponder. Powered by a cad-celled battery carefully hidden in the bow locker and continually charged by the ship's generator, it continued to sing out its 100 khz song. Unlike the cocaine stash, no one onboard knew it existed. Currently outside the range of the shorebase tracking stations, its antagonizing tune was effectively drawing two enormous creatures to the boat from hundreds of miles away. SEA NYMPH's contingent knew one fish was close by.   That a second, even larger visitor would soon be arriving was beyond their wildest fears.

A bulkier transducer, connected to the University's sound modulator, still hung in the water along the starboard side.   It stopped transmitting when the twin GM's were killed for Chad's fatal dive. For the past two hours only the transponder on the bow had been sending its message into the depths. As Captain Mason restarted his engines and swung the damaged ship's bow onto its westerly course, the more powerful, rear modulator sprang to life, saturating the sea with low-frequency sound.

* * *

The great male was biding his time. The tiny morsel he'd eaten two short hours before made no impact on already satisfied hunger. The oversized monstrosity wasn't here because of hunger, his food supply flourished several thousand feet below. That *all-consuming sound* dominated the great fish, demanding his presence. Gliding in and out of the milky substance tainting the water, those savage, noise-generated urges remained temporarily suppressed. Unpleasant pain due to the pulsations was also numbed for the time being. If the prehistoric beast had been human, the false ecstasy of a hallucinogenic high might have been enjoyed. For him, the rich concentration of the whitish drug was simply delaying the inevitable. For two hours, he never ventured deeper that 100 feet from the placid surface, always within a 500-yard radius of the beckoning source. The sound still reigned him in; a gigantic, lethal weapon waiting, its hair-trigger cocked, but momentarily restrained.

Cells along dual lateral lines registered instantly as starters on the ship above turned the vessel's engines over. Heading away from the boat at the time, all sensory systems in the great fish instantly went to full alert. He spun in the clear water, well below the mind-destroying milk. Electrical fields around his quarry intensified from the circuit generated by the welding machine and hull. Seconds later, a crippling blast of sound filled the ferocious creature's watery domain. A temporarily restrained trigger released.

Accelerating rapidly, over sixty feet of refined killer shot upward toward the amplified sound-source emanating from the SEA NYMPH. The milky material polluting the clear ocean water had lessened considerably and traces of light filtered through. Intent only on destroying the source of the unrelenting noise, his keen eyesight detected flashing lights dancing off the slowly spinning bronze propellers. There was no maliciousness in the beast's actions. Driven by instincts evolved over millions of years, forty-seven tons of muscle and power vaulted forward. Jaws agape and eyes rolled back in their protective posture, his multiple rows of ivory-white, razor-edged, seven-inch teeth hit the port wheel and rudder of the creeping SEA NYMPH. The rudder shaft buckled at impact and the prop was torn loose as the craft's stern cleared the water. Gripping the hull with massive jaws, the prehistoric remnant mouthed the boat, shaking it violently. The starboard propeller continued to spin.

Distress, not pain, alarmed his nervous system as the starboard prop, spinning like a table-saw blade, sliced deeply into the right side of his head. It cut through his eye, causing a snotty-gray mucous to spew forth. Quickly working through iron-like skin and muscle, the right lateral line was completely severed. A split second's time and several centuries of refinement vanished as half the creature's sensory system was rendered useless. Almost angrily, he released his grip and dove.

Adjusting both pectoral fins, the frenzied behemoth curved in a sharp circle and fired himself upward again. This time he keyed on a second sound-source and a brilliant, flashing light toward the front of the hard-shelled creature, again heaving the boat viciously into the air. Mouth spread wide, the great fish's trajectory brought him up directly beneath the flashing light. Jaw muscles tightened as claw-like teeth raked over the hard surface, gouging tracks in the aluminum and easily cleaving off a lone protruding appendage hanging beneath the hull.

Those incredible senses detected blood, forcing a tight, downward pass from the thing above as significantly damaged vibratory sensors perceived the halving of his prey. *He had split the SEA NYMPH in two!*

Pursuing the smaller portion, the colossal shark focused on a relatively small and bleeding Bill Parsons, who dropped into the water when the bow separated. Spurting blood from the stump left when his leg was bitten off seconds earlier, he sank helplessly through a white cloud and uncountable downward drifting packets. The seven-foot tail twitched, those prodigious jaws opened and closed and the SEA NYMPH's engineer, accompanied by a hundred powdery packages, vanished forever.

The great fish spun and flung himself against the SEA NYMPH's separated bow-section. Huge jaws grabbed the corner and edges of its hard shell as he drove it through the water. Dragging it beneath the surface was impossible, even for a denizen as large as he, buoyancy prohibited sustained submersion. In futility, the gigantic shark tossed and battered the bow-section over the mid-Atlantic Ocean's calm surface with Scott and Red trapped inside.

For almost an hour, the unbelievably large creature bashed, mouthed and bit the object, continually driving it before him. Over a mile from the original attack-site, stout aluminum succumbed to the devastating battering. The hull was finally breached and water jetted inward through tooth-induced holes as the giant fish jerked the floating coffin under for longer and longer periods. Sensing the small creatures struggling inside, he gnawed unmercifully on the failing shell, determined to get at them. Unexpectedly, his attention was diverted. The beast's functional left side detected *another*! Pivoting near the surface, the obscene monster propelled himself toward his victim's larger half.

FRIDAY, JULY 24TH, 09:03 HOURS

In the rear bilge, Mark and Cookie were working arduously on the inlet to the water tank, sealing off two of its vent lines. The lone vent on one of the empty fuel tanks was also plugged. Racing against time, the 120 plus degree temperatures in their confined area drained energy from them. Sweat saturated their shorts and flooded their eyes. Diesel fumes reeked and a thick bilge-sludge coated and burned exposed skin. On hands and knees, Mark struggled vainly to get the male plug started in the female port beneath the tank.

Cookie, wiping salty sweat from his brow, cursed as traces of diesel found his right eye. Crouching, he held the open-end wrench Mark needed to tighten the fitting if he ever got it started. His filthy companion was straddling the two-inch steel rudder shaft. To their left, the drive shaft from the port propeller to the gear box squeaked unpleasantly as it slowly revolved. On his right, so close Cookie was almost touching it, rotated the starboard shaft.

"Got the motherfucker," Mark complained. "Shit man, that was one tough bastard to get to." Almost cracking a grin, he looked over his right shoulder at Cookie and asked for the wrench. "Let me have her Cookie, we'll make a goddamned mechanic out of. . ."

His comment died on his lips as a colossal force struck the hull beneath their feet. Cookie collapsed like a wet rag on top of Mark, ricocheting off him into the starboard drive shaft. Searing agony flared as his back hit the spinning steel while SEA NYMPH was being tossed into the air. A shrill squeal saturating the humid space around them was momentarily accompanied by brittle fracture and snapping sounds. Pain rocketed through him as Cookie watched the port drive-shaft snap and pivot in seesaw fashion toward his helpless body. Three-inch steel smashed through Mark's left shoulder, neck, and cheek, blowing his head apart like cannon shot

The shoulder was driven into his chest as his cheek followed his jawbone out the side of his head.

Sweeping the first mate's body with it, unforgiving steel crossed the space between the two men. Petrified, Cookie watched a dragged corpse's right hand clutch frantically at its disfigured head and neck. The fractured steel missed the cook's right leg, but nailed his left. Knee pinned against a structural support, the rampaging shaft caught Cookie's leg just below that restriction. Like rifle shots, the major bones both snapped. Excruciating pain engulfed him as his skin, ligaments, and muscles were sheared. The grown man watched hypnotically as most of his left leg accompanied a twitching Mark and the deadly steel pendulum to the end of its sweep.

Clutching at his mangled stub, a viscous, red liquid spurted in great gushes between interlaced fingers. Cookie's anguished scream filled the damp air. With time only to clutch and scream, another seizure struck the dying boat. The one-legged man was flung through the air, striking support beams, tanks, and equipment before eventually coming to rest on Mark Boudreau's remains. Whipping back toward the port side, the broken drive shaft's pointed end looked upward just as Cookie rebounded off the potable water tank. The shaft's end penetrated an appendectomy scar and plowed through a nicotine-contaminated lung. Cold steel impaled a still strong heart, shattered a collar bone, and shoved several vertebrae out his neck. For a split-second, the combined flesh and bones, so recently a cook and a ship's engineer, flailed about wildly on a three-inch shaft. As the shaking subsided, unrecognizable meat hung limply.

* * *

Jim and Bill had already removed a hundred bags of white powder from that *illicit drug room* near the bow, creating just enough room for one man to squeeze into the newly discovered hold. Working along the badly damaged boat's starboard side, the SEA NYMPH's engineer resembled a miniature *Pillsbury Doughboy*, his body caked with a pasty film of the stuff people kill for. Perspiration meandered aimlessly down his body as mental strain and oppressive heat opened sweat ducts. "Shit man, could be a lot worse," he admonished himself, sitting alone atop a multi-million dollar stack of drugs. "Those poor guys in the back hold must be cooking."

"What'd you say, Bill?" Jim Gaffney asked. "Need something?" His question floated down from above, reminding Bill he wasn't alone.

Sneezing violently three times before he could reply, his system futilely tried to cleanse itself of the vaporous powder. Lifting the welding shield carefully off his saturated brow, he grinned upward. "Nothing Jim, just thinking out loud. Tons of money down here and ain't a cent of it mine. Bloody hot too. Feeling sorry for myself, 'til I got to thinkin' about Cookie and Mark in the rear bilge. God knows it's hot as hell down there. Least I got a little ventilation. Plus I'm a little bit pissed at that fuckin' tanker busting 'Lizabeth and Mary's picture. What the hell. Time to quit jackin' my jaws and get busy."

"Okay, Bill," Jim replied. "I'm here if you need anything. Just give a shout mate." His forced attempt at a reassuring grin went unnoticed as Bill's attention returned to his task.

"All right, let's see just how good a welder you really are," Parsons muttered to himself. "These plates got to hold this baby together for one long fuckin' time." His right hand, in its stiff leather glove, repositioned his welder's head gear, flipping down the rectangular face plate with its polarized glass window. He wiggled his ass, unable to alleviate discomfort from wet shorts riding up his crack. Readjusting his legs in a hopeless attempt to prevent cramping and direct contact with the encroaching sea, Bill positioned the first aluminum plate. It was an insignificant piece of metal for such a demanding task. He held it firmly against an area of the hull's interior he had just wiped down and touched the end of a silver-colored electrode protruding from the welding torch in his right hand to the edge of the plate. "Here goes nothing," he mumbled and a brilliant light flared on the far side of the dark protective eye shield.

In thirty seconds, a six-inch root-pass was run between the plate and the rear section of the hull. "Not bad, not bad at all," Parsons bragged, complementing his own efforts.

Sweat continued pouring down Bill Parsons' face, stinging his partially blinded eyes. "Damned Arab tanker," he muttered quite loudly to himself, "ramming us like that. Damn, that burns." Grimacing, fiery pain knifed through his right eye as his powder-covered index finger wiped it. Glaring at the sticky paste through blurring eyes, he cursed, "Fuckin' coke!"

His mood mellowed and a slight grin crossed his face as he thought about Mary and Elizabeth. "God they're pretty. My baby girls, decked out like Angels in those white Christening dresses their mamma bought. God, I miss 'em. Miss their mamma too.

"Has it only been two weeks?" his diversionary thoughts continued, momentarily obscuring the current situation. "Can the twins really be fifteen-months already? And me, turning the Big Three-Oh that same Sunday? Going to church too. Oh well, screw it all! Back to work!" Lowering his welding shield into place, Bill again touched the tip of his welding rod to the hull. A sunburst moved along the second plate he was installing. "A little weld here, little weld there. 'Fore ya know it, SEA NYMPH will make it home okay."

Breaking the monotony, he found himself humming a tune from that recent Sunday service. *"Jesus loves me, this I know. For the bible tells me so. Little ones to . . ."*

The same collision which initiated Cookie's flight also halted Bill's work. An unseen monstrosity assaulted the ailing hull and his chamber of pain became an instant hell-hole of horror. Acrid welding smoke and suffocating narcotic dust thickened the air, choking the ship's engineer. The impact flipped him onto his back, his landing cushioned by packages of cocaine. He was flung forward again, slamming face first into unyielding metal. The welding shield deformed against the skin and bone behind it, crushing his nose and driving four top front teeth inward before they snapped off. His nearly-unconscious body slid down the ship's interior wall, leaving a path of smeared white paste.

The treacherous crack lengthened at each end and the gash widened momentarily. His right leg slid through the opening and the cool water beneath him became the fires of hell. Infinite pain roared through his calf and thigh as saw-tooth edges bordering the crack bit nasty incisions into living flesh. Time stopped as the entrapped man was shaken unmercifully. Pulverized by bursting bags of white powder, he was immersed in the shrill, terrifying sound of tearing metal. Finally, movement ceased and a deathly stillness prevailed.

Choking on cocaine-saturated air, while drowning in a flood of his own blood as his broken nose and shattered mouth lost their liquid contents down his throat, consciousness remained. Oblivion wouldn't mask his dilemma or alleviate his pain. The crack closed around his right thigh in an unfriendly, toothy grasp as the shaking stopped. Wicked fangs penetrated the major muscles and the cold, lifeless gums of the split hull applied abhorrent pressure to the wound. In front of the imprisoned ship's engineer flashed the blinding light of the welding torch. Pinned by myriad bags of cocaine, electrical contact continued between the welding apparatus and the boat. The air around him was contaminated with the crackle and pop of the welding process and the numbing fragrance of burning cocaine smoke. Receding pain, wavering judgment, and quiet prevailed, temporarily.

Hell returned with a vengeance. Inhalation of intoxicating smoke was dulling his reactions but also heightened his nervous system. The ravaged vessel beneath him cleared the water when something struck it on the opposite side of his imprisoning shell. Countless waves of pain flashed through him as the fore and aft sections closed, metal teeth and gums penetrating to the bone. A piercing squeal knifed through the stagnant air as oversized, obscene tools-of-death ripped through the thin plate supporting him. Killing fangs closed rapidly on a captive leg dangling helplessly outside.

"*Christ Almighty! Help me!*" Hopelessness and terror merged in Bill's pathetic plea. His family filled his thoughts as he pleaded, "*Oh God, I'm dead! Lord, take care of my girls! Please take care of my girls!*"

Inches away, prehistoric muscles closed enormous jaws, quickly drawing opposing rows of cruel, unrelenting teeth together. As the fangs meshed, serrated edges ripped easily into already-mangled flesh and bone. Agonizing consciousness flared. Numbing fingers searched futilely for his protruding leg, trapped beneath those tightly clamped lips of the lengthening crack. As incredible muscles snapped the huge jaws together, Bill's bladder failed and he released an unending stream of excrement.

Jaws overflowing with rows of deadly teeth rendezvoused. The ivory guillotine snapped shut and a single severed leg slipped quietly into a dark and cavernous maw. A dissipating hint of pink briefly tainted the milky water beneath SEA NYMPH.

Tearing metal was the last sound Bill Parsons ever heard. His shrunken body was freed when the great shark fell back into the sea and the shattered SEA NYMPH crashed down. The damage initiated by that unidentified tanker six hours earlier propagated swiftly around the hull. Fore and aft sections separated grotesquely, dumping the false bulkhead's cargo into warm, tropical waters.

Tepid, restless water engulfed him and, surrounded by dissipating powder and intact plastic bags of a deadly drug, Parsons' remaining leg and arms flailed hopelessly as he settled slowly toward oblivion. Unseen in the cloudy water, two enormous jaws closed around him. *Dear God, please take care of my girls,* was Bill's final, unspoken plea.

Death came instantly as a million years of evolutionary perfection and incalculable pressure crushed Bill's spinal cord. The lifeless body of the father Mary and Elizabeth Parsons would never see again accompanied several hundred pounds of pure cocaine down the waiting gullet.

Terrible teeth gnashing and its gigantic body convulsing, the deadly creature's attention turned elsewhere.

* * *

"Here's one more life jacket," Red stated in the confines of a well-stocked locker room at the vessel's bow. "That's an even dozen for the ten of us." He passed the latest count on to Scott and tossed another fluffy orange vest to the base of the ladder. "Whistles and lights on all of 'em. Latest issue money can buy."

"We've already hauled enough emergency drinking water and food rations back to the bridge," Scott stated calmly. "The rest will have to stay." Panning the wide-beamed flashlight around the forward storage locker, he silently complemented the ship's crew on the provisions they had laid in. "Coke running must be plenty profitable," he mumbled to Red. "That bastard Breaux sure didn't short-change himself any outfitting this boat. Hope we don't have to use all this stuff we're moving around."

"My gut feelin' says the worst is yet to come," Red replied, nervousness showing in his southern drawl.

Standing with his right foot on the ladder's bottom rung, Scott's head almost reached the brilliant white sunlight at the compartment's single opening. A swinging hatch cover stood at attention, adjacent to the forward edge of the circular thirty-inch hole. Isolated beams of daylight peaked through the two stout, permanently-closed, plexiglass portholes located on each side of the raked bow. Strewn beneath the ladder were emergency supplies including a dozen more Coast-Guard-approved life vests. Red continued apprehensively, "Let's get this crap moved. See if we can help with anything else, 'fore that overgrown shark starts fuckin' around some more."

"Okay Red," Scott replied. "Soon as I get a hold of these two, I'll have 'em on deck." Bending over, he grabbed the final two life vests with his right hand and slung the straps over his shoulder.

"Got 'em. See ya in a second."

Starting up the ladder, he extended his left arm and curled his fingers over the vertical lip surrounding the hatch's opening. As his grip tightened, SEA NYMPH's nose dove when the giant shark made its first attack on the stern. His foot slipped from the ladder-rung and he was left dangling by one arm, his feet kicking a few inches above the plated floor.

The hatch cover teetered briefly, then plunged downward in an accelerating arc. As his fingers relaxed so he could drop to the floor, the hatch opening darkened and the lid slammed shut. "Shit!" he screamed as pain rifled through his hand and left arm. The axe-like motion of the hatch cover's outer edge cruelly fractured four fingers at the first knuckle and nearly severed the middle and index fingers. Damage done, the cover bounced slightly, releasing the shattered fingers. Scott fell, landing on Red, who was knocked to the floor by the collision. Fiercely squeezing the pain-drenched area with his right hand, he lay helplessly across his friend while an unseen monster literally shook the boat.

"Christ Scott! Big bastard's back?" Red bellowed from beneath him. "Must've hit the stern."

Tears cascaded down Scott's face, excruciating pain exploding in what, seconds before, were functioning fingers.

Red got a quick glimpse of Scott's hand from the corner of his eye and could taste his friend's blood leaking on his face. He knew the damage was serious. "Scott, what the . . .?"

"Hatch cover slammed on my fingers! Think I cut a couple of 'em off! God it hurts!"

"Slide off me if you can," Red asked, his breathing strained. "I'll take a look-see. Can't do a thing from down here." Only then did Scott realize Red was pinned beneath him.

Using his elbows, Scott pushed himself to his knees and leaned back against the ladder. "Shine that light over here. I'll check the damage."

The flashlight rolled back and forth next to Red's head, its swinging beam indiscriminately illuminating littered gear. He grasped it while struggling to his feet. For the time being, the vessel bobbed imperceptibly on the calm ocean. Dropping to his knees, he directed the beam of light onto Scott's left hand, still tightly enclosed in the right. Outside of his right fist, the middle finger looked much too long and the tip appeared purple in the faint light. Blood was dripping down both arms, which had come together prayerfully in front of a rapidly-paling face. Inwardly, panic clawed its way toward the surface.

"Scott," Red instructed sympathetically, "let go of it so I can see what's what."

Pain mushroomed when Scott relaxed the fierce hold. Whimpering like a baby, he watched two of his fingertips hang uselessly from their upper joints. Blood continued to flow without restraint, and Scott was about to be sick.

Darkness hid the fingers for a moment as Red guided the light's beam about the compartment, searching for one of the first-aid kits they'd seen during their plunder operations. Miraculously, Scott's fingers didn't hurt as much when he couldn't see them. Out of sight, out of mind.

"There's one!" Red sighed in relief as his light located a kit. "Should have some small splints, tape, and bandages in it." The red cross embellished on a small blue and white box was clearly illuminated. A single beam of light emanated from his left hand and his right arm extended as he reached for the box. Scott's rattled emotions were almost under control again when . . .

The bow section surrounding them exploded upwards. What felt like a runaway freight train hit the vessel's bottom. Red somersaulted through the air, crashing into unyielding aluminum plate on the port side of the hull. Scott was vaulted forward, landing on his crippled hand and driving abused fingers forcibly into his chest. Indescribable pain flooded him before blackness cloaked his senses. In the distance he could faintly hear the squeal of oversized teeth attacking metal. As the SEA NYMPH's bow section shivered and shook, Red laid stunned and moaning.

What seemed like an eternity later, the motion finally quieted and Scott's black cloud lifted. The bow section had been separated from the rest of the boat. The tip of the bow behind him pointed skyward and he rolled helplessly toward the stern with Red sliding limply after him. The clanging hatch cover overhead drew his attention as the shortened vessel continued to roll. When it stabilized, Scott was staring at a water level through one of the starboard portholes. Panic spawned fear burned his throat as the rising water level reached the next glass, rapidly approaching the open hatch, leaving a clanging, finger-smashing hatch cover that was unlatched. It had to be closed to seal the only entrance to this oversized, floating casket. Helplessly, Scott waited for water to reach the hatchway and pour its wet death into their waiting laps.

Eventually, the bow section stopped bobbing and the hungry sea lapped noiselessly against it a yard below the lip of the opening. Laying on the plated underside of the top deck, boxes and life jackets were cluttered around them. Scott squeezed his distressed fingers again while trying unsuccessfully to revive his red-haired friend. Outside it was silent, except for the remote sound of idling diesel engines. Scott believed hours had passed since the violent attack which separated the SEA NYMPH began. In reality, it was only minutes.

"What the hell's going on Scott?" Red yelled in the darkness. "Where are we? What's happened?" Before Scott could reply, the bow section was again thrown into the air as the giant shark assaulted it, clamping onto the opposite side of the plate they were leaning against. This time, Scott's injured hand was driven into Red's nearby stomach. Escape from reality flirted briefly, but passed him by. Pain did not. The despicable beast shook them relentlessly then let go. A heartbeat later, the attack was repeated. Again and again.

Rotated slightly by each ruthless barrage, the first splash of heavy seawater fell ominously from the opening above them. Red, finally realizing the hatch cover had to be closed or they'd flood and drown, dragged himself toward the opening. But IT was still there, its gigantic jaws clamped to the bow shaking them like a rag doll. Bruised, bloody, and banged to hell, a petrified Red Dickson struggled toward that loathsome hatch.

Water pouring in, Red clamored to hold onto the top, now the bottom, of the ladder. Twice he wrenched the hatch cover tight, only to have the hull's angry motions rip it from his hand. The shaking suddenly stopped and the point swung up out of the water. The level fell below the hatch-opening and gravity pulled the cover shut. Using the almost-horizontal ladder like monkey bars, he hung from the second rung by his left hand while his right quickly engaged and tightened both latching dogs. *Safe,* as long as that mean sonuvabitch outside didn't pierce the hull; as long as their dwindling air supply held out. Red Dickson's attention returned to his injured friend.

"Sorry Scott," he apologized. "I know it hurts like hell." Compassion governed his voice as he splint the broken fingers. "Hang in there another second or two and I'll be finished."

The big bastard outside had left them alone for almost thirty seconds; an eternity after forty minutes of nonstop crashing about the ocean's surface. As if playing a game, Megalodon tossed their battered container around; tossed it, rammed it, bit it, shook it. Anything to get at them. Inside, Red and Scott were beat to hell. Bloodied and bruised from head to toe, there wasn't a square inch of plate nor a structural brace the hold's two prisoners hadn't hit many times over.

On the plus side, if there was one, the ocean was still outside. The down side included trapped air already fouled by stinking body odor, a dramatic increase in carbon dioxide levels, and the incapacitating stench of regurgitated food. Red Dickson's last few meals floated around them. Vomit clung to walls, to boxes, and to both men. Scott's contribution to the compartment's soiled contents was eminent.

"That'll give it some support and should stop the bleeding, if you'll just quit banging it around," Red told Scott, oblivious to the situation. Concentrating on doctoring those poor fingers, Red's own blood dripped slowly from all the bangs and scrapes covering his once-supple body. Dark purple splotches and nasty welts decorated his face, neck, and arms. And, the shark resumed his relentless assault.

Twenty minutes later the harrowing grating sound had pushed both captives to near-insanity and an indication of their approaching doom appeared. Scott looked at his watch, a force of habit, which read 10:07:52. The unmistakable sound of fatigued metal yielding pricked four uneasy ears. As the beast outside hit them yet one more time, a weld-seam in their tomb finally gave way. Minute streams of water geysered forth and the water's influx increased, adding salt to Scott's painful wounds.

"No choice, Red. We gotta get out." Scott's film-covered time piece changed from 10:15:03 to 10:15:04. The water level crept steadily upward and other jets cascaded into the rapidly reducing air space. A nasty crack now ran the entire width of an *unbreakable* porthole. Bow pointed to the sky with boxes and life jackets floating on upchuck-layered water already reaching their chests, Scott added, "If we stay in here, we'll drown like rats. We've got to get out."

"Like you say Professor," Red concurred. "There ain't no choice. Damned if we don't and maybe damned if we do. Hell, we may not be able to get out now." Scott's eyes followed Red's gaze to the farthest porthole. The water outside was already past the hatch cover's bottom.

Scott yelled what his friend already knew, "Red, if that water gets any higher, we're dead meat." Hydrostatic pressure may have already made opening the hatch cover impossible.

Certain death continued to batter the small section of the SEA NYMPH that trapped them. Ignoring the squalid water, Red Dickson dragged himself ever so slowly toward the hatch. Death was the two men's dominant companion inside. If they could get outside, a very big if, something even worse awaited. But they had no choice. They would have to chance it. Reaching above his tangled mass of auburn hair, Red hung onto the top ladder rung and loosened the first latch.

Chapter Eighteen

MAY DAY! MAY DAY!

Peter Smith reached for the shiny lever as he started to stand up. Before he could flush, the monster struck the SEA NYMPH's stern for the first time.

Sitting back down, the rigid chrome piping and flush lever on the commode dug painfully into his lower back.

"What the hell was that?" Doc exclaimed, grabbing his back. Quickly answering his own question, "Fucking shark! Back for the main course." Staggering upright, he yanked on his underwear and shorts, flipped the lock, and bolted out the door, only to be halted by the flailing legs and arms of two young women at the base of the stairs.

"What happened?" the girls' shrieked in unison.

Springing up, he grabbed Rachel's hand and jerked her roughly to her feet. Karen was already back up and moving by the time Doc snapped his reply. "The bloody shark's back! Let's get to the bridge!" The vessel was rocked savagely and a faint scream from the aft bilge reached them as they scrambled up the stairs like a single living organism, in spite of the boat's irrational gyrations.

"Where's Jim?" Rachel cried. Alarm bells were going off everywhere and Captain Mason was clinging to the *barber-style* captain's chair on the bridge. He finally hit the kill switch on the port engine and its high-pitched noise ceased immediately.

"Something happened to the port engine," Mason said angrily to no one in particular. "Damn thing over-revved, I mean way up in the red. The shaft must have sheared off." As he spoke, the violent shaking stopped.

"Please, does anybody know where Jim is?" Rachel repeated, looking frantically toward the stern where the attack probably occurred, and then toward the bow.

"He's on the foredeck!" Doc exclaimed, pointing toward the bow. He hollered through the open window, "Jim! Jim! You okay?"

A flippant, behind-the-back wave without turning around was Jim's only acknowledgement. He was intent on the drug-filled hold below him, trying to talk to Bill, who had been welding on the crack. Straightening up and facing them, Jim cupped his hands and yelled,

"Bill's leg's caught! I've gotta help him! Someone give me a . . ." His words died in the air as he was flung toward the bridge, landing painfully on his face. Once more, the boat had been lifted from the water by a violent collision.

Knocked to his knees, Doc clamored back to his feet. With blood dripping from his nose he mumbled incoherently, "We got us one pissed off sonofabitch down there."

The boat rocked ruthlessly as four people clung to anything they could. With Jim Gaffney sprawled helplessly over an orange-colored life raft and its survival gear, frenzied vibrations shook SEA NYMPH and the sound of failing metal curdled the humid morning air. The erratic motion subsided and the vessel bent downward, forming a valley where Jim had been standing. The back of the bow and the front of the rear section rose as one before separating with an obscene tearing sound.

Gaffney immediately pushed himself toward where the bow should have been. Looking over the edge, his hands gripped a jagged roughness which burned from the heat of failing metal as he stared down into a sea of white. Behind him, the welding machine buzzed and crackled angrily, trying to short itself out. Several feet below, twin rubber leads vanished beneath a layer of white jell coating the water. Eight yards in front of him, Scott could be heard whimpering, berating his injured fingers as Red's southern drawl tried vainly to comfort his friend. Between them was nothing except slowly sinking packets of cocaine. There was no trace of Bill Parsons.

Time seemed to hesitate in a quiet stillness. Then, hell returned with a vengeance as twenty feet of angry shark cleared the water so close to Jim that he could count the separate denticles making up its sandpaper-like skin. Yard-long feelers dangled around its deadly mouth and the gray-brown skin of its head seemed to be coated with gigantic acne. Over forty feet remained beneath the murky water, and twin welding leads dangled from its expansive jaws as it crashed into the remote bow.

Jim was paralyzed, laying on his belly and gripping the hot edge of ripped aluminum. His mind journeyed back to a similar, but smaller, creature as it destroyed the BILLFISHER PERSONIFIED. Once again, he relived those agonizing minutes. Once again, Kenny slid steadily toward a gaping maw and its glittering ivory knives of death. Once again, hopelessness closed in.

"Gaffney! Gaffney!" Captain Mason shouted. "Get your ass

back here!" His order cut through Gaffney's cloak of dread. "Come on Jim," Mason affirmed. "Nothing you can do up there. For God's sake, we're going down. Rachel needs you!"

His wife! The mention of her name jolted Jim back to reality and he pushed away from the shortened bow. Rising to his feet, he took a final look at the monstrous beast called Megalodon methodically destroying two good friends. Before turning away, he whispered toward the retreating bow section, "Good luck and God speed mates." Spinning around and racing for the bridge, Jim stated, "Got to save what we can."

"May Day! May Day! This is the SEA NYMPH, Whiskey Victor Charlie 6647! We're breaking up, repeat, breaking up. Coordinates . . ." Mason's plea for assistance went unanswered. The survivors could only hope someone received their message. Dropping the microphone, Mason issued his instructions. "Doc, you and the girls grab Gaffney and get all the supplies you can into the two life rafts. I'll be back in a minute. Got to go below and get Mark and Cookie. Get moving." Without waiting for a reply, he vanished down the stairway in search of his crew, unaware that Megalodon's attack had already sealed their fate.

* * *

Technology's unrelenting eye missed nothing. The initial attack loosened its mounting, but the color video camera on the masthead had simply spun a few degrees. It now pointed sternward toward the floundering vessel's port side and continued panning back and forth. The bow separating from the rest of the boat was on tape. A giant shark's attacks on the buoyant section were recorded for posterity. James Gaffney's brief presence provided size perspective as he watched helplessly before turning back toward the wheelhouse. The trusty camera continued to pan, unerringly recording the distant activity in front of the boat. It also captured unbelievable pictures of another creature approaching from the southeast, directly behind the slowly settling stern.

FRIDAY, JULY 24TH, 10:10 HOURS

The all-seeing eye momentarily panned the glassy slick trailing the boat. It seemed to follow a deliberately-approaching and impossibly-large shadow. The shadow brushed the surface and materialized into an expansive grayish-brown back with a wide, triangular dorsal fin over six feet high. Three feet of its tail moved rhythmically above the calm water. The greatest of all fish swam effortlessly toward the badly damaged vessel. Disturbed when the compelling noise she had tracked faithfully for so many days stopped, olfaction and electrical sensitivity continued drawing her forward.

The sound modulator's powerful pulsation ceased when the port engine was killed. A mile away, the partially-disabled male was finally stripping the hidden transducer from Red and Scott's potential coffin. Except for the uninteresting hum of the idling starboard engine, the warm, salty waters harbored only the sea's normal sounds. Broken seals around the port propeller shaft were leaking traces of blood and body fluids from the aft bilge into the ocean. That slight scent, supplemented by the hull's electromagnetic field, sucked her ever forward.

Part of the giant female's approach was not recorded when the obedient camera swung toward the bow before panning back to videotape the new arrival. She did not rush, since nature's endowments included precision and caution. Deep inside, her mate's sperm had recently penetrated several ovulated eggs. The regeneration of cells, a miracle repeated for millions of years, assured continuation of the species. While nurturing the fetuses, caution would govern her every action. The instinct to preserve her young would prevail, overshadowing everything else. Still, she came on.

Thirty yards from the stern, she raised her head above the water. Coal black eyes the size of basketballs saw an unfamiliar object floating before her; eyes appearing to direct their intent gaze into an unblinking lens 130 feet away. Moments later those eyes observed a frail creature with a distraught look crossing the deck and suddenly seeing what approached from the sea. She wasn't malicious or blood-thirsty. There was no craving for wanton violence. Over 10,000 generations of inbred instinct and survival swam deliberately toward the doomed SEA NYMPH.

* * *

"Oh my God!" Mason prayed. "Oh sweet Jesus. Hail Mary, mother of our Lord." Those long forgotten recollections of childhood Catholicism, learned as a child, percolated inaccurately to the surface. Nothing could have prepared him for what awaited in the rear of the stinking, steaming bilge. A single, indistinguishable mass of battered flesh and bone greeted the captain. A stack of bloody meat, skewered on a motionless steel shaft, was all that remained of Mark and Cookie.

"Can't tell them apart, except for their clothes," Mason mumbled. Legs failing him, he dropped to his knees and threw up in the rancid confines of the rear bilge. Grabbing a handrail next to him, Captain Mason pulled himself to his feet and prayed briefly. "God have mercy on them and on the rest of us too." His crew was far beyond help. Wiping his chin with the back of his hand, he quickly surveyed the damage. *SEA NYMPH was a goner.* He turned and bolted from the depressing scene.

Mason cut his inspection short. Not exiting by the stairs, he instead clamored up a steel ladder and pulled himself through an open overhead hatch on the starboard side of the afterdeck, eight feet behind the wheelhouse. As he instinctively checked the waterline to see how quickly his boat was settling, movement astern caught his eye.

"It can't be!" his weather-beaten, defeat-conceding lips cried. "Look out! Look out!" he screamed, panic controlling him completely. *"Fucking Jehoshaphat! Another one!"*

The new leviathan's head was incredibly enormous and a mass of scraggly, four-foot feelers covered its rancid-skin. Its eyes were ominous, coal-black masses that seemed to bore into Mason's soul. For precious seconds, he could not tear his gaze away from their hypnotic stare.

Beneath those eyes spread the epitome of terror, a satanic grin half the width of Mason's foundering vessel. Its lips were stretched back tightly and the ghastly white gums, hinting at pink, were evilly exposed. Protruding from those gums were unending rows of gigantic, yellowing-ivory teeth. Each was a triangular, foot-long instrument-of-death with a needle-sharp point and saw-like edges. "This can't be real," Mason said aloud. "Nothing alive's that big." Panic overcoming him, Mason screamed and bolted across the cluttered, slippery deck.

* * *

Doc left the seemingly safe confines of the bridge to help Jim. The girls remained, manning the radio with repeated distress calls. Mason's scream devastated all four, projecting a hopeless feeling through the cadre of observers. As the monstrous creature reached the stern, they witnessed the captain break from the starboard rail and flee toward the port side of the cabin. Jim and Doc could only see his head and shoulders outlined against that background of black eyes and ivory teeth. Several feet higher in the wheelhouse, Rachel and Karen were subjected to a much better view. They saw his khaki shorts and tan-colored deck shoes, connected by abnormally white, hairless legs, unused to the tropical sun. They watched Captain Mason take his third stride, accelerating rapidly, just as that thing - *that shark* - bit viciously down on SEA NYMPH.

The stern plunged under several tons of attacking monster. Grabbing stationary objects, four of those remaining onboard retained their balance. A solitary figure starting his fourth stride stumbled, fell forward, and struck his head on the inoperative RCV's cage. The deck's slope increased, creating an uncontested path across slick, wet aluminum plating to the horror waiting at the stern. Momentarily stunned, the lone figure slid toward his doom. Beneath the shadow of that huge head, Mason unfortunately regained his senses.

The cabin's superstructure prevented Doc and Jim from seeing what happened next. Karen Korinski and Rachel Gaffney were not so lucky. From their front row seats on the bridge they watched the massive jaws open and those black eyes roll back. The great mass of rotted flesh, flopping feelers, and deadly teeth clamped down on the boat. As the upper row of teeth left the deck, visible indentations crossed the rigid plate in an arcing line. Captain Mason, his arms grappling and his legs kicking helplessly, slid across that newly created benchmark just as the fierce jaw slammed back down.

The huge snout briefly obscured the women's view, but nothing could camouflage the sickening scream from beneath the creature's head. Rachel averted her eyes, but Karen could not. As the upper jaw raised those lethal teeth for the second time, Mason came with it, hanging from a pair of gigantic, white prongs. Desperation flowed pathetically from his rapidly-glazing eyes to the pretty twenty-one year old witness. For an instant she was level with the captain as the upper jaw reached its apex and his gurgling scream coursed through the morning air.

Ribbons of red streamed down the front of his white, button-down shirt. Matching white points glittered at the leading edge of each rapidly growing dark-red stream. Ragged tears formed in the shirt around each ivory wedge and razor-like knives protruded from beside each nipple. His head back, eyes vacant, and his suddenly silent mouth agape, Mason's arms stroked the empty air. He hung there, impaled by deadly fangs, only a few feet and a single pane of glass away from Karen.

The vessel surged violently while Karen's stare continued and Rachel returned her gaze. With two white points receding into his shirt, the captain's life-blood flowed freely and the monster shark released his quivering body. Mason dropped with a distinct *splat!* and lay motionless in full view of the two girls. The boat's erratic actions continued as the great jaws closed again and the uninvited creature slid beneath the calm water, its gruesome feelers leaving a mop-like trail of blood.

The rear deck was clear, except for a dark blue captain's cap and the diluting smear of red across damaged plating. Captain Mason and the second unbelievable creature were gone. The camera's watchful eye continued to monitor and record.

FRIDAY, JULY 24TH, 10:39 HOURS

Less than sixty-five feet of the SEA NYMPH remained. Her rear deck was badly awash and sinking was eminent. A mile away, the water around her amputated, thirty-foot bow section was also still. It, too, was sinking. Suddenly, the great fish reappeared. With her dorsal fin towering above an expansive back, the creature circled the dying vessel. Four survivors watched from the meager protection of the bridge, horrified by its hundred-foot length. That such a creature could exist astounded and appalled them. But there it was. The *thing's* circles continued to expose it to the trusty VCR camera a short distance above the quartet.

Their escape supplies were stockpiled in front of the bridge. Two six-man life rafts were roped together. The first was filled with a conglomeration of life-saving and survival equipment including several gallon jugs of drinking water, packets of C-Rations, dried food stuffs, and a few cans of assorted juices from the galley. Towels and clothing, five flash lights, six flares, a single mirror, three knives, and a red handled hatchet were also carefully stowed. Completing the first raft's cache were two battery-powered marine radios. In the second raft were six life vests and a half-dozen more jugs of fresh water. Doc and Jim scavenged the boat for less than fifteen minutes to accumulate the stuff. Along with two very distraught young women, they could only watch and wait.

* * *

The huge male's final attack breached the battered remnants of the boat's pointed hull. Continued aggression would have expedited its end, along with the two men trapped inside. Only the damage to his right side delayed detection of the rapidly-closing female a couple of miles to the east. His last attempt to crush the hard-skinned prey finally silenced that maddening sound. With silence came awareness of another shark nearby and the previous hour's obsession was forgotten.

The giant creature wheeled, targeted his quarry and sped toward it. His recently damaged senses distorted the incoming vibrations, making a beeline to the target impossible. Swimming in a *limping* tack, he favored his unimpaired left side. Nearing the colossal female, the distorted perception caused by his damaged eye proved costly.

Catapulting himself upward, the lesser-sized male attacked from beneath. The monstrous female sensed his presence and instinctively evaded. Her unanticipated movement and the male's damaged senses nearly caused him to miss her entirely. Grazing her left side, sixty-plus feet of misshapen and angry Megalodon cleared the water. Crashing down with an ear-shattering splash, the giant fish's roles reversed. Her defensive posture switched to attack and one hundred feet of prehistoric female shark charged a male that was half her size.

The SEA NYMPH and its small inhabitants were conveniently forgotten as two mammoth denizens of the deep went after each other. Fatal wounds to any other creature in the sea were only scratches to these combatants and, for several minutes, the battle raged at the surface. In one precarious moment, both specimens collided with the bowless boat. As quickly as they hit it, the two were suddenly tearing up the surface while inflicting minimal damage to each other a hundred yards to the west.

The male realized he was overmatched. For the first time in over 500 years, he fled from something. Pectorals tilting, the great beast dove, driving himself downward toward the sanctuary below with rapid strokes of his powerful tail. Fin attitude and frequent changes in his body posture created an erratic path and gave the pursuing female no clear shot. Deeper and deeper he went, with her in hot pursuit. Almost 2,000 feet down she broke off the chase. The desire to destroy her fellow fish diminished and she halted abruptly, swung around, and began retracing her course. The defensive male continued his dive, a lacerated lateral line confusing his incoming signals.

FRIDAY, JULY 24TH, 11:08 HOURS

The SEA NYMPH's already acute angle of float suddenly changed. Her stubby bow rose and a few remaining objects slid to the rear wall of the wheelhouse. She was going under.

"Got to go. The fickle bitch is lost," Jim confirmed. "Come on honey, let's get out of here." With his right arm around his wife's quivering shoulders, he urged her to her feet using gentle, reassuring pressure, assurance not felt by himself. Silence shrouded the perishing ship as four desolate souls left the bridge and deployed two tiny life rafts.

"Just a second," Doc stated. "One last thing to do." He grabbed one of the knives, turned, and sprinted for the afterdeck. "Gotta cut the damn TV box loose," he shouted over his shoulder. "It'll prove what the hell happened out here." The invading ocean lapped at Doc's knees and covered the rear deck. Escaping air burped and belched from below and two large patches of bubbles were breaking up the calm surface near the submerged stern. The fiberglass box strained the four ropes tying it to the deck in its attempt to float away. Doc could read the name and address imprinted upon it.

IF FOUND, PLEASE CONTACT:

DR. SCOTT THOMPSON
UNIVERSITY OF MIAMI
CORAL GABLES, FLORIDA, USA
PHONE (305) 244-3474

CALL COLLECT - REWARD FOR RETURN

One stride from the box, there was a tremendous blast of air and the deck sank from beneath his feet. SEA NYMPH gave up her brief but valiant fight. Ignoring terrified shouts from behind, Doc dove, his right hand gripping the fillet knife and his left hand extended toward the nearest line on the orange box. Groping fingers closed on the taut, quarter-inch nylon rope as the uninvited sea closed in.

Traces of diesel and warm saltwater burned his eyes as he was dragged under. Frantically sawing on the rope in his hand until it parted, Doc pulled himself along the box until he reached the second rope and renewed his cutting efforts. By the time he got to the third rope, the ship had totally submerged. Twenty feet below the surface, the indistinct sounds of imploding containers reached his ears, aching from rapidly increasing pressure. A quick swallow granted him momentary relief. Finally the third rope separated, but one remained.

Lungs rebelling and eyes burning, Doc's ears resumed their adverse reaction to the ever-increasing pressure. Starving for air, he clung to that final rope as sixty feet of water covered him. The glinting blade in his right hand moved back and forth relentlessly across the taut remaining obstacle. *He wasn't going to make it!* The surface, with its life-giving air, was just too far away and Doc had already been under for three minutes.

"Let it go! Let it go! Let it *go!*" he begged himself, blackness taking hold and saltwater flooding his throat. Ignoring his own pleading command, he hung on and just kept cutting away as his decent continued. With his lungs screaming in oxygen-starved agony, his eyes clinched shut, and his ears imploded. A gray darkness settled over Doc Smitty.

Chapter Nineteen

THE SURVIVORS

RED AND SCOTT

A struggling Red Dickson managed to force open the bow section's hatch. Scott's left hand was out of commission and Red hauled him bodily through the small circular opening, before tossing several life preservers and other meager provisions out of the rapidly flooding coffin. Clinging to the cache of orange vests, Scott heart sank when the remnants of SEA NYMPH's bow suddenly vanished beneath the surface with Red still inside. Unbridled relief replaced his anguish when that distinctively colored hair popped through the surface amidst an upwelling of bubbles and debris.

Already wearing life jackets, the two men struggled to connect seven other vests and two cushions together to create an impromptu life raft. Scott's fractured fingers inhibited his effort and shared apprehension slowed their progress as they awaited the monstrous killer's eminent return. Just why it didn't finish them off would remain a mystery forever. Meanwhile, Red continued to cut and tie nylon cord and Scott continued to get in his way.

Their survival supplies rested insecurely on the flotation devices lashed together between them. Each item was tied to the makeshift raft by nylon cord. Two knives, a single flashlight, four flares, three tins of C-Rations, and six one-gallon jugs of drinking water were all that stood between them and death. Not much, but the stash would probably give them a few days, or until Scott's giant fish returned for an encore.

As the day wore on, the midday sun brutally cooked their exposed features, their lips blistered and their skin reddened. Splashing their faces with seawater provided relief. However, the cure was temporary and proved worse than the illness. When the wetness evaporated, it left a crusty layer of salt which added greatly to their discomfort. Speaking infrequently, they waited impatiently for the sun to go down, or for that huge unwelcome visitor to return with its teeth and fury.

Scott's trusty Omega showed 18:47:30 as the diffuse reflection of the falling sun crystallized into a distinct shape. Inspired by the beauty and invigorated by reduced solar radiation and subsiding temperatures, the duo stared hypnotically at the western horizon. Twin balls of fire crept perceptively closer together. Vertical nipples protruded and quickly touched, creating an hourglass.

"God, that's unreal," Scott mumbled. Awed by the serenity accompanying the sunset, his troubles were temporarily forgotten. "First time I've seen an hourglass at sunset. Before, it's always been when the sun was coming up.

"Makes you forget where you are, doesn't it?" Red replied an arm's length away, quickly adding, "Almost."

In the stillness of dusk, twin tits vanished and orange balls became a shrinking ellipse before merging briefly into one brilliant circle and then flattening. Seconds later, a blazing fire rimmed the shallow curvature of the earth and the sun was gone. A multi-hewed glow spread upward into the rapidly increasing darkness. Overhead, the planet Venus appeared in the western sky, the *first star* of their first night adrift. High overhead, the vapor trail left by a European-bound jet dissipated, leaving cottony proof that they weren't alone.

The glow faded rapidly with fingers of light shrinking toward the vanishing horizon. Night fell and countless stars burst forth, adorning the sky with infinite points of light. Fear and hopelessness returned with a vengeance. No breath of wind disturbed the slick waters. Not a sound reached their ears as they searched the quiet night for other life. Woeful cries for help went unanswered. In the darkness accompanying 10:30 PM, Red fired the first flare.

FRIDAY, JULY 24TH, 20:38 HOURS

The peaceful-blue, glass-flat ocean, glistened deceptively as it merged with a cloudless sky. The scorching tropical sun's relentless heat finally began to subside before the meeting of sky and water became discernible. Blinding and impossible to look at during its daytime tour across the heavens, the sun's hostility quickly diminished as its glowing yellow hue was replaced by spectacular burnt orange.

"Pain and fear can attack man's faith and courage, but nothing stems the perfection and beauty spawned by nature," Scott mumbled. Captivated by the gorgeous scene before him, he carefully sipped a trace of water from the plastic jug secured to one of the orange life vests.

"What'd you say, Prof?" Red asked quietly, trying to turn toward Scott. "Couldn't make it out." A barely distinguishable movement of warm water about Scott accompanied Red's effort.

"Nothing important, Red. Amazing isn't it, how frail man really is when confronted with nature's majesty and splendor?" Glancing to his right, Red appeared vague and dreamlike as Scott's eyes slowly recovered from their fixation on the rapidly descending orb. "How you doing big guy? Looks like we made it through the first day. Now we get to try the night."

"Hang in there, Scott, we're gonna be okay." His longtime friend feigned confidence and hope, but his voice was unable to hide their hopeless plight. "Doc and them had time to get into the rafts 'fore she went down. They'll find us."

JIM, RACHEL, KAREN AND DOC

The final rope separated. Launched like a missile, the orange crate he labored so valiantly to save raced upward, attempting to return the favor. That fourth rope was enveloped in a death-grip as buoyancy catapulted the crate toward the distant surface and a semi-conscious Peter Smith went along for the ride. Would he reach the surface and its life-giving air in time?

Above, Jim Gaffney was treading water, face down, watching a blurred image of the boat below as it sank into the black abyss. The charter boat skipper was devastated by grief. Doc was gone. He'd been down for almost four minutes. The stupid, lovable, ridiculously-dedicated sonofabitch had gone and drowned himself trying to prove that his friend's obsession was real. Jim cried aloud, his tears mixing with the ocean's saltiness.

Then, an orange object materialized, coming at him like a runaway train. Maneuvering evasively, he barely avoided the crate as it popped to the surface beside him. "At least we got what he died for," complained the Australian, little consolation at the loss of such a good friend.

"Help!" came a gurgling cry. "Goddamn it, somebody help me 'fore I drown." Next to the bobbing orange crate a few feet from the remorseful Gaffney was a familiar face.

"I can't believe it!" Gaffney screamed in gleeful joy as he saw Doc. Jim's surprise and his relief showed in an ear-to-ear grin. Doc, coughing, choking, and even laughing as he gulped down lung-fulls of precious air. "Give me a hand before I go back under."

Rachel and Karen maneuvered the linked rafts over to the swimmers and assisted Doc and Jim aboard. There was barely enough room for the four survivors in the small raft crowded with salvaged supplies. The noonday sun was directly overhead as they settled into the raft.

The four survivors knew that the rest of SEA NYMPH's crew had perished with her. In the area where the boat sank, there were no signs of any survivors. They had watched in horror as the displaced bow section sank almost a mile from them shortly before the rest of SEA NYMPH succumbed. Now they could only hope and pray that Red and Scott had somehow managed to escape. They'd seen Captain Mason and Bill Parsons killed by those sharks. And Mark Boudreau and Cookie were both still below deck in the stern when the boat disappeared, so they had to be dead too. Yeah, along with Chad Brown, all the others must be dead. But not Red and Scott. Somehow the four survivors could feel that their two friends were out there somewhere.

A few hours later, the westerly movement of the sun finally let Jim and Doc orient themselves. Taking turns, they started paddling toward where they believed the bow had sunk. They hoped and prayed that Red and Scott were still alive. Trailing behind like an obedient puppy was the orange crate.

Protected from the sun's direct rays by towels and hats, their sojourn was somewhat tolerable. Not knowing when, or even if, rescue would come, they rationed supplies from the start. The only immediate concern of all four was the search for Red and Scott. They knew the general direction they should take, but an error of a few degrees in course selection would cause them to pass their friends by without detection. It was a very large ocean. Except for themselves and their makeshift craft, it was also a very empty one.

* * *

Exhausted and scared, Rachel had slipped into a restless sleep at mid-afternoon, only to be awakened by Karen's coughing a short while later. Fearfully scanning the water around them, the

mirrored sea remained vacant in all directions. She could not believe
that only half-a-day had passed since that tanker started their
troubles; it seemed more like a lifetime. And just six hours had
elapsed since the pair of huge sharks disappeared. Dread crept
along her spine as she visualized their size. Fear clogged her throat
every time she shut her eyes and saw Captain Mason, hopelessly
impaled by monstrous teeth. She couldn't stop wondering, "Where
did the sharks go?"

"Oh my God! They're back!" Karen shrieked against the back
of her right hand which was pressed tightly against her cracking lips.
She saw it first and blurted out, "Behind us! Over there! Its fin. *Oh
God! NO!"*

The others looked in the direction she was pointing and their
fearful eyes confirmed her statement. Slicing through the glassy
calm surface and heading directly for them was a large dorsal fin.
"I think it's the smaller one," Jim stated with rising emotion. "Must be
underneath a little, not all of its fin is out." Against that creature,
there was simply no defense.

Then the fin vanished, but an ominous shadow still
approached. "Sit still. Don't excite it," Jim's said quietly. His
instructions weren't needed. Fear-induced rigidity was already
governing all their actions. Closer and closer came the shadow,
carrying a gruesome death with it. Enormous and unhurried, it had
all the time in the world.

Karen whimpered, then slowly wet her pants. Her breaking
point was approaching more rapidly than the denizen in the clear
blue water. Doc put his arm around her, trying to offer unfelt comfort
and hope. Perceiving the insidious tremble welling up from deep
inside her body, he squeezed a little tighter.

An immense shape neared the pair of rafts. The shadow grew
more distinct as it rose toward the surface. Ten yards away, the tip
of its dorsal fin again touched the air. Swimming death approached
almost casually. The glare of the setting sun made it impossible to
see clearly, only that it was immense, whale-like. The illusion of light
spots fluttered across its back. The entire dorsal fin cleared the
water and its broad head emerged into view. Onward it came.

Jim's eyes bulged, captivated by the gigantic creature. Then
his shoulders squared and a huge smile spread across his face as
his heart started beating again. "It's a whale shark mates! A
beautiful, bloody WHALE SHARK." Relieved laughter accompanied
his revelation and the others quickly joined in. "A marvelous

plankton eating sonofabitch," he added. Oh you wondrous, beautiful beast. Welcome to our world."

Forty-five feet long, the harmless fish circled them inquisitively, following the floating rafts for most of an hour. Then, it slipped into the depths and was gone. Dread tempered their initial relief. The appearance of the massive, though harmless, fish, emphasized the existence of the other, not-so-welcome, inhabitants of the sea. Like an all-consuming black cloud, the knowledge that either or both of those could return at any moment shrouded the rafts. In spite of their fear, Doc and Jim continued taking turns paddling. Two missing friends still needed finding.

* * *

"God, I'm sorry," Rachel sobbed. "I'm trying Jimmy. I just can't stop my shivering and crying. I'm so scared.

"That's all right, honey," her husband comforted. "Nobody's ever been through what we've just experienced. I'm proud of you. Jim offered her a partially-filled water jug. "Here honey, have a sip. Drink it slow now. Take it easy."

Nightfall was spectacular, accompanied by the sky's brilliant color changes. A jetliner passed silently overhead as the sun was disappearing from view. Looking like a silver speck, its presence was given away by a white vapor-stream trailing behind. With darkness came increased fear and loneliness. Not knowing where their friends were, even if they were still alive, created unbearable depression. Their collective spirits sagged. It would be so easy to give up. Two long, terrifying hours after sunset, Doc saw it.

Lighting the southwest sky like Fourth of July fireworks, the glow from the flare appeared larger than it was. "There! A flare!" Doc's cry startled his three companions. Only he was facing in that direction and the burning alarm was fluttering downward without a sound. Had he dozed off, it would have probably gone unseen. "It's got to be them!" he barked enthusiastically. "Red and Scott are alive!"

Grabbing the paddle, Doc stroked wildly toward the receding glow. "Take it easy Doc, that's at least a couple miles away." Jim cautioned Smitty, snapping him back to reality. "It'll take the better part of a day to go that far in this contraption. Anyway, it's my turn to paddle."

Changing positions in the raft with Doc, Jim took a bearing on the North Star's position relative to the dying messenger-of-light. Moments later, the beacon was gone, but firm, methodical strokes were springing from the paddle and adrenalin was pumping hope through four hearts. No one on the two rafts noticed the gentle rise and fall produced by long ground swells rolling in from the east. The faint blush of a breeze out of the same direction was also lightly rippling the calm water.

* * *

Scott's mind was tangled as hallucinations began to take over his tortured body. He backed up, feinted, and screamed, anything to avoid the slashing teeth, flailing barbels, and blood-filled water. Mutilated bodies floated by, accompanied by the excruciating screams of two nameless, long-dead fishermen. Then Bobby Catchman and Chad were being torn to pieces and devoured, eaten alive. Scott wrenched away from the searing, unimaginable pain accompanying his digestion and learned that restful sleep was an impossibility. Each closing of his eyes produced the brutal visions and cold realization that the surrounding water contained a million kinds of horrid deaths.

Scott thought he'd known fear before, but that was a mistaken belief. Compared to those long empty hours spanning the time till dawn, previous nightmares paled into cartoon-like dreams. That sparkling flare sank much too swiftly toward the upreaching horizon and disappeared, extinguishing any meager hope that remained for survival. The creature haunting him throughout his adult life was toying with them. Scott knew it was nearby. He could feel it. What was it waiting for? Why try to escape? Giving up was so much simpler, so much quicker. Without realizing it, the still-functioning fingers of Scott's right hand began to untie the straps on his life vest.

As he reached the final strap, a vision appeared, figures floating in space above him. Blinking, Scott hesitated in his efforts to find eternal peace. Two cherubs flickered into focus and a glowing, angelic face materialized between them. The aberration addressed him, speaking words he felt more than heard, words from an endless tunnel, from an infinite distance.

"Scott my darling," the angelic face pleaded, so clear he could see the tears trickling down. "You have to come back to me. Never give up. I need you. We need you."

"Daddy, daddy, please come home," the other two shapes echoed as well. "Please come home. We love you." A teenage boy and a younger girl chorused the heart-wrenching plea. The Cherubs became Kristine and Tommy. Then Louise hovered between them. The emptiness of their absence impaled Scott. Fear remained, but desire to survive reignited, blazing forth like that bursting flare. Somehow, he would get back to his precious family. He suddenly knew he would. With that thought in mind, and their likenesses burning in his consciousness, the life vest's comforting support slipped away. Warm water covered Scott's head and filled his eyes.

* * *

"See anything yet?" Doc asked in despair. "I know we've been going in the right direction, toward where that flare was last night. I just know it."

"Take it easy Doc," Karen pleaded, "we'll find them. We've just got to." The pretty coed glanced over her shoulder at him before returning here attention to the approaching horizon. Jim was finally asleep, curled up with Rachel in the second raft.

"Damn weather seems to be turning to shit on us," Doc grumbled, taking notice of building swells that grew shorter and steeper by the minute. Small whitecaps dotted the once-flat surface of the ocean. A steadily increasing breeze chilled their backs as they continued westward. "At this latitude, the only thing that'll kick up the sea is a tropical depression," Doc added in despair. "Shit, that's all we need."

The increasing motion was taking its toll on Jim and eventually woke him when a three-foot wave broke over the sleeping couple. "Damn it Smitty, why'd you let me sleep?" he complained before asking, "See our mates yet?"

"Nothing Jim. I'm wondering now if we're on the right heading." Doing a slow 360 with his eyes, Doc never let the paddle rest.

Five hours later, the sun's heat had intensified toward mid-day unbearability. Fluffy white clouds raced toward them from the east, forebodings of impending bad weather. The swells continued to steepen and the sea was now marred in all directions by whitecaps falling off of building waves. Tandem rafts were no problem on a pond-like ocean. Now, their stability and ease of propulsion was lessening exponentially with the angry, stirring water. Several times, Doc glanced at the orange box following faithfully behind them. Tempted to cut its tethering rope, he hadn't been able to cast off the visual proof of what happened. They were just going to have to drag that extra weight a little longer.

Four pairs of eyes searched in all directions as Rachel took her turn with the short-handled oar. An empty world surrounded them. Not a hint of other life; no birds, no fish, no people, *no nothing*. Radical motions increased steadily as the weather deteriorated. A supreme effort was now required just to sit in the bobbing craft.

The seas continually increased and the minutes crawled by. Temperatures spiraled upward as the sun edged ever higher into the blue sky, pock-marked by fleeting clouds. Several dolphin took refuge beneath their craft. Fading into the blue depths, the fish's brilliant colors reflected scattered light rays as they descended. The four survivors shared a can of Vienna sausage and a swig of water from a partially filled jug.

Directly overhead, the noon sun beat down unmercifully; perspiration evaporating as quickly as it seeped through salt-encrusted pores. The seas built steadily but the random movements of their rafts became less and less objectionable. Fear and a nausea returned with each backhanded slap by a breaking wave. All eyes continued to search the sea's expanse, but there was still no sign of Scott and Red. The desolate sea remained sterile, devoid of other human life.

Jim Gaffney's eyes were much more attuned to visual sea searches than those of his companions. For almost fifteen years, his livelihood and very survival had depended on the sea. Successful fishing evolved from continuous and careful observation. His eyes were trained to detect anything out of place. Color was the most recognizable event in an otherwise blue-green world. Jim caught that first glimpse of color.

*   *   *

Crippled fingers on Scott's left hand slid uselessly down the rough, canvass covering of a tethered vest. His scream died in a watery realm, not reaching a dozing Red Dickson. The Georgian nodded peacefully, apparently unaware of his friend's peril. Numb legs unable to kick and his right hand groping empty water, all contact with the makeshift raft vanished. Not wanting to die, Scott's descent into vast nothingness began.

Pain, blessed pain! The roots of Scott's hair held as a calloused hand twisted its strong, athletic fingers in his blond countenance. Scott's sinking direction changed, his choking face broke the surface, and there was air.

"Going somewhere, Prof?" Red asked with obscene casualness, seemingly aware of Scott's intentions. "Sorry to change your plans, but I think I'll keep you around a while longer." That welcomed southern drawl was unmistakable. "What's the matter, can't keep a life vest on? Guess I'd better tie it for you."

Scott could have kissed his friend. Instead, he gulped down moist air and felt his love for this man grow to new levels. Friends like Red were irreplaceable.

The redhead lashed the two of them together with ten-feet of strong nylon cord after replacing Scott's life jacket and securely knotting the straps. Scott could say nothing to this gentle friend sharing a common fate. They passed the time speaking quietly and reassuring each other, saying anything to keep their strained minds off the void surrounding them, knowing the unspeakable horrors it housed. Tension filled the hours preceding daylight before both lapsed into exhausted, restless sleep. A northbound tanker passed in the night, only eight miles to the west. Neither had any inkling it was there.

Scott's motion altered, waking him as the sun's ascent was accelerating. Increasing waves spanked his face and the life-vest-raft rose and fell noticeably with each arriving swell. Far to the east, a tropical wave had been born. Her first fingers reached out to them, a docile preview of what was to come, should she decide to intensify.

* * *

Light stings and nondescript pain winked off and on over every square inch of Scott's battered body. Rubbing in response to messages sent by damaged nerves, he realized that a multitude of open wounds were weeping invitations into the sea. "A chum line," he muttered. "That's all we are, a bloody, human chum line." Still Red didn't stir, his strong chin resting peacefully on that broad chest. Spoken comments didn't disturb his fitful slumber as Scott spat angrily, *"Pumping our blood into the ocean. The proverbial welcome mat, that's all we are."*

Red coughed and mumbled, salt water splashing up his nose from the increasing seas. But he didn't waken.

A bible verse from the book of Jonah entered Scott's thoughts. Was it a premonition of things to come? *"Now the Lord had prepared a great fish to swallow up Jonah. And Jonah was in the belly of the fish three days and three nights."*

SATURDAY, JULY 25TH, 11:30 HOURS

"About half-full," Scott commented, screwing the blue plastic top back into place.

"Or half-empty, depending on your point of view Prof," Red ventured in response. "Shit man, at this rate we can last a couple of weeks in this big ole swimming hole."

Very funny, pecker-head," Scott snarled at the humor transcending their despair with Dickson's off-the-shelf remark. A slight chuckle rolled painfully up Scott's throat and escaped as he grinned reflexively. His burned lips cracked and caked-on salt identified multiple new abrasions. "Great fun Dickson. Even your hick-style humor now causes me pain. Do me one small favor please. Shut the hell up before you kill me. Please . . .."

Red's intense facial reaction cut Scott's dialogue short. Turning painfully, he struggled to follow Red's stare.

"Scott! Scott! A ship! *I think I see a ship*!" Red's eyes widened perceptively as growing excitement permeated his voice. "Over there, long way away, but it's there. A ship, *big fuckin' ship*! Look Scott, damn it, look! Goddamn it, Thompson, don't you see it? Say something, damn it, say something!"

Desperately, Scott strained to see whatever his friend was pointing at, whatever Red saw. Twisting around, pain reminded him quickly of his ongoing exposure to a merciless tropical sun. The badly burnt skin on his neck wrinkled and cracked, exposing more damaged tissue to the onslaught of the salty waters. Temporary hope and elation plummeted like the breaking waves around them. He could see nothing, only a sea filled with massive swells and littered with frothy white caps. There was just nothing there.

"Where Red?" he pleaded. "Slow down, man. Show me. Tell me. Where do I look?" Scott knew Red had seen something.

"There! Over there!" Red's right arm was again extended toward the horizon, his index finger as rigid as a wooden spike. "Look now, you can see it, when we crest the wave! *There! There!* See it?"

And Scott *did* see it. From atop the current swell they rode, a long wave that raised them up just a little higher, he could make out the superstructure of a large ship. Suddenly, the helpful wave

slid by and the sea was again vacant. But Scott had seen a ship.
Once again there was *hope!*

"Yeah, Red, I saw it. I *did* see it!   We're gonna be saved!"
Excitement filled his reply and his reborn desire to live increased a
hundred-fold. Hope consumed him as Scott replied with absolute
conviction, "I see it big-guy, I see it! But it's a long ways away.
Seven or eight miles. Probably more."

As Red's eyes were burning holes through Scott, something
mysterious and secretive peeked through, undermining his excited
gaze. An uncontrollable chill ran through Scott, a deep despair over
something unknown.   Then the illusion passed and Red was
shouting again.

"A flare, Scott!" he screamed. "We've got three of 'em left.
The sonuvabitch is headed right at us. She's got to see a flare."

Red was right, Scott knew he was. A lifelong scrounger, Scott
hesitated to use anything he was hoarding. But if there was ever a
time to be extravagant, it was now. A wry smile creased his brittle
lips again, the excitement of possible rescue screening out the minor
pain. "Go for it partner," he instructed calmly. At the same time
thinking to himself, "And let's hope she's friendly, not another
Algerian ship."

Unkept auburn hair was hanging carelessly from his friend's
head, down his face, partially covering Red's intense green eyes.
The eighteen-inch-long flare, looking like a stick of dynamite, was
held tightly in a strong right hand. The graceful fingers of his left
gripped the *rip-cord-type* ignition device. From between the strands
of red, those keen, athletic eyes drilled a hole past Scott to the
southwestern horizon. Those eyes, totally oblivious to the man
watching them, were unaware when contact was broken. Turning
slowly and painfully to face the direction their salvation would come
from, Scott heard that distinctive southern drawl state, "Just a minute.
Gonna wait 'til I see her one mo' time. Gotta be sure. Gotta be
sure."

The next swell didn't carry them high enough to see the ship.
Seconds, then minutes marched by, as a series of smaller swells
came and went. Then, the seventh wave approached, towering
above its predecessors. Scott felt like they would never reach its
peak, but slowly the mass of water slipped beneath their insignificant
selves. Red's hands were rock solid, the direction of his frozen gaze
never faltering. Suddenly, the steepness flattened and they rode the
mountain's top.

"There she is! Oh, you beautiful lady!" The words had not even cleared Red Dickson's cracked and bleeding lips when his muscles tightened and the flare burst forth. Two pairs of prayerful eyes followed its upward trajectory, waiting for the release of its life-saving light.

"Nothin' man! Nothin'!" Red muttered in disbelief. "It's a dud, a *fuckin' dud*. The sum-bitch didn't go off." Two spirits plummeted as the almost-invisible speck decelerated and began its fall back to the sea.

Scott tore his eyes from the malfunctioning projectile and glanced at the remaining two flares lashed to the orange canvas in front of him. "Try another."

Before Red could reply, an almost inaudible bang echoed overhead accompanied by a puff of smoke below the missile's apex. A brilliant white light that could not possibly be missed was hovering in the sky beneath the blistering sun. It slowly commenced its descent, proclaiming their presence to the outside world, as symbolic as the *Star of Bethlehem.*

"Someone on the ship has to see that," muttered Red through gritted teeth. "They'll have to help us. It's the *law of the sea.*

Already holding another flare, Red just stared silently at the heavenly glow heralding their presence. "If she sees it," he stated flatly, "no, *when* she sees it, it'll take her a good twenty or thirty minutes to get here." His comment was professional, a matter-of-fact statement. "And she'll be tough to maneuver. Heard it can take ten miles for a supertanker to stop when its got a full head of steam."

"Red, it's Doc and the others," Scott was shouting. Looking eastward past Red's straggled hair, he could see an orange object rolling into view on the blue horizon. "Red, there's the raft, behind you. They're coming! They're coming! Must see the flare? Thank God! *We'll all get saved!"*

Red acknowledged Scott's excitement with a slight nod, but didn't look around, just kept staring upward at the descending light. Again Scott detected that faraway look in his friend's eyes that seemed to house some deep personal secret, an ominous and important something, knowledge not shared. Scott picked up a few of Red's incoherent words as a faint smile was evident on his lips. "As long as you and Doc Smitty are okay . . ." Red continued staring upwards at the dulling light, but his eyes were looking somewhere beyond. Toward heaven maybe? Or to hell?

* * *

Cresting waves crashed into the frail rafts, occasionally rolling right over their four exhausted bodies. The fifteen-foot rope behind them slackened and tightened, slackened and tightened. Each time, the rafts would swing, making propulsion and steering that much more difficult.

"Got to cut the VCR crap loose Doc," Jim Gaffney stated. "No sense towing it any longer." The Australian fisherman's comment made sense, but Peter Smith still ignored him.

"Can't, Jim. Not yet. Got to hang on to it," Doc stated flatly. "It'll prove what happened, even if we're not here." He tossed a quick glance over his right shoulder at the brilliant orange crate, dutifully following in their wake. "It's not that much trouble to haul," he added in justification. "We'll make it." Changing the subject he asked, "Do you still see them?"

"Not in the last few minutes," Jim allowed, "but I know that flash of color was Scott and Red. It had to be."

Jim's eyes were glued to the southwestern horizon and his back was toward Doc who kept on paddling in the deteriorating conditions. Blue-green and frothy, the building seas continued to roll under, and even over, their sluggish vehicles. An orange container continued to trail behind, doing its best to impede their progress.

"There! I saw some orange." Rachel pointed, right of dead ahead.

"How far Rachel?" Doc pleaded more than asked. "Could you tell how far?" Cresting on a mountainous facade of foaming white water, his eyes answered for her. A quarter-mile to the west. Half-a-mile at most. A splash of orange surrounded two heads bobbing on the turbulent waves. Even from that distance, Red's hair was unmistakable. Sliding over the back of the mammoth sea, the glimpse of color that was his friends vanished. High above, a brilliant light burst forth in the rapidly darkening sky. They could only see its glow for a few seconds, until the first stinging sheet of rain lashed down on four exposed raft riders and obliterated their guiding star.

"Where the hell'd that come from?" Jim asked everyone's question. "Rachel, you and Karen get under those towels. Doc and I'll keep after them."

From a foreboding sea to a full-fledged gale, nature suddenly unleashed her fury. Wind gusts blew the tops off of already dangerous seas. Torrents of bruising, tropical rain lashed down upon them. Legions of wind-driven droplets attacked like a swarm of stinging bees. The horizon disappeared in all directions and visibility dropped to a few yards. Two rafts lurched violently, threatening to pitch their occupants into a furious ocean. Doc dropped the paddle and fell forward into the bottom of the raft where he and Jim hung on for dear life.

As the starboard raft dropped over the shear edge of a twenty-foot wave running out from under them, a vast chasm opened below. It was all over. A void below it, the leading raft with Rachel and Karen cowering inside, toppled. Jim sprawled toward his wife, her petrified scream piercing the din of the storm. Just as the second raft commenced its tumultuous decent, a saving hand, like the finger of God, halted their slide. From across the wave, a singing rope vibrated near its breaking point. Both rafts hesitated long enough for the vicious peak of water to slide by beneath them, closing the yawning abyss.

"What the hell?" Doc was able to spit out, regaining a little of his composure. "What . . . what happened? Thought we were goners for sure."

"Your bloody crate," Jim mumbled thankfully, his voice quivering at their near demise. "Mate, that fucking box of television shit you wouldn't cut loose acted like a goddamned sea anchor; saved us from going over that watery cliff."

And as quickly as it had started, the rain ceased. Like waterlogged kittens, two female figures slinked out from beneath soaking wet garments. Slight smiles betrayed a subdued gladness just to be alive. Off to the starboard, a brilliant whitish light still hovered before them, though much nearer to the horizon. The squall lasted all of three minutes; three long terrifying minutes when death's proximity grabbed at, but missed, four shipwrecked friends.

Then Jim spotted the reason for the flare. "A ship! That's why they shot the flare," he shouted with joy and excitement. "Rachel honey, look! A bloody ship!"

From near the crest of the massive wave now lifting the rafts, a pile of water much less angry than those of mere moments before, they all saw the huge ship. Clearly visible on the horizon, less than five miles away, it seemed to be bearing down on the life-giving light. At the same time, they all swung their gazes toward the descending flare, its light paling as its energy waned. Beneath it, in the churning blue, green, and white of the mid-Atlantic floated their comrades in science. The auburn head was looking away from them, occupied by the approaching vessel. A smaller, darker figure peered in their direction, his right arm flailing away in recognition.

Doc lifted the paddle and waved back. Offering any hope he could to that forlorn figure in the water, he was now certain that they were all going to make it.

Quickly, the blade reentered the salty sea and completed a stroke. The ship and their friends disappeared again as the wave swept under the rafts and they fell into the ensuing valley. Moments later, the following wave lifted them again. The ship, now definitely homing in of the remnants of the fast-dying flare, rose into view. Again, the two bodies in the roughened water materialized, floating on a prodigious swell before sinking from sight.

"*Oh my God! No! Not now! Not now!*" Karen shrieked in disbelief. She saw the dark blue shadow first, just seconds before her companions. "Look, Scott! Look out! Behind you!" She shouted at the top of her lungs, but her pathetic warning died long before it could reach him. She was joined by three other voices, crying out their alarm. Four voices, still much too far away to be heard.

But their panic was transcended across a quarter-mile of vacant, turbulent ocean. All sound dissipated in the wind, but its imperativeness extended out, touching the unwary Scott and his companion. Red ripped his gaze from the life-restoring ship. Smiling pleasantly, he looked past Scott at the orange picture on the not-so-distant wave. Sensing the disquieting message being transmitted by four frantically yelling people, two water-logged heads swung in unison.

With X-ray-like vision, the tethered companions looked through the closest wave. Only fifty yards away, a cobalt blue shadow was stalking them. Extending above it, a sickle shaped growth cut the surface. Moving toward their right, the illusion of safety created by separation quickly evaporated. They had unwanted company, a visitor of unmistakable identity.

* * *

Diminutive traces of blood had controlled its every movement for over two hours. Erratic motions transmitted through the water provided guiding impulses that aided the direction of its methodical search. The unfamiliar scent was unmistakably blood and aroused its feeding instincts. A brief flurry of motion excited the series of delicate fibers running the length of a twelve-foot body. Amplified on its left side, its heading adjusted accordingly and it proceeded due east. Greater blood concentration drew it to the surface where bodily temperature controls kicked in, reacting to an infinitesimal increase in water temperature. Over 900 pounds of sinew and muscle rose and fell effortlessly with each successive swell.

A fraction of Megalodon's size, this shark had evolved as one of nature's most efficient predators. Scientifically known as *Isurus Oxyrinchus*, the common name was *Mako*. One of the mackerel sharks, it was closely related to the great white, a distant cousin of its prehistoric ancestor. Graceful and streamlined, the Mako was probably the world's fastest shark. Like the white, its homocercal or equally lobed tail and horizontally flattened keel manifested power, expanding into the musculature of its tail structure. The dorsal fin and back were the darkest of blues, a color termed rich-ultramarine. A snowy white underbelly was distinctively separated from the dark blue by a brilliant band of silver. A female, she was a strikingly beautiful fish.

Her conical snout was uniquely pointed and spear-like as it preceded her through the water. Dark eyes, set like circular pieces of coal on either side of her head, seemed intensely intelligent. They were larger than the eyes of most other sharks and this enhanced vision complemented other senses when she stalked her prey. Set in the white underside of her bullet-like head was an awesome set of jaws. Her two-inch teeth were exceptionally long for her size and resembled curved knives with flat, razor-sharp cutting edges on both sides, not serrated like those of her kin. *Grasping fingers* best described their appearance protruding outward from a slowly opening and closing mouth as she followed the meager, bloody trail. Flattened forward surfaces amplified the knife-like impression. One of creation's perfect killing machines, she was a creature of shear terror, *a mechanism to fear*.

On the downslope of a swell, her rigid dorsal fin felt dry air and a magnificent blue back glinted brilliantly in the sun. Almost at once, water covered her again as she submerged. The scent was suddenly much stronger, the potential quarry much closer. Her feeding instinct percolated to a higher level. Her stiff-bodied swimming style was extremely effective as she proceeded through the gin-clear water using short strokes of a thick, powerful tail. As the blood scent proliferated, the frequency of her strokes accelerated.

Her potential quarry was only a scant three-hundred yards away. Feeding on any fish in the sea, her strength, armaments, and prowess permitted no real enemies. Her senses heightened in response to the increasing content of blood, but she remained in control. Cool, almost calculating, in moments her vision would come into play. There was no need to rush. She wouldn't hurry, nor would she commit to a dangerous situation. Only when she was sure of what she was stalking, would it be feeding time. Then, and only then, would she attack. Altering her easterly direction toward the north, she started to circle. Ensuing circles would shrink as she closed on and identified her target.

The strong tail slowly cut the water. Saber-lined jaws opened and closed as she mouthed the scent which increased with each stroke. Every action of her powerful body was attuned to ages of inbred survival and feeding techniques. While not definite, attack was highly probable. Then, for the first time, she saw it.

Chapter Twenty

RESCUE

His silver hair was tussled as the thinning strands emerged from beneath Captain Fred Melin's navy-blue cap with its circular orange emblem. The dim light overhead on the bridge's battleship-gray ceiling reflected dully off a silver-dollar-sized bald spot on his scalp. Six-foot-three in his prime, the ship's master appeared shorter as the rigors of time hunched a proud back and shoulders. The tanker's aging bridge was his one true domain. He hadn't left it in over a day, except to use the toilet; ever since the May Day signal was picked up. Steel-blue eyes drooped in weariness, but continued their ceaseless search of the limitless horizon. The huge ship was throttled back to fourteen knots as the desolate, roughening waters continued to sweep by beneath him. Although anticipation was fading, hope still remained. For three hours, a faint rendition of the International Distress Signal was guiding him. Now, that directive had ceased. Fatigue threatening to overcome him, ancient memories surfaced.

Born in Sweden, he'd been eleven-years-old when he entered the U.S. illegally through Canada with his widowed father almost a half-century before. Shortly thereafter, the senior Melin vanished and young Fred was left to fend for himself in New York's slums and wharfs. Maturity came rapidly out of necessity and the teenager found himself thrust into World War II via the Merchant Marine. At nineteen, on his third transatlantic run, the young Swede's Liberty Ship GOD'S GRACE ran afoul of a German U-Boat's torpedoes and was sunk.

Fred Melin survived four miserable days in the frigid North Atlantic. In the process, he watched twelve of his shipmates succumb. Frostbite took the better portion of his right hand's index finger and both little toes. That terrifying experience indelibly carved the young man's character with permanent compassion for anyone lost at sea.

His education came through self-teaching, a high school equivalency exam, the Merchant Marine Academy, and a life at sea.

Fred married a tiny Norwegian girl he seldom saw and who gave him no children. She passed away quickly, but painfully, from cancer in 1982. He continued to sail the world, a captain of his own vessels since '59. Nothing spectacular, nothing memorable, life had passed him by. As legacies went, his was short and not-so-sweet. However, since the sinking of the GOD'S GRACE, Captain Fred Melin would never abandon anyone lost at sea.

Reality flooded back as a distress flare erupted beneath the overhanging clouds six or seven miles off the starboard bow. The first mate took a bearing as Melin altered his course. Engines were backed off even more, and instructions were given to prepare for *man overboard* recovery operations. The 990-foot length of the GULF LAKE CHARLES responded slowly to his commands. Heavily laden with Brazilian crude, her destination was the Gulf Oil refinery at Port Arthur, Texas. Captain Melin and his crew would make this detour first.

The scene played out before him. As the Very-Large-Crude-Carrier's engines responded to their changing gears, her gigantic wheels reversed their spin and the ship slid obediently toward two groups in the choppy sea while gradually slowing down. Closest to them were the two men in the water, tethered to a makeshift raft of life preservers. Melin trained his powerful binoculars on them. The larger of the two was truly distinctive, sporting a brilliant crop of red hair. His intense eyes seemed to be staring directly into Captain Melin's polished lenses. They were less than a half-mile now, but it would still take ten minutes before he could rescue them. "If only these big ships responded faster," he mumbled to himself. "But you can't hurry tonnage of this sort."

A couple hundred yards further away, two men and two women were clinging to a pair of bucking life rafts, infuriated by the fifteen-foot seas which went unfelt onboard the LAKE CHARLES.

"They must know we can see them," he mumbled to himself. "They're wasting an awful lot of energy waving those paddles and flags." These thoughts and others flashed through Melin's mind as he kept his field glasses trained on the four people momentarily. Realizing their attention was centered on the two in the water and not on his ship, he panned his view back toward the first two men. Efficiently sweeping the waters in his search for them, experienced eyes glimpsed the change of color, a darker spot in the frothy blue water. Instinctively, he recognized the different shade for what it was, the mariner's most fearsome enemy. *The Mako!!!* The large shadow was bearing down on the pair in the water.

Captain Melin could only watch. Haste would prove disastrous. His huge vessel was a lethal weapon if not controlled properly. If only the shark would delay its attack for a few minutes more. The vivid blue back with its scepter-like fin briefly broke curdling water atop the whitecap-crested swell. Its spectacular shape and brilliant colors literally screamed with efficient brutality. Blood slowly welled in Melin's mouth as clinching teeth bit into his lower lip. Helplessly, the drama unfolded as the nub of his missing finger rubbed his bristled jaw. He sighed with relief as the massive bow of his vessel finally towered over the potential victims. He was in time.

Engines full astern, he sensed the reaction of his ship halting as ordered. Within the visual confines of the binoculars, the imposing blue shape faded with depth and was gone. Two hundred yards from his position on the starboard wing of the bridge, two faces grinned at the hovering giant. The smaller one was waving gratefully. A funny type of smile creased the red-haired one's face. Melin sensed something secretive behind that mask. Before he could put his finger on it, the auburn hair and pleasant face vanished.

* * *

Scott could hear Doc shouting as the raft came within earshot. A towering gray hull, randomly splotched with muddy-brown streaks of rust, blotted out the southwestern horizon. She looked to be at least a thousand-feet long and a hundred-feet high. Salvation was taking an imposing shape. There was a capless man on the starboard wing of the bridge, obviously the ship's captain. Black field glasses at his eyes focused on Red and him. A day-and-a-half in hell was more than adequate. In minutes they would be plucked from that nasty sea and hoisted to safety. Scott's buried memories of the oil patch returned with the personnel basket being dropped over the side from a ship's crane just forward of the bridge's superstructure.

"Just a couple more minutes big guy," he said quietly to Red. "Going to feel good to be dry again. Wonder where the damn Mako went? Guess it was just curious."

"No sweat, Prof. We're home free now." Dickson's quiet reassurance buoyed Scott. "Then it'll be their turn, nodding toward the approaching rafts. She's American this time. Thank God," he added. "Has to be, with a name like GULF LAKE CHARLES."

Glancing over his shoulder toward the northeast, Scott could see the rafts approaching. The wind-blown seas and towering swells were rolling in from the same direction, intermittently hiding them from view. Their friends and the rafts reappeared like clockwork, each time a little closer.

"Good ole Doc. He's towing the damn video crate. Not only do we live, but we also prove Megalodon's real." Scott squeezed Red's left shoulder with his good right hand and then looked back at the descending basket. Waving both hands appreciatively, he gave a grateful thumb's up signal with his operative one. While Scott should have been ecstatic, apprehension swept over him.

"Where'd that damn shark go?" he asked himself. "And just what the hell happened to Megalodon?" Behind loosely closed eyes, he instinctively offered the Lord's Prayer. *"Our Father who art in Heaven, hallowed . . ."*

"Say something, Scott?" Red asked. Without waiting for a reply, he added something foreboding. "Great to be saved. Just wish I had more time to enjoy it."

Interrupting his quiet prayer, Scott looked at Red's familiar face less than four feet away. Before he could say anything, something rough brushed his slowly kicking feet, making him flinch. "What the hell . . ." Red Dickson wasn't there. A split second later, Scott was sucked beneath the surface, a tremendous strain on the now-taut nylon cord connecting him to his friend.

* * *

Sound vibrations and smell led her home. The concentration of blood in the water had increased dramatically. Her target was very near. Driven more by instinct than hunger, she didn't rush. Then she saw it; outlines though, not colors. Her vision could only distinguish shades of light and dark. Like all sharks, this great predator was color blind. The accurate lenses of her eyes identified several erratically kicking appendages at the turbulent surface. While capable of feeding easily amongst the cresting waves, the Mako was far more comfortable submerged. Pectoral fins trimming slightly, her powerful caudal stroked stiffly and drove her downward.

For immeasurable seconds, then minutes, she circled eighty feet below four inviting legs. Indecision confounded the large fish. The intrusion of a very large shape extending downward almost to the depth she was prowling disquieted her. And an irritating dull throb emanated from this new creature. Reaction came in the blink of an eye. One of the small, bleeding creatures above was transmitting a message of pain and hopelessness, distinctly more attractive signals than those of its companion. Hanging vertically for a split-second, she zeroed in on her choice. Nine hundred pounds rose, graceful as a ballerina, powerful as a ballistic missile.

Her massive jaws opened, fangs like an aroused lion's claws curved inward. One of the flailing extremities entered her beckoning maw as her left side was brushing against the other creature's legs. Unleashing age-old power, knife-like teeth in opposing jaws meshed. Her motion halted and momentum shifted. The Mako quickly sank several feet and then bolted through the clear water, now blemished by the pinkish cloud spreading from the morsel in her teeth. Momentarily, she felt resistance to her motion. Her strength intensified and she shook violently. Quickly, flesh and bone parted and the dragging force disappeared. Only the flesh in her mouth remained. She quickly swallowed before circling back.

* * *

Red Dickson was treading water beside his longtime friend as they watched the descending basket. Their elevator to safety approached. But for him, it was just a short stop on his way to oblivion. Behind him, he could hear Doc Smitty barking instructions and gleeful squeals from the two girls awaiting rescue. He wondered where Mason and the SEA NYMPH's crew were. Did they make it too? But Red's path was preordained, destiny having already thrown his lot. Watching the man on the ship's bridge signal instructions, Red was overcome with self-pity.

"First my knee. No telling how long I could have played, how good I could've been," he mouthed bitterly. "Damn, if that wasn't enough, then I lose Jane. Now, with all the money in the world and these great friends, the 'Big C.' Fuckin', inoperable cancer." This knowledge filled Red's head, feelings he had shared with no one, although he desperately wanted to. As the basket hit a cresting wave, his mind snapped back to the present. "Wish I had more time to enjoy it."

His right foot was shoved from beneath and an upward force jolted his entire body. A terrifying shiver coursed through him as Red somehow realized what was happening. Tremendous pressure crushed down on his right thigh above the knee and on his left ankle. Before any sound could clear his throat, searing pain exploded in his legs, an all consuming pain even greater than he had experienced that night in Shea Stadium when he destroyed his right knee. As some tumultuous force dragged him under, stifling his agonized scream in a rush of seawater, Red Dickson knew exactly where the Mako was.

The pain was immediate and unbearable, but consciousness wouldn't desert him. Red recognized the taut cord connecting him to Scott. His friend was being dragged down too, would suffer the same fate because of him. At that moment of despair, his only concern was for Scott, not himself. A vision of Scott's family quickly flashed through his mind and then vanished. His descent continued, with Scott Thompson in tow.

Without warning, the pain lessened and the pressure about Red's leg and foot subsided. The combined buoyancy of the two men's life vests thrust them toward the surface. Red kicked strongly with both legs, marveling that they were responding at all. Reaching the surface, he knew for sure. *It was the Mako!* Then there was total blackness.

"Red, Red! Oh Christ, Red!" Scott screamed, concern blending with his panic. "What's wrong, Georgia? You okay?" His functional right hand reached out and touched Dickson's limp chin. But only momentarily. Startled for a second time by a painful scraping sensation and massive impact on his legs, his friend was jerked away again. Instantaneously, Scott followed as the connecting line came tight.

* * *

The Mako returned for another taste. Zeroing in on the longer extremity in the discoloring water, she ignored the two other flailing legs. Brushing them aside, those viscous teeth struck again. Momentum carried her ten yards before her progress slowed. Furiously shaking her steel-blue, streamlined head, flesh and bone again shredded and parted in her mouth. A second stub, even shorter than the first hung motionlessly below her floating prey. Pulsating purplish spurts contrasted against a pale-blue whiteness of ragged bone. Diluting quickly, the immediate surrounding water turned pink. Decreasing volume testified to the rapidly-fading pump that was Red's heart. Mouthing the morsel, her taste buds dulled with its unfamiliar texture and flavor. Interest waning, the large fish glided slowly away, to circle and survey the proceedings from a respectable distance.

Twin stumps of flesh wrapped around jagged white shafts jutted from beneath the orange vest. Seconds before, those missing legs were providing the ballast needed to keep the vest upright. Suddenly top heavy, what was left of Red's dying body pitched forward, submerging his face and exposing the results of the brief, but brutal attack. Two vehicles arrived at the same time as Scott struggled in vain to upright his inanimate friend.

Red's blood was on Scott's face, running down his neck and spilling everywhere. His left hand was useless, but the right reached futilely down the unconscious man's length, grasping for the jacket's top. Gagging, vomit and gore rose uncontrollably in his parched throat. Raw flesh and bone clung to Scott's vest as grotesque stubs pointed upward on each side of his head. Fragmented edges of twitching bone entered Scott's open mouth, slicing shallow cuts along his left cheek. All the while, less and less of Red's priceless liquid squirted against his sunburned skin.

"God help me!" Scott cried pathetically. "Goddamn it, Red! I'm trying buddy. God knows I'm trying!" Miraculously, two strong hands gripped Red's life jacket.

"I got him Scott," Doc's steady voice reassured him. Red's face was lifted clear of the water, hidden from Scott on the far side of his auburn head.

"Look out for the basket, Scott." Rachel's comforting voice said from close by, but he didn't know what she meant. Then something heavy banged into the back of his head and shoulders.

"Cut the rope, Jim," Doc commanded. "Got to get him in the raft, stop the bleeding. God, I hope we're not too late."

A persistent force on Scott's waist evaporated. He heard Jim Gaffney say, "That's got it. Pull him in, Doc."

"Oh God! Look at his legs!" Karen groaned. Her ashen face collapsed as she quickly turned away. Dry heaves and the sobs of her crying echoed against the imposing hull of the giant ship which now laid alongside the shattered contingents.

"Pull him in." Doc's orders continued as he and Jim dragged an inert Red Dickson over the edge of their raft.

"Rachel, throw me those towels!" Doc demanded. "Quickly girl, quickly." Dr. Peter Smith's professional aura took control of the scene. "That's it, good girl. Jim, unscrew those paddle handles. Hurry man, we got no time."

Twisting the towel, Doc applied a tourniquet to the repulsive stump nearest him, blood still flowing freely from the mass of paling flesh around the protruding white bone. "Rachel, twist another towel like this and get started on the other leg," he ordered. "That's right. Don't be afraid of hurting him." He took the handle of the first paddle from Jim, slipped it into the tied towel and rotated it like a fan blade. Two turns and the flow of blood slowed noticeably, then another turn and it halted. Rachel grabbed that handle and held it as Doc's attention shifted. He quickly repeated the process on what remained of Red's right leg.

For the second time, the heavy object struck Scott's back. With its impact, reality finally returned. He'd been mesmerized by Doc and Rachel bending over his friend. From his position in the water, all he could see of Red was the orange life vest's front and his two grotesquely shortened appendages. Turning slowly, he surveyed nearly two-tenths of a mile of supertanker and the oversized personnel basket hanging from its deck. It was that basket which was assailing him from behind.

Jim was grasping the basket's edge and pulling the pair of rafts over to it. Scott's thoughts turned to the large Mako that had just mutilated one of his best friends. It was still here, nearby. Why hadn't it come back after the second attack? He also visualized the two monstrous creatures from the day before. *Megalodon! How far away were they?* Somehow, he wasn't afraid for himself. Somehow Scott knew *it was finally over.*

* * *

Three ropes were secured to the bottom of the basket as Jim, Scott, and one of the ship's crew clung to the wide-meshed sides. The GULF LAKE CHARLES engines idled quietly below decks while the winch on her davit easily lifted its makeshift load. The bulky basket cleared the water, carrying its grateful occupants. The life rafts and the fiberglass box of video gear were also saved. The rescue operation was taking place on the starboard, upwind side of the ship which offered no shelter for the survivors from the vicious seas. Plus, reflected waves off the huge hull only increased the sea's treachery.

"Hope he'll be okay," Jim said wishfully. "Jesus man, did you see those legs?" Gaffney stood up well during the heat of battle. With the end in sight, the pressures were now taking their toll as the

Australian fisherman asked, "Think Doc can save him, Scott? Can Red survive without legs? I mean, will he even *want* to?"

Scott looked into the eyes of the younger man an arm's length away. "Doc'll do what he can, but I'm afraid we're too late. Red lost an awful lot of blood." With that, Scott's chin fell against his heaving chest and he wept openly.

Doc and Jim quickly moved Red's limp body to the center of the basket. Less than ten minutes before, Doc and the two women were lifted off the water and accompanied poor Red on a hundred-plus-foot journey to the tanker's deck. During the entire rescue operation, Doc was vigilantly tending to his fallen comrade's wounds. The basket was swung onboard and the ship's beam remained vacant for a couple of minutes. Scott and Jim bobbed awkwardly in the rafts alongside as those minutes dragged by, tethered by a half-inch rope lowered from above. Finally, Rachel's concerned face reappeared overhead, quickly followed by the returning basket which carried the lone seaman.

* * *

"I've got a pulse. It's very faint, but it's definitely there." Doc's face told the story. Red's unconscious form was covered by a sheet as it lay on a padded, stainless-steel table in the ship's infirmary. Clear tubes filled with life-giving blood ran from a needle in the crook of his right elbow, through some bottles and valves, and down to a second needle in the ship's second officer's arm.

Doc commented, "He's strong, but he's got one hell of a hill to climb. Only the good Lord knows if he's up to it. I've done all I can medically. All we can do now is pray."

Chapter Twenty-one

JOURNEY'S END

Scott listened intently to Mr. Fitzmacon's eloquent oration from the neatly typed legal document. His injured left hand was immobilized by a plastic cast which extended from just below the elbow to the tips of his two remaining fingers. The fingers of his right hand were intertwined with those of his wife. She was sitting rigidly in a front row seat, next to Kristine, who was between her mother and Tommy. Unashamed tears glistened on the cheeks of all four members of the Thompson clan. Seated on Scott's left was Dr. Peter Smith, his utter seriousness making him seem out of place. Jim and Rachel Gaffney occupied two of the stiff-backed chairs in the rear of the group attending. Several others, including all of Red Dickson's family, were also present, bringing the total in the spacious conference room to eighteen, including Mr. Fitzmacon and his assistant.

The burnished brass placard on the elegant mahogany entrance door they came through almost one hour before, was imprinted with the name of the attorney.

Pausing for a moment, Larry Fitzmacon surveyed the room, his eyes resting momentarily on the Thompson family directly in front of him before returning to the legal size pages in his hands. He resumed his reading, the baritone voice resonating with authority to those present.

"To my friend Scott David Thompson and his wife Louise, both of whom I grew to love, I bequeath a cash gift in the amount of ten million dollars, to be shared equally and utilized as they see fit. Scott, thank you for all the years you shared with me. Wherever I end up, I know I will miss you. Louise, next to my dear Jane who I will now have rejoined, I loved you as much as was possible for me.

"To John Thomas Thompson and Kristine Louise Thompson, I establish Irrevocable Trusts for each in the principle amounts of two million dollars. Broward National Bank shall be named Trustee and shall invest the funds as it sees fit, except that forty percent of the value of each trust shall be maintained in five-year or less Certificates of Deposit. Interest and other proceeds from the trust shall be dispersed for educational and/or health related needs, if any, of

Tommy and Kristine. I can only say thank you to these fine young people. If I had ever been blessed with children of my own, I would have wanted them to be just like you two.

"To my good friend and physician, Doctor Peter Smith, I bequeath the cash amount of three million dollars and the entirety of my land holdings on Key Largo. Thanks for the great times and catch one for me buddy.

"To my more recently acquired friend James Gaffney, I leave a cash gift of one million dollars to be utilized as he sees fit. Thank you for the Blacks, skipper.

"Finally, I hereby bequeath and establish a Trust of fifteen million dollars which will perpetually fund the CARCHARODON MEGALODON RESEARCH FOUNDATION. I direct that the principal amount shall remain intact, except as specified in the trust document, and that all income and interest derived therefrom shall be used to further man's knowledge of this magnificent creature. I appoint Dr. Scott David Thompson as the sole Director of this Foundation and leave him full authority over its operation. Give them hell Scott. And if you haven't already, find that sonuvabitch Megalodon."

* * *

Scott was shell-shocked at the reading of the Last Will and Testament of William "Red" Dickson. On July 26th, two weeks before, Red died onboard the GULF LAKE CHARLES. All of Doc's efforts were fruitless. Their treasured friend never regained consciousness and the loss of blood and accompanying shock was just too much to overcome. In reality, Red didn't want to live in this shape and had just let go.

Red's statement in the beginning of his Will did not alleviate the pain those present were suffering at his passing. Apparently he had contracted a form of blood-cell-cancer that was inoperable. Five weeks before departing on that Venezuelan fishing trip he learned of his illness. Unbeknownst to anyone, he put his considerable estate in order and executed these papers and just went fishing. Finding Megalodon and being with his two closest friends kept his mind off the inevitable. According to Fitzmacon, Red Dickson was worth more than one-hundred-twelve-million dollars.

The bulk of the estate was divided among Red's relatives. A significant cash stipend was left to the family of Jane Kent in Australia and several million dollars went to various charities. He also bequeathed the International Game Fish Association five hundred thousand dollars.

Leaving the Attorney's office, eleven days after William Dickson was laid to rest in a Broward Memorial Garden's plot which Red also arranged for, Scott Thompson said it all. "Goodbye again old friend. We'll all miss you." Free flowing tears and a cracking voice halted him there.

*   *   *

The Miami Herald ran a two-column article on August 1st, 1987, which was picked up by the wire services and appeared in 143 papers across the country. The following is an excerpt from that article.

. . . *expedition was made up of seven persons and a ship's complement of four. The MV SEA NYMPH was reportedly rammed by a Libyan tanker with the full knowledge of its crew. The foreign ship did not stop and made no effort to assist the damaged vessel. The damage to the ninety-four-foot SEA NYMPH disclosed a hidden cache of what may have been illicit drugs, namely cocaine. In connection with that accusation, an investigation of the vessel's owner, a Mr. Malcolm W. Breaux of Golden Meadow, Louisiana, is being initiated by appropriate Federal and State Authorities. This reporter has learned that Breaux, nicknamed "Bubba," left the country before law enforcement agents could locate him and is currently in hiding somewhere in Central America.*

The five survivors, identified earlier in this article, claim that the vessel was attacked by two gigantic shark-like creatures, one of them over a hundred-feet long. The damaged SEA NYMPH was literally torn apart by the assault of these two leviathans, which also killed a young University of Miami student, the vessel's captain, and a member of her crew. Two other crew members went down with the vessel, their exact fates are unknown.

Reportedly, video tape documentation of the entire episode was recovered with the survivors. This evidence is now in the hands of local authorities. According to off-the-record statements from Professor Scott Thompson of the University of Miami and Dr. Peter Smith, a renowned Florida orthopedic surgeon, the TV record substantiates all of their claims. Professor Thompson added that the giant sharks were not malicious, but reacted to certain sound frequencies discharged into the water. Such frequencies were being transmitted from the now sunken vessel in an effort to confirm the existence of these sharks.   He identified the giant fish as Carcharodon Megalodon, a supposedly extinct ancestor of today's great white shark. In addition . . .

The article ended shortly thereafter.   On August 6th, the Associated Press put an article on the wire which was picked up by almost every major newspaper in the country and by several overseas publications. Quoted in its entirety,

By The Associated Press - BERMUDA

Tragedy occurred in the waters 300 miles west of this beautiful island country on the morning of Wednesday, August 5th. A fleet of forty-seven open-ocean sailboats departed New York Harbor at dawn on July 31st in the inaugural New York to Bermuda Cup Race. These sleek vessels ranged in length from fifty-three to seventy-two feet and were equipped with state-of-the-art navigation and communications gear. The boats were spread out over ten miles of gentle ocean on the night of August 4th.

According to stories relayed from participating vessels via satellite hookups, as many as ten of the yachts were attacked by giant shark-like creatures sometime before dawn. At least two of the monsters continued their wanton attacks until after midday on the 5th. Several different boats verified this, as did the captains of two passing tankers. Attempts to help the vessels were moderately successful. However, the exact extent of the damages and the loss of life are unknown at this time.

No more than two of the giant sharks, if that is what they were, showed themselves at any one time during the assault, which reportedly ended at about 2:00 PM, local time. One shark was estimated to be over a hundred-feet long. The smaller shark appeared to be between seventy and eighty-feet long and carried massive lacerations of recent origin on the right side of its head. All reports indicate that the two or more sharks were very selective in their attack patterns. The monsters ignored most of the sailboats, as they proceeded only to select a few.

An unconfirmed report has it rumored that several of the boats participating in the race carried state-of-the-art location monitoring devices. It also seems that only the boats equipped with these devices were attacked. Appropriate officials within the Navy Department have been asked about this accusation, but declined comment.

Coincidentally, a recent article picked up by another wire service has disclosed a similar incident. That attack reportedly

occurred off the coast of Brazil late last month. Six people were killed, including Baseball Hall of Fame member Red Dickson. According to University of Miami Professor Scott Thompson, one of five survivors, giant sharks called Carcharodon Megalodon were attracted by U.S. Navy developed LRLFST's, Long-Range Low-Frequency Sound Transmitters. The Navy also declined comment on that incident.

The surviving sailboats should reach Bermuda sometime today. An air-sea rescue effort has been initiated to search the area for any survivors. The giant sharks, Carcharodon Megalodon were reportedly unharmed during the attacks and were last seen at approximately 2:15 PM local time when they simply disappeared.

* * *

Except for nature's suppression during brief mating periods, the giant female never encountered other's of her kind without the triggering of aggression. This time, the incessant vibrations had driven her crazy. Fortunately for her and the smaller male, attention was focused on the sources of the ingratiating throbs. Dozens of hard-skinned creatures slithered silently across the slight chop on the surface overhead. Eleven of them were screaming that intolerable noise into the depths. The previous one-hundred-million years had born witness to the instinctive, uncontrollable dispatch of anything in the sea responsible for similar emissions. *Nothing had changed.*

The male sensed her presence. He also found his attention completely occupied by the noisy creatures trespassing in his realm. *Destroy! Destroy!* Silencing the painful noises engulfed his being. His mission commenced.

From several hundred miles, the two gargantuan creatures had been drawn to this noise, the similar noise that drew them to the SEA NYMPH weeks before. The depths they left would never see the faintest ray of light; external pressures there were 150 times greater than what they now experienced at the surface. The epitome of survival, the optimal killing and eating machines did not care. Adapting to changing environments and conditions predicated their survival and two massive throwbacks to the days of the dinosaur closed on forty-seven sailboats. Eleven of them, courtesy of Uncle Sam's sonic device, were destined to perish that morning.

She destroyed six, her massive body dwarfing each quarry. All living things aboard the sleek ships were devoured. The smaller male dispatched five others. Only the ones emitting that sound were attacked. The many remaining things were without interest to the beasts. Recent lacerations, which damaged the extraordinary senses along the right side of the head and body of the male, adversely affected his abilities. Three living creatures, of insignificant size, were missed. Clinging to inedible debris, three cowering humans observed the holocaust. These three were left when the giant fish's mandated task was completed.

Quiet and stillness prevailed. Evolution's requirements were satisfied. Again, nature sent the magnificent specimens in separate directions, avoiding conflict between themselves. They would meet their kind again in the next year or two, to breed and thus insure continuation of the species. Meanwhile, she would give birth to two young. Nature's brilliant handiwork would dictate their destiny.

Silence filled the sea, except for natural noises belonging in her depths. The enemy was vanquished. Effortlessly, a male and a female Megalodon slipped into the eternal darkness and endless pressures of their chosen home. The QUEST FOR MEGALODON was over.

ABOUT THE AUTHOR

Tom Dade was born and raised in Fort Lauderdale, Florida. He is a direct descendant of Major Francis Langhorn Dade who was massacred by Chief Osceola in 1837 to start the Seminole Indian War and for whom Dade County, Florida and Dade County, Georgia are named. Tom grew up in and on the waters of South Florida during the '50's and 60's, spending much of his formative teenage years sport fishing, shark hunting, skin and scuba diving, working charter boats, and doing salvage work for commercial diving companies.

He attended the University of Florida for three years before transferring to Florida Atlantic University's fledgling Ocean Engineering program at Boca Raton. He graduated with FAU's first class of Ocean Engineers in April 1967 and became the initial OE to enter the "Oil Patch". While at FAU, he was selected to spend one summer working with the late Ed Link on his diving research efforts. Returning to Florida Atlantic, Tom earned one of FAU's first MS degrees in Ocean Engineering in '72.

Tom's exposure to the sea continued with a career in the Oil Industry that has now spanned 26 years, 5 states, and 2 foreign countries. Holding down a variety of technical and supervisory positions with two major oil companies, managing a major commercial diving company's Gulf of Mexico operations, and working as an engineer and manager with oil field contractors, virtually all of his assignments have been offshore related.

Utilizing this wealth of experience and a little God-given talent, Tom has emerged as an exceptional writer, demonstrating the ability to place his readers in the marine environment and have them see, feel, and experience much of what he has been through. In QUEST FOR MEGALODON, he has tapped the possibility of a supposedly extinct ancestor of the Great White Shark somehow surviving in the depths of present day seas. Based on his knowledge of the oceans, Tom is convinced that this giant shark, scientific name Carcharadon Megalodon, may still exist.

Tom's worldwide travels slowed in 1982 when he returned to Lafayette, Louisiana where he had started his "Oil Patch" career in 1967. He still resides there with his wife, the former Lois Thiel, also an F.A.U. graduate (class of '67) who is an elementary school teacher. They have one son, Tommy, Jr., who just graduated from Troy State University in Environmental Sciences, and a daughter, Regine', born in Scotland and presently completing her junior year at Teurlings Catholic High School in Lafayette.

Tom's active interest in the outdoors continues with a yard full of endangered Alligator Snapping turtles up to 80 pounds, which he and young Tommy are trying to breed to prevent extinction of the species. He also enjoys "too infrequent" fishing and diving trips to the bountiful waters of offshore Louisiana. In his "spare time" Tom plays a little tennis, watches some TV, and writes.

To order a personally autographed copy of
QUEST FOR MEGALODON *by mail, send*
check or money order for $15 (tax, plus S&H) to:

MEGALODON
% SWAN PUBLISHING
P.O. Box 53743
Lafayette, LA 70505

Mastercard or Visa orders call:
(318) 981-6647

Libraries, bookstores or quantity
orders:

SWAN PUBLISHING COMPANY
126 Live Oak, Suite 100
Alvin, TX 77511
(713) 388-2547